INTERIOR
CASTLE

D1320106

INTERIOR CASTLE

BY

TERESA OF AVILA

Bridge-Logos
Alachua, FL 32615 USA

Bridge-Logos

Alachua, FL 32615 USA

Interior Castle
by Teresa of Avila

Printed in the United States of America.

Library of Congress Catalog Card Number: 2007943556
International Standard Book Number: 978-0-88270-464-7

Scripture quotations are from the *King James Version* of the Bible.

G616.316.N.m712.35240

Prayer in my opinion

is nothing else than an

intimate sharing between friends,

it means taking time frequently

to be alone with Him

who we know loves us.

TABLE OF CONTENTS

THE SECOND MANSION

THE THIRD MANSION

THE FOURTH MANSION

THE FIFTH MANSION

THE SIXTH MANSION

following these favors. Humility produced by them. How the Lord comforts such a soul. Mysteries learned.

THE SEVENTH MANSION

SELECTED EXCERPTS FROM
The Way of Perfection

FOREWORD

*Let not your heart be troubled: ye believe in God, believe
also in me. In my Father's house are many mansions: if it
were not so, I would have told you. I go to prepare a place
for you. And if I go and prepare a place for you, I will
come again, and receive you unto myself; that where I am,
there ye may be also (John 14:1-3).*

There is a sanctuary inside every child of God. A secret
garden overflowing with the beauty and fragrance of the
indwelling Lord. A haven of peace that encourages intimate
communion with Him, who loves us. He draws us into His
heavenly vineyard to sip the wine of His love that removes
the taint of bitterness from our tests and trials. All the while
He fills us to overflowing with His life and places us, where
and when He wills, to bring forth the living water of His life
from the heart of our beings, for a thirsty, sinful, lost without
hope, and dying world.

Saint Teresa walked the dark path of trials in her early
years, yet kept moving forward toward the inner light that
was drawing her into a relationship with the Lord that
changed her life, the lives of many in her day, and continues
to do so.

In the journey to the center of the soul, Saint Teresa has
used the illustration of the bride and the Beloved in the Song
of Solomon to describe the betrothal and the spiritual union

of the soul with the Lord. Each step of the journey brings about a purging of fleshly desires and things of the world from the soul earnestly seeking divine union with God.

The Lord has placed every child of God on this pathway; for some of us it can be a very long journey, but if we surrender our will to His divine will, we find in our weakness we can do all things through Christ who strengthens us.

We have carefully and sensitively revised this book to enhance the readability and aid in the comprehension of certain words and phrases that have changed through the years or are no longer in usage. A glossary has been provided in the back of the book to define certain words of either archaic or theological nature.

As you read this book and walk your own inner pathway, there may be many curves, deserts, valleys and mountain tops you can relate to in your own past, present and future experiences.

As I wrote this foreword, the Scripture from John 17, the Lord Jesus' prayer to His Father for all those the Father has given Him, continually came to my mind.

"As thou hast sent me into the world, even so have I also sent them into the world. And for their sakes I sanctify myself, that they also might be sanctified through the truth. Neither pray I for these alone, but for them also which shall believe on me through their word; That they all may be one; as thou, Father, art in me, and I in thee, that they also may be one in us: that the world may believe that thou hast sent me. And the glory which thou gavest me I have given them; that they may be one, even as we are one: I in them, and thou in me, that they may be made perfect in one; and that the world may know that thou hast sent me, and hast loved them, as thou hast loved me" (John 17:18-23).

Beverlee J. Chadwick

*This Introduction to the Interior Castle was written by
Benedict Zimmerman, Prior, O.C.D. at St. Luke's Priory,
Wincanton, Somerset, England, on July 1, 1905, and
then revised on December 25, 1911. It is here reproduced
essentially as he wrote it, with only minor editing.*

INTRODUCTION

Saint Teresa began to write the *Interior Castle* on June 2,
1577, Trinity Sunday, and completed it on the eve of
St. Andrew, November 29, of the same year. But there was
a long interruption of five months, so that the actual time
spent in the composition of this work was reduced to about
four weeks—a fortnight for the first, and another fortnight
for the second half of the book.

The rapidity with which it was written is easily explained
by the fact that the Saint had conceived its plan some time
previously. On January 17, 1577, she had written to her
brother, Don Lorenzo de Cepeda, at Avila: "I have asked
the bishop—Don Alvaro Mendoza—for my book (the *Life*)
because I shall perhaps complete it by adding those new
favors our Lord has lately granted me. With these one may
even compose a new work of considerable size, provided God
grants me the grace of explaining myself; otherwise the loss
will be of small account."

She never asked for permission to write anything, but
waited until she received a command from her superiors,
which, in this case, came from Father Jerome Gracian,
superior of the Discalced J. Carmelites of the Provinces of

Andalusia and Castille, and from Don Alonso Velasquez, canon of Toledo, afterwards bishop of Osma. The French Carmelite nuns in their new translation, quoting the Año Teresiano, and Father Gracian's Dilucidario, as well as his additions to Ribera, show the exact share of Fr. Gracian and Dr. Velasquez in the preliminaries of this work.

The Saint was not in good health at the time; she repeatedly complains of noises in the head and other infirmities, but, worst of all, she was weighed down by troubles and anxieties resulting from the action of the superiors of the Order and of the Papal Nuncio against the nuns and friars of the Reform. Matters became even more serious when, in October, the nuns of the Incarnation of Avila proceeded to the election of a new prioress. Notwithstanding the prohibition of the provincial, fifty-five electors recorded their votes in favour of the Saint and were immediately declared excommunicated. The whole work of the Reform seemed on the brink of ruin; the Saint, as well as all her friends, was in disgrace, subject to obloquy and ill-treatment.

No trace of these trials is to be found in the *Interior Castle*. Saint Teresa possessed the power of concentration of thought in a marvelous degree. The early mornings and late evenings were devoted to the composition of the book, while the rest of the day was taken up by the affairs of the Order. Mother Mary of the Nativity, a member of the community of Toledo, where the book was begun, declared afterwards that she often saw her writing, generally after Holy Communion, her face resplendent, with such rapidity and so absorbed in her occupation that she seemed undisturbed by, and in fact quite unconscious of, any noise that was made.

A somewhat similar incident is reported by Mother Anne of the Incarnation, but it appears to be wrongly brought into connection with the composition of the *Castle*. The nun in question had belonged to the convent of St. Joseph at Segovia at an earlier period, but there is no evidence that St. Teresa visited this place in the course of the six months during which she composed this work. The Bollandists, indeed, maintain that it was commenced at Toledo, continued at Segovia and completed at Avila (about 1541), but their sole authority for including Segovia is the passage in question, which, however, must refer to some other work of the Saint.

The sister, passing St. Teresa's door, saw her writing, her face being lit up as by a bright light. She wrote very fast without making any corrections. After an hour, it being about midnight, she ceased and the light disappeared. The Saint then knelt down and remained in prayer for three hours, after which she went to sleep. Reports were heard from the same witness, that entering her cell one day to deliver a message, the holy Mother was just beginning a new sheet of her book. While taking off her spectacles to listen to the message, she was seized by a trance in which she remained for several hours. The nun, terrified at this, did not stir, but kept her eyes steadily on the Saint. When she came to, it was seen that the paper, previously blank, was covered with writing. Noticing that her visitor had discovered it, Saint Teresa put the paper quietly in the box.

Another nun, Mary of St. Francis, left the following declaration: "I know that our holy Mother wrote four books, the *Life*, the *Way of Perfection*, the *Foundations*, and the *Mansions*, which I have seen her writing. Once, while she was composing the last-named work, I entered to deliver a message, and found her so absorbed that she did not notice me; her face seemed quite illuminated and most beautiful. After having listened to me she said: 'Sit down, my child, and let me write what our Lord has told me ere I forget it,' and she went on writing with great rapidity and without stopping."

Mary of St. Joseph says she heard from Mary of the Nativity that Father Jerome Gracian commanded the Saint to write the *Mansions*; she, however, begged to be excused, because so many books having been written by holy and learned men, there remained nothing for a woman to write. At length she yielded under obedience. This nun (Mary of the Nativity) was frequently in the Saint's cell while she was writing and she noticed her resplendent face and the almost preternatural velocity with which her hand travelled over the paper.

Writing to Mother Mary of St. Joseph, Prioress of Seville, on November 8, 1581, St. Teresa gives her a message for Father Rodrigo Alvarez, S. J.: "Our Father (Jerome Gracian, then provincial) tells me that he has handed you a book written by me, which perhaps you do not feel inclined to read yourself. Kindly read to Father Rodrigo Alvarez, at his next visit, the last *Mansion*, but under the seal of confession, as he asks this in his superior wisdom. This is only for you two. Tell him that the person he knows has arrived at this Mansion and enjoys the peace there described; that she is entirely at rest, and that some grave theologians have assured her that she is on a safe road. In case you could not read these pages to him do not send him the book, for it might lead to unpleasantness. Until I have his answer on this matter I will not write to him. Give him my compliments."

At the end of the original manuscript, before the Epilogue there is a notice in Father Alvarez' hand-writing to this effect: "The Mother Prioress of the convent of Seville has read to me this seventh *Mansion*, whither a soul may arrive in the present life. Let all the saints praise the infinite goodness of God, Who communicates himself to His creatures so that they truly seek His glory and the salvation of their neighbor. What I feel and judge of this matter is that everything that has been read to me is conformable to Catholic truth and in accordance with Holy Scripture and the teaching of the Saints. Whosoever has read the doctrine of the Saints, such as the books of St. Gertrude, St. Catharine of Siena, or St. Bridget of Sweden, and other saints and spiritual writers, will clearly understand that the spirit of Mother Tireza [sic] of Jesus is true, since it leads to the same effects as are to be found in the saints; and because this is in u8n my judgment and opinion, I have hereunto set my name, this, the 22nd day of February, 1582. P. Rodrigo Alvarez."

The work was copied, probably under the supervision of the Saint, who introduced many changes; when completed the original was handed to Father Jerome Gracian and to the Dominican, Fray Diego de Yanguas, for approval. Both, particularly the former, made numerous corrections, which Fuente, not without reason, calls impertinent, scratching out whole sentences and adding others.

The book thus revised must have enjoyed a certain celebrity, though not to the same extent as the *Life*, to which St. Teresa herself preferred it. On December 7, 1577, scarcely a week after its completion, she wrote to Father Salazar, S.J.: "If Señor Carillo [Salazar himself] came, the person in question [the Saint] thinks he would find another jewel which in her opinion is superior to the former [the *Life*]. This one reflects nothing foreign to itself, but is resplendent in its own beauty. It is enriched with more delicate enamels than the former, the workmanship, too, is more perfect. For, as the person in question says, the jeweler was less experienced when he fashioned the previous one. Moreover, the gold of the new one is of better quality than that of the former, though the precious stones are not so well set. It has been done, as might be expected, according to the designs of the Jeweler Himself." Later, on January 14, 1580, she wrote to Father Jerome Gracian: "The book I have written since seems to me superior [to the *Life*]; at least I had more experience when I wrote it."

One day, speaking with Mother Mary of Jesus on spiritual matters, she said that our Lord had communicated so much to her since she had reached what she described in the seventh Mansion—the spiritual Marriage—that she did not consider it possible to advance further in this life, in the way of prayer, nor even to wish to do so.

The book was eagerly read by those who were able to obtain copies. At the archiepiscopal Seminary at Salamanca it was read publicly after dinner; the students, contrary to custom, sacrificing the recreation rather than miss so edifying an instruction. The result was that several entered the religious life, one becoming a Franciscan, two others, who had already taken their degrees, joining the Discalced Carmelites. We also know of a lady who became a Poor Clare through reading the *Interior Castle*.

The process of Beatification contains the following evidence of Don Francisco de Mora, architect to Philip III: "The same prioress (of a convent of Dominican nuns) being concerned about my salvation gave me a book in manuscript, called *The Mansions*, by Mother Teresa, hoping I should derive some benefit from it. I fear this was not the case, but it made me acquainted with Teresa of Jesus, the foundress of the Discalced Carmelite nuns, of whom I had not yet heard, but for whom I now felt devotion."

In August 1586 it was decided to print Saint Teresa's works, the Augustinian Fray Luis de Leon being selected as editor, as he was unconcerned in the quarrels raging round the Reform. Accordingly, the manuscript of the *Interior Castle* was handed to him. When Luis de Leon undertook the editing of St. Teresa's writings he received a long letter from Don Diego de Yepes, afterwards Bishop of Tarazona, a former friend and confessor of the Saint, in which he records his personal recollections. I shall only insert here what he says about the *Interior Castle*:

> This holy Mother desired to see the beauty of a
> soul in the state of grace, a thing greatly to be coveted
> both for the sake of seeing and of possessing it. While
> this desire lasted, she was commanded to write a
> treatise on prayer, of which she had much personal

experience. On the eve of the Blessed Trinity, while considering what subject to choose for this treatise, God, Who disposes everything in due season, fulfilled her wish and furnished a suitable subject. He showed her a most beautiful globe of crystal, in the shape of a castle, with seven rooms, the seventh, situated in the center, being occupied by the King of glory, resplendent with the most exquisite brilliancy, which shone through and adorned the remaining rooms. The nearer these lay to the center, the more did they partake of that wondrous light. It did not, however, penetrate beyond the crystal, for everything round about was a mass of darkness and impurity, full of toads and vipers and other venomous animals.

She was still admiring this beauty which, by the grace of God dwells in the soul, when, Lo!, the light suddenly disappeared, and the crystal, wherein the King of glory was still residing, became opaque and as dark as coal, emitting an intolerable odor; the venomous animals, formerly held in check outside, obtained admittance into the castle. The holy Mother wished that every one should behold this vision, for she thought that no one having seen the beauty and splendor of grace, which is forfeited by sin and replaced by such repulsive misery, would ever dare to offend God.

She told me this vision on the same day, for in this as well as in other things she was so communicative that on the following morning she said to me: "How I forgot myself yesterday! I cannot think how it could have happened. Those high aspirations of mine, and the affection I have for you must have caused me to go beyond all reasonable limits. God grant I may have derived some profit therefrom." I promised her to say nothing about it during her lifetime, but since her death I should like to make it known to all men. From this vision she learnt four important matters.

First, she came to understand this axiom, which in this form she had never heard of in her life, that God is present in all things by His essence, presence, and power. As she was deeply humble and submissive and obedient to the doctrine of the Church and the teaching of the learned ministers of God, she never rested until her revelations had been approved of by her superiors and by theologians, and were shown to be conformable to Holy Scripture. She went so far as to say that if all the angels of heaven said one thing, and her superiors another, though she could not doubt that the former were true angels, yet she would hold what was told her by her superiors, because faith comes through these and there remains no room for deceit, whereas revelations coming from angels might be illusionary.

With such regard for obedience, she asked me one day at Toledo—probably at the time when she saw the vision of the Castle—whether it was true that God was in all things by His power, presence, and essence, to which I replied in the affirmative, explaining it as best I could on the authority of St. Paul, particularly where he says "the sufferings of this time are not worthy to be compared with the glory to come that shall be revealed in us" (Romans 8:18). Laying stress on these words, "shall be revealed in us," she was so overjoyed that I was quite astonished. Though in a way it seemed to me a kind of curiosity, I could not help thinking there was some mystery about it, for she said: "This is the very thing."

Secondly, she was greatly surprised at the malice of sin, since, notwithstanding the presence of God in these various ways, it prevents the soul from partaking of that powerful light.

Thirdly, she derived such humility and self-knowledge from this vision, that from that moment she never thought of herself in all the good she was doing; for she learnt that all the beauty of the soul emanates from that resplendent light, and that the powers of the soul and of the body are enlivened and strengthened by the Power established in the center, whence comes all our good, so that we have but a small share in our good works. All the good she did, she from this moment referred to God as its principal author.

Fourthly, she derived from it the subject of the book she was ordered to write on prayer, comparing the seven rooms of the Castle with as many degrees of prayer, whereby we enter within ourselves and draw nearer to God. So that, penetrating to the depths of our soul and gaining perfect self-knowledge, we reach the seventh room where God Himself dwells, with Whom we become united by as perfect a union as is possible in the present life, being made partakers of His light and love.

I will say no more of this vision and the Mansions, because your Reverence must by now have seen this admirable book, and must know with what accuracy, with what majestic doctrine, with what lucid examples she describes the progress of the soul from the gate to the very centre. It is clearly seen in this treatise how she communicated with our Lord, and how His Majesty vouchsafed to place her in the centre and to unite her with Himself, as she puts it, by the bonds of marriage and an inseparable union.

After the publication of the *Interior Castle* in 1588 at Salamanca, it became not only more widely known, but also more and more appreciated. Francis Suarez, the great theologian of the Society of Jesus, says in his deposition in the process of Beatification that he had read some of St. Teresa's works, particularly the Mansions, which contain an absolutely safe doctrine and give proof of a wonderful spirit of prayer and contemplation.

Thomas Hurtado, professor of theology at Seville, speaks as follows:

As often as I read the books of the holy Mother, I admire the wonderful manner in which God instructed her in mystical theology for the sake of souls giving themselves truly to familiar intercourse with His divine Majesty. But where I most regret my inability of expressing in fitting terms my sentiments towards this excellent teacher is when I look at, and refresh myself in that Castle with its seven rooms; for there is seen the effect of infused knowledge such as St. Denis received from St. Hierotheus (This is an allusion to the famous Mystical Theology attributed to Dionysius the Areopagite, and long considered the chief authority on this subject.), and both from St. Paul, and which has been committed to writing in the famous book of Mystical Theology. Hence comes, as from a fountain-head, notwithstanding the obscurity (to our manner of thinking) of its language, the doctrine of the great masters of the spiritual life such as Hugh of St. Victor, St. Bernard, Ruysbroek, Tauler, Gerson, and many others whom I pass by.

Nevertheless, I will boldly say that no one has given us water more limpid from that Apostolical and Areopagitical well than the holy Mother Teresa, who, in her books, but chiefly in the Mansions, has cleared up in simple language the most difficult questions of this divine theology, and has brought forth light from darkness, as it is written: "God, who commanded the light to shine out of darkness" (2 Corinthians 4:6). Who has ever been able to show as clearly as our Saint how God takes possession of the soul, how He unites Himself with its substance, whence comes to the intellect the light of faith, to the will the ardor of love, and to the senses the jubilation over His works?

No one has ever turned theory into practice in a more convincing or more catholic manner. The most profound secrets of this supernatural wisdom are here treated with such ease, so amiably, so delightfully, they are illustrated by such nice and homely examples, that instead of awe-inspiring obscurity, we find lovely flowers and the sweetness of love, through which, as through an avenue, the soul passes onwards.

When God made known His exalted doctrine to St. Dionysius and other mystical writers, He made use of their own language and pen. But St. Teresa in the Mansions is like the light of dawn whose rays are not intercepted by the clouds of this world; like a soft rain from above, whereby the soul grows and profits by its communications with God. Until the teaching of this great door became known it seemed as though God were inaccessible, being surrounded by darkness, through which Moses and some other persons had to pass when approaching Him; but they neither explained the manner nor showed the way whereby they came to the enjoyment of the sweetness of the Spouse.

Now, however, this way is clear and patent to all, having been pointed out in the Mansions, in language so straight and so methodical, and no longer such as could not be understood, or required further explanation. In my opinion this holy writer derived not only the substance of her teaching from infused knowledge, but even the words with which she explains it.

Likewise Don Alvaro de Villegas, canon of Toledo, expressed his opinion that the *Way of Perfection* and the *Interior Castle* contain "heavenly doctrine." The weight of the subject-matter, the propriety of the comparisons, the force of the expressions, the consistency of the teaching, the sweetness of her well-chosen, vivid words, the clearness of the arguments, all this proves that she was guided by her heavenly Spouse, in Whom are hidden the treasures of the wisdom of God; and that the Holy Ghost, Who more than once was seen resting on her head like a dove, was dilating these works. Villegas does not believe that any one could read them, as such books ought to be read, without becoming himself a master of the spiritual life. For they are like heavenly dew, rendering the soul fruitful in the matter of prayer. These testimonies could be easily multiplied.

It would be a mistake to consider the *Interior Castle* a complete treatise of mystical theology. Like St. Teresa's other works, it is intensely personal: she describes the road by which she has been led, being well aware that others may be led in a different way. In the heavenly Father's house there are many mansions, not only seven, and many paths lead to them. What gives the work such high value is, that it is the result of a most searching inquiry into the various phases whereby a soul is gradually transformed into the likeness of God Himself. Here St. Teresa is always at her best. She takes nothing for granted, even her own personal experiences are admitted only after having been fully investigated and found to be consistent one with the other, and conformable to the teaching of the Church and the words of Holy Scripture.

Mystical theology is generally divided into three parts, respectively called the purgative, the illuminative, and the unitive life. In the first, man is cleansed from sin and habitual imperfection by the use of the sacraments and by voluntary mortification of the passions. The mind is purified by sedulous meditation on the last end and on the Life and Passion of Christ, which must ever be the great model of the Christian. This first portion of the way to heaven can be covered by the help of the ordinary means of grace, without any direct and extraordinary intervention of divine power. The second part differs in many ways from the first. It comprises the passive purification of the soul and the passive enlightenment of the mind. By sending it keen interior and exterior trials and sufferings, God completes the cleansing of the soul in a manner far surpassing any voluntary effort of man. By raising it to the stage of contemplation He gives it fresh light on the mysteries of our Redemption. The mind is then no longer compelled to strain the memory, the reason, and the will, in order to dwell upon the great truths of religion and to derive some personal benefit therefrom, for these truths are now more or less permanently before it and fill it with holy thoughts, sometimes giving it consolation in trouble, at other times striking a warning note against imperfection. Again, the subtraction of sensible consolation, and the interior aridity arising therefrom, leave a terrible blank in the soul, showing it that, without God's help, it is mere nothingness. This apparent estrangement from God is the keenest trial that can befall a soul, but also the most powerful means of cleansing it from the least, the most subtle imperfections.

Emerging from this state of probation, the soul enters upon the third stage, in which, though perhaps in the midst of severe suffering and sharp persecution, it knows itself to be a chosen child of God, to Whom it is united by perfect conformity of the will. Such phenomena as revelations, visions, locutions, and even more wonderful manifestations, like the wound of love, spiritual betrothal and nuptials, are incidental rather than essential to the second and third stages. Some great contemplatives have never experienced anything of the kind, while, on the other hand, some of these occurrences may sometimes have been merely the work of an exuberant imagination, or even the result of diabolical illusion.

They should, therefore, never be wished for, or cherished, but rather shunned and ignored, in as far as that is possible. If they are real and come from God, they will do their work without the co-operation of the soul. The danger of self-deception is so great that a person laboring under such phenomena should offer every resistance, and the spiritual director should exercise the utmost vigilance. St. Teresa is very eloquent on this point and undeceived many would-be contemplatives, while her disciple, St. John of the Cross, is even more thorough-going in the deprecation of spiritual favors. Among the numerous marks whereby the trained theologian may discriminate between real and imaginary phenomena, there is one about which Saint Teresa speaks with wonderful clearness. If they proceed from hysteria, the imagination alone is active and the higher powers of the soul are torpid; if, however, they come from God, the intellect and the will are so intensely active, that the lower powers and even the body lose all strength for the time being.

It will be noticed that the first two Mansions belong to the purgative life, the third and fourth to the illuminative, and the remaining three to the unitive life. Compared with similar works, the treatment of the first stage must be called meager. True, in her *Life* and in the *Way of Perfection*, St. Teresa has dealt with this subject somewhat more fully. Indeed, the last-named work was designed as a treatise on Christian Ascetics, dealing with the purgation of the soul by mortification and the enlightenment of the mind by meditation. There, too, appears the first idea of the Mansions, and Fuente remarks that the passage in question may be taken for the parting of the ways between the two works.

However, this is not the only, nor, indeed, the chief reason why St. Teresa is so reticent about the preliminary stage of the contemplative life. The fact is that she herself did not pass through these experiences. By God's grace she was preserved from childhood from grievous sin and gross imperfection. Though she never grows tired of bewailing her faults and unfaithfulness, these avowals must be taken *cum grano salis*.

While yet a child, she sometimes gave way to vanity in dress and wasted her time in reading romances. As a young religious, she was sought after by friends and relatives who took pleasure in her attractive conversation. This proved further loss of time and caused distractions. Owing to acute suffering, she for some years left off the practice of mental prayer, though she faithfully performed all her religious obligations, as far as her weak state of health allowed. This is all. The war of the flesh against the spirit, the insubordination of the lower parts of nature, the fickleness of the will, which so often thwart the most noble aspirations of a soul, were unknown to her. Under these circumstances, we cannot be surprised to find her entering upon the journey towards God at a point which in many cases marks but the closing stage.

As to the remaining parts of this book, [much of it covers] the same ground as her *Life* and the *Relations*. With her singular gift of introspection and analysis, the Saint studied her own case from every point of view, so as to make sure that her extraordinary experiences were due to no illusion, and offered no obstacle to the safety of her soul. Although the *Interior Castle* contains little that we do not already know from her other works, it is superior to them by reason of its logical order and the masterly treatment of the most recondite matters of mystical theology.

While ostensibly dealing with general facts, St. Teresa in reality records her personal experiences. How definite these were, how little room there remained for the freaks of the imagination, will appear from the fact that she nearly always repeats the very words she had used in her *Life* and in the other reports of her interior progress, although she did not have these writings before her eyes, nor had she ever seen them since they first left her hands. Every one of her experiences must have produced a profound impression to be remembered so minutely after an interval of years.

There is that in the *Interior Castle* which reminds one of Dante's Paradiso. In the one and the other, the soul, purified from earthly dross, is gradually being invested with new and glorious qualities, and is being led through regions unknown until it arrives at the very threshold of the throne of God. Not even the boldest imagination could have designed so wonderful a picture of a soul adorned with graces at once so varied and so true. In one case we know, the poet has drawn abundantly from the treasury of the Angelical Doctor, putting in verse the conclusions of the scholastic theologian. In the other case we can follow, chapter by chapter, the influence of the teaching of St. Thomas Aquinas.

St. Teresa had never studied it herself, but her directors and confessors were deeply versed in it and solved her doubts and perplexities on the lines of the greatest of the school men. The *Interior Castle* might almost be considered a practical illustration of certain parts of the Summa Theologica [also Theologiae], as it describes the progress of the soul through every stage of perfection. When we have reached the second chapter of the seventh Mansion, there remains but one thing: the Beatific Vision, and this is reserved for the next life.

After the publication of the *Interior Castle* by Luis de Leon, the manuscript came into the possession of Father Jerome Gracian, who, after having made a copy of it which is still extant, presented the original, on the occasion of a visit to the convent of Seville, to Don Pedro Cereso Pardo, a great friend of the Saint, and a benefactor to the convent. When his only daughter took the habit there, the precious manuscript was part of her dowry. Doña Juana de Mendoza, Duchess of Beguiar, a novice in the same convent, had it bound in silver and precious stones. It is still there, and the present writer had the privilege of seeing it.

It comprises a hundred and thirteen leaves in folio, but originally there must have been some more leaves which at a later period were torn out. These, it is presumed, contained the headings of the chapters. Unlike the *Life* and the *Foundations*, the text of the *Castle* is divided only by figures, without indication of the contents of each chapter, but the arguments which have come down to us are so entirely similar to those of the two works named, that it is impossible to consider them otherwise than the genuine work of the author. In the present translation they have been inserted in their proper places.

On the occasion of the tercentenary (300 years) of Saint Teresa's death, a photo-lithographic edition of the original was published under the direction of Cardinal Lluch, Carmelite of the old observance, Archbishop of Seville: *El Castillo Ynterior ó Tratado de las Moradas, escrito por Sta. Teresa de Jesús. Litografia de Juan Moyano* (Seville) 1882. The present translation, the third in English, has been made directly from this autograph edition.

Criticisms which have appeared in various papers, or have been privately conveyed, have been gratefully received and acted upon in the second and the present edition. It would have been easy to multiply quotations from the works of other writers on mystical theology. Thus, the influence of the *Imitation of Christ* by Kempis (Published as a Pure Gold Classic by Bridge-Logos Publishers), and of the *Life of Our Lord* by Ludolphus the Carthusian can be distinctly traced in the Interior Castle. Both these works, as well as some

Spanish books, were held in such esteem by St. Teresa, that she ordered the prioress of each convent to keep them at the disposal of the nuns.

In conclusion I venture to express the hope that this new translation will be found helpful by those who feel called to a higher life.

Teresa of Avila

1515–1582

The Ecstasy of St. Teresa of Avila
by Giovanni Lorenzo Bernini
stands in the Cornaro Chapel
of the Church of St. Maria della Vittoria
in Rome, Italy

ST. TERESA OF AVILA
1515-1582

The year 1478 birthed three hundred and fifty-six years of unending upheaval, torture, death, and countless other horrors in Spain until the year 1834. It was called the Spanish Inquisition. In the year 1492, Queen Isabella of Spain commissioned Christopher Columbus to sail to the uncharted waters of the Western World, thus opening the West to European colonization. Then in the year 1517, Martin Luther started the Protestant Reformation.

In the midst of all this change, and two years prior to the Reformation, came little Teresa de Cepeda y Ahumada to point the way from outer turmoil to inner peace. Born in 1515 to bless the lives of her parents, Don Alonso Sanchez de Cepeda and his wife, Dona Beatriz Davilla y Ahumada, in the town of Avila, Old Castile, Spain.

Teresa's Early Years

Beatriz was determined to raise her extroverted daughter to be a pious Christian. At the age of seven, Teresa was so fascinated by accounts of the lives of saints, that she and her brother Rodrigo left home to go to the Moorish Territory in hope of being beheaded by the Moors. Fortunately, her uncle saw them as they were leaving Avila and brought them home, thus foiling their planned martyrdom. By the time Teresa was twelve she became interested in books on chivalry and an awareness of her natural beauty began to bloom in her young mind. She began to take an affectionate interest in her cousins. The affectionate interests grew in a few years to fancies of marriage. Her father was very disturbed by these thoughts of marriage in his favorite daughter and opposed them. Early in her fourteenth year and in the midst of her growing-up crises, her mother died. The effect on Teresa was devastating, for her mother Beatriz had been very close to her, reading to her and spending long periods of time with her. In her loneliness and need for a mother's attention, Teresa appealed to the Virgin Mary to be her mother. Seeing his daughter's need for guidance, her father sent her to a convent to be entrusted to the care of Augustinian nuns at Santa Maria de Gracia in 1531.

Seeds of a Vocation Planted

Under the influence of Dona Maria de Brinceno, who was in charge of the lay students at the convent school, Teresa was helped to recover her early piety. She began to have thoughts of being a nun. In the year 1532 she became ill and returned to her family to live with her sister in Castellanos.

Teresa became interested in the letters of St. Jerome; reading these letters led her to decide to enter a convent, but her father would not consent to it. Rodrigo—Teresa's brother, confidant, and companion in her early life adventures—had just sailed to fight in the war on the Rio de la Plata. She persuaded another brother to leave home and flee with her to a monastery so they might both receive a religious habit. She had a friend, Juana Suarez, in a Carmelite Monastery, so Teresa decided to join her friend in the Carmelite Monastery of the Incarnation at Avila on November 2, 1535. Teresa's father resigned himself to this development.

The following year she receive the habit and gave herself to prayer and penance. Just a short time after her profession, Teresa became very ill and did not respond to medical treatment. Her illness continued to worsen, so her father decided to take her to the village of Becedas, to a woman who professed to be a healer; however, Teresa's health did not improve. Teresa left Becedas in the fall of 1538 to go to the home of her Uncle Pedro de Cepeda in Hortigosa. While living at her uncle's home, she received his gife of a copy of the *Tercer Abecedario* of Francis of Osuna. This book and the Letters of St. Jerome were paving stones in her life path. She commented, "I did not know how to proceed in prayer or how to become recollected, and so I took much pleasure in it and decided to follow that path with all my strength" (from the autobiography of St. Teresa).

Teresa did not regain her health in Hortigosa; indeed, she grew more ill. Her father brought her back to Avila in July of 1539, and on August 15th she lapsed into a coma so deep she was thought to be dead. However, after four days she began to revive, but was paralyzed in her legs for three years. After a time of healing, which she attributed to St. Joseph, she experienced a time of struggle and seeking for understanding in her spiritual life. She did not cease to pray, but she could not understand that the use of the imagination could be dispensed with as she sought to contemplate, and that she could go through her soul directly to contemplation. During this period of time—that lasted eighteen years—she had transitory mystical experiences.

Teresa had a strong need in her life to be appreciated by others. This finally left in her conversion experience when the presence of an image of the sorely wounded Christ freed her from this egoism that had hindered her spiritual development. Then at the age of thirty-nine, she began to enjoy the vivid experience of God's presence within her.

3

However, some of her friends tried to convince Teresa that this experience was the work of the devil, because she had become very peaceful in her relationship with the Lord and more relaxed than was thought proper, according to the ascetical standard of the time. A close friend helped by encouraging her to continue in mental prayer and keep her thoughts on Christ Jesus. In 1555, her confession was heard by Francis Borgia; he told her that the Spirit of God was at work in her and that she should concentrate on the Passion of Christ, not resisting the ecstatic experiences that came in prayer. Nevertheless, as her divine favors increased, so did the distrust of her friends.

When her director, Pradanos, left Avila in 1558, the new director Baltasar Avarez, caused her much distress. Either from his cautious attitude with her, or a desire to search her spirit, he told her that others were convinced that her raptures and visions were the work of the devil and that she should not communicate so often. Another priest, after hearing her report of a vision she had repeatedly had of Christ, told her it was of the devil and that she should laugh at the vision while making the sign of the cross. However, the Lord never failed to comfort her and in August of 1560, St. Peter of Alcantara counseled her: "Keep on as you are doing, daughter; we all suffer such trials."

St. Teresa's Work as a Reformer

The objective of St. Teresa's reform was to reform the spirit of the Primitive Rule of St. Albert. Prayer was the heart of her reform. Her teachings still inspire many today and are along these three main lines:

Firstly, God is sought for His own sake, He is worthy of all our love and adorations. Before Him all created things are nothing;

Secondly, contemplation of God is inseparable from obedience to His will. The only possible union with God is by conforming our will to His, and without this fundamental union, any other mystical experiences are suspect.

Thirdly, union with God in prayer leads to an ever-increasing desire to serve Him by furthering His plan for salvation and by working for the establishment of His kingdom here on earth.

Teresa's work of reform began with herself. She made a vow to always follow the path of perfection and resolved to keep the vow as well as she could. However, the atmosphere at the monastery was not favorable to the type of life of perfection that she aspired to. A group of like-thinkers assembled with her one evening and decided to take their inspiration from the primitive tradition of Carmel and the discalced reform of St. Peter of Alcantara. They proposed the foundation of a monastery of a hermitical type. The plans were accepted by her confessor and spiritual advisors in the beginning; however, when the townsfolk heard the plan, they rejected it with a great outcry against it. Teresa's confessor followed suit, changed his mind, and disassociated himself from the project. Additionally, her spiritual advisors sided with the townspeople.

Six months later, there was a change of rectors at the Jesuit collect, and Teresa's confessor, Father Alvarez, gave his approval of the planned project.

With no further delay, Teresa had her sister Juana and her husband buy a house in Avila and occupy it. This strategy was necessary to prevent difficulties with the nuns at the Incarnation while this building was being made ready to serve as a convent. Teresa was sent to Toledo by the Carmelite provincial at the request of a wealthy and noble lady. While in Toledo she was visited by St. Peter of Alcantara, who offered to act as a mediator in obtaining permissions from Rome for the foundation. She also received a vision from the holy Carmelite Maria de Yepes, who had just returned from Rome with permission to establish a reformed convent.

She provided Teresa with a new light on the question of the type of poverty to be adopted by her own community. While at Toledo, Teresa in reluctant obedience completed her first version of a book her confessor had commanded her to write.

After returning to Avila at the end of June, 1562, permission was received for the foundation of the new convent. The following August 24th, Teresa's new monastery dedicated to St. Joseph was founded; Maestro Daza, delegate from the bishop officiated at the ceremony. Four novices received the habit of the Discalced Carmelites. There was strong opposition from the townspeople and from the Incarnation. The prioress at the Incarnation commanded Teresa back to the monastery to be rebuked by the Carmelite provincial, Angel De Salazar, who was indignant at her for putting her new convent under the jurisdiction of the bishop. However, after hearing her reasons and account of the circumstances, he came into agreement with her and even promised to help quiet the disturbance and gave her permission to return to St. Joseph's when things had quieted down with the townsfolk and the prioress at Incarnation.

On August 25th the council met to discuss the new foundation, and on August 30th the townsfolk met. The only opposition was from one person. A lawsuit came before the royal court, but by the end of 1562, the founder, Teresa of Jesus, was authorized by the provincial to return to the convent of St. Joseph. Five years of peace then came into Teresa's life. During that time she wrote "The Way of Perfection" and "Meditations on the Canticle."

Foundations Established

In April, 1567, the Carmelite general, Giovanni Battista Rossi (Rubeo), visited the convent and approved Teresa's work, and commanded her to establish two houses for men who wished to adopt the reform. The following convents were established:

Convent at Medina del Campo, August 15th, 1567

Convent at Malagon in 1568

Convent at Valladolid (Rio de Olinos) in 1568

Convents at Toledo and Pastrana in 1569

Convent at Salamanca in 1570 and at Alba de Tormes in 1571.

As St.Teresa journeyed to Toledo in 1569, she passed through Duruelo, where John of the Cross and Anthony of Jesus had established the first convent of Discalced Brethren in November, 1568. In July 1569, she establishd the second monastery of Discalced Brethren in Pastrana. The founding of these foundations was followed by a period of time in which St. Teresa served as prioress at the Incarnation monastery in Avila. She was appointed to this position, much to her dislike. Not only that, she also faced opposition from the townspeople of Avila. In spite of the negatives, and with the help of St. John of the Cross, who served as confessor for the nuns, she brought about great improvement in the spiritual condition of the community. The establishing of convents continued through 1576. St. Teresa said this of her method of governing in the convents, "You know, I no longer govern in the way I used to. Love does everything. I am not sure if that is because no one give me cause to reprove her, or because I have discovered that things go better in that way."

In 1576, a series of persecutions began by the older Carmelite order against Teresa. She was forbidden any further founding of convents, and she was condemned to voluntary retirement in one of her convents. She chose St. Joseph's at Toledo. Her friends and subordinates were subjected to further trials. Finally, after several years of her pleading letters to King Philip II of Spain, the charges brought against her by the Inquisition were dropped. Pope Gregory XIII allowed a special provincial for the younger branch of the discalced nuns and a board of four assessors was set up for the reform.

During the last three years of her life, St. Teresa founded convents at Villanueva del la Jara in northern Andalusia (1580), Palencia (1580), Soria (1581), Burgos and Granada (1582). Seventeen convents (all but one founded by her) and just as may men's cloisters were established due to her reform activity of twenty years. St. Teresa also left a legacy of writings that represent important benchmarks in the history of Christian mysticism. The works include *The Way of Perfection, Interior Castle,* and her autobiography, *The Life of Teresa of Avila.*

Her final illness came upon her during a journey from Burgos to Alba de Tormes, Salamanca, Spain where she died on October 4th, 1582. She was sixty-seven years old. A nun who stood by her bed describes the hours just before the death of Saint Teresa: "She remained in this position of prayer, full of deep peace and great repose. Occasionally she gave some outward sign of surprise or amazement. But everything proceeded in great repose. It seemed as if she was hearing a voice which she answered. Her facial expression was so wondrously changed that it looked like a celestial body to us. Then immersed in prayer, happy and smiling, she went out of this world into eternal life."

When the bells of Avila tolled for her, the townsfolk said: "The Saint has gone to heaven." Her feast day is celebrated on October 15th.

St. Teresa was beatified by Pope Paul V on April 24, 1614, and she was canonized by Pope Gregory XV on March 12, 1622. St. Teresa and St. Catherine of Siena were recognized by the Roman Catholic Church as Doctors of the Church in 1970 along with St. Therese of Lisieux in 1997.

References

Saint Teresa of Jesus (http://www.carmelite.org.uk/Saints.html)

Teresa of Avila – (http://en.wikipedia.org/wiki/Teresa_of_Avila)

The Teresian Carmel (http://www.ocd.or.at/eng/teresa.htm)

St. Teresa of Avila (http://www.ccel.org/t.teresa/)

St. Teresa of Jesus (http://www.ccel.org/ccel)

Reform of Saint Teresa (http://www.carmelite.org.uk/carmway.html)

Dark Night of the Soul by Saint John of the Cross, Revised and Rewritten by Lloyd B. Hildebrand, Published by Bridge-Logos Publishers, Alachua, Florida, 2007.

The Convent of Santa Teresa, Avila

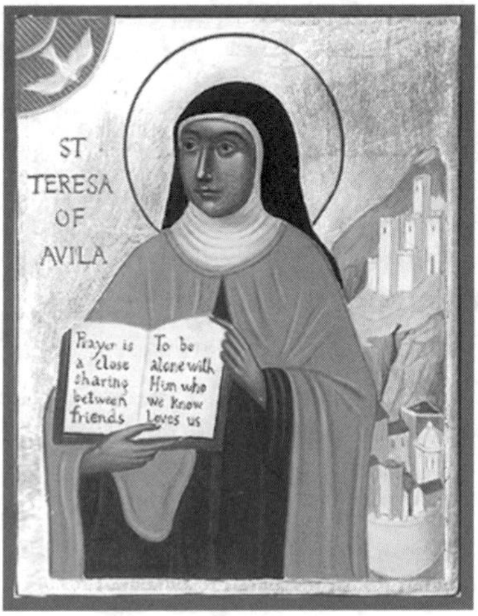

Text on book reads:

"Prayer is close sharing between friends …
To be alone with Him who we know loves us."

Text on scroll reads:

"My beloved is the mountains,
strong islands and resounding rivers."

ST. JOHN OF THE CROSS

St. John of the Cross was born on June 24, 1542, in Fontiveros, Spain, close to Avila, Spain, the birthplace of St. Teresa. He was the youngest child of parents who were silk weavers in the city of Toledo, Spain. Life was a struggle for these parents just to provide for their family's basic needs. St. John's father, Gonzalo, died shortly after his little son Juan (St. John) was born. This left the little family in dire need. Juan's mother Catherine continued looking for work to take care of her family. This resulted in moving from town to town until they moved to Medina del Campo, a market town that was thriving. Catherine continued to work as a weaver and taught this trade to her oldest son, Francisco, during their moves from town to town looking for better work to support themselves. Eventually, John, was sent to boarding school in Medina del Campo to study reading, writing, and catechism, in preparation to learn a trade.

Juan worked at various trades, but was not successful in any of them. Then the governor of a local hospital took him into his service as a hospital orderly, and while in this position he worked with many of the poor of the town with great love and devotion. This prompted the governor of the hospital to help Juan further his education by enrolling him in a school run by the Jesuits, called the Society of Jesus.

After graduating, Juan felt the call on his life to enter a religious order. Juan entered the Carmelite Order at Medina del Campo, Spain, in 1563. In 1564 he made his profession and continued his studies at the University of Salamanca and the Colegio de San Andres, majoring in philosophy.

A major influence of Juan's life was a professor at the university, Luis de Leon. Juan learned biblical exegesis, Hebrew, and Aramaic under his teaching. Professor De Leon had translated the Song of Solomon from the Old Testament into Spanish; this had a profound influence on the theology of St. John of the Cross in later years. Juan served as a Prefect of Studies revealing his leadership abilities and was a very devoted monk, spending much time in solitude in prayer and doing penance. After completing his preparation and studies, St. John was ordained as a priest in 1567. While in his monastery in Santa Ana, he met St. Teresa who was building a new Carmelite monastery for the nuns. Meeting St. Teresa of Avila was no doubt arranged by God, for she and John seemed to have the same goals and desires to be in service to the Lord.

After St. John had spent an additional year in study, he accompanied St. Teresa on a trip to learn more of the manner of life practiced by the nuns in Vallado. It was at this convent that St. Teresa taught St. John about the lifestyle of the sisters. He continued working with St. Teresa as her helper in founding monasteries all throughout Spain. He served in many roles over the years and lived a very simple life by choosing to live in an old decrepit, abandoned farmhouse with a lay brother, Anthony de Heredia. It was around this time that John began to call himself "John of the Cross." He worked in various roles in the following years until summoned by St. Teresa to be a spiritual guide to the nuns in the Incarnation of Avila. He and St. Teresa worked diligently and overcame the economic and spiritual stagnation the convent had fallen into. The nuns grew in grace and knowledge of the Lord under the guidance of St. Teresa and St. John of the Cross.

Soon to follow were the tension and problems between the Discalced Carmelites and the Calced Carmelites. John became a target of the opposition, was arrested, and put into a very cold, damp cell. Torture was the rule of the day for this man of God; but in spite of the beatings, he never changed his views of the religious life. Much of his time in prison was spent in composing poetry that he later penned on paper. He finally escaped this prison of horror and went into hiding with the Discalced Nuns of Toledo. After his escape from prison, St. John continued his reform work with the Carmelites.

In the year 1591, he came down with a an inflammation and fever, and the Prior of the monastery was not friendly to John at all. In fact, he put him in the worst cell he could find. John grew increasingly ill, and ulcerations spread from his legs to his back, where a very large tumor began to grow. He develop gangrene in his leg and on December 14, 1591 at the age of forty-nine, he went to be with his Lord.

His spiritual writings were published posthumously in 1618. His works include:
- *The Ascent of Mount Carmel*
- *Dark Night of the Soul*
- *Spiritual Canticle*
- "Love's Living Flame" and various other poems and letters and minor works.

THE CARMELITES

The Carmelite Order of the Roman Catholic Church originated during the Middle Ages. The place of origin is said to have been on Mount Carmel, where some hermits lived in caves and spent their lives studying the Scriptures, praying, and doing manual labor.

The organization of the Order consists of three different divisions or orders:

The First Order—the active/contemplative friars.

The Second Order—the cloistered nuns.

The Third Order—laypeople. Unlike members of the first two orders, members of this third order can marry. They participate in the order by liturgy, prayers, ministries, and contemplative prayer.

There are offshoots of the order as well, such as the active Carmelite sisters.

The Carmelites learned much from the example of Elijah, the servant of the Most High God. Elijah loved experiencing the presence of God, he took refuge in solitude, and spent much time in prayer and ministry to others. This is the mission of the Carmelites as well. In the same way that Elijah experienced the living God and was able to practice His presence, the Carmelites endeavor to do the same.

St. Teresa acted on the encouragement of General Rubeo, who had visited Spain and greatly approved of her establishment of convents for nuns and also granted her permission to establish two convents for reformed friars within the province of Castile. General Rubeo was well aware of the opposition St. Teresa had experienced at Alba, so he put stringent regulations on the work to avoid problems. However, most of the convents that St. Teresa established were done under very obstinate oppression.

Saint Teresa and Saint John of the Cross worked together in the Teresian Reform Movement. This is when the "Discalced Carmelites" name began to be used to represent monks and nuns who were devoted to the strictest rule of the order, the same rule the hermits on Mount Carmel followed. The "Calced Carmelites" appealed to Rome, resulting in a major dislike of the Reform Movement. Among the friars, Teresa found two very willing helpers, the prior Anton De Heredia and St. John of the Cross, who had recently completed his studies. They entered a time of severe and untold hardships on their pathway, but along the way postulants and former brethren joined in the work. The papal nuncio, Hormaneto, favored the work of reform. Much opposition arose for the little group that ended with the friars commanded to return to their proper convents, and St. Teresa received an order to choose one of her convents to live in and abstain from further establishment of foundations. The Discalced friars, however, did not do as they were commanded.

A new nuncio was appointed who worked vigorously against the reform and the reformers. He excommunicated all the capitulars, and St. John of the Cross was seized in the convent of the Incarnation at Avila where he was confessor. He was taken to Toledo and put into a dungeon and very cruelly treated. Other friars who were taken were imprisoned in other prisons. The persecutions lasted for almost a year, then King Philip II intervened. The reform had proven to be stronger than the opposition, and it was given legal standing by the establishment of a special province for the Discalced friars and nuns. The first provincial was Jerome Gratian, who throughout all this period of reform had been the chief support of St. Teresa.

St. Teresa had a very definite objective in mind when she set up her first convent, not only to reintroduce the contemplative life, but she also knew many souls were being lost daily through heresy and unbelief. She also wanted her sisters to pray and offer mortifications for the conversion of heretics and infidels. She was delighted when St. John of the Cross and his brethren went village to village giving instruction to those ignorant of Christianity. Her joy was filled to overflowing when, in 1852, missioners of the order were sent to the Congo.

Brother Lawrence, who wrote *The Practice of the Presence of God*, was a Carmelite friar during the seventeenth century. Here is a quote from his classic book that describes the devotion and contemplative lifestyle of the Carmelites:

"You must know that the tender and loving light of God's countenance kindles imperceptibly within the soul that ardently embraces it, a fire of love to God that is so great and so divine that it is necessary for the person who is so affected to moderate the outward expression of their feelings. Great would be our surprise, if we knew what communion the soul holds at these times with God. He seems to so delight in this communion, that to the soul who would willingly abide forever with Him, He bestows favors past numbering." (From *The Practice of the Presence of God* by Brother Lawrence.)

References

Order of Carmelites (http://www.carmelites.net/tradition/index.html)

Catholic Encyclopedia: The Carmelite Order (http://www.newadvent.org/cathen)

The Practice of the Presence of God by Brother Lawrence, Published by Bridge-Logos Publishers, Alachua, Florida, 1999.

PROLOGUE

Seldom has obedience laid upon me so difficult a task as writing this book about prayer. The main reason for this difficulty is I do not feel that God has given me the power, or even the desire, to do it. My other reason is a physical one. During the past three months, I have suffered from noises and weakness in my head. This has made it very painful for me to write, even on necessary business affairs.

However, obedience has the benefit of producing power that makes impossible things easy. Therefore, my will submits with a good grace. Although my nature seems greatly distressed and repugnant to this task, for God has not given me strength to bear the constant struggle with illness as I perform my many duties. May He, who has helped me in other more difficult matters, aid me with His grace in this, for I trust in His mercy.

I think I have very little to say that has not already been written in my other works of obedience. In fact, I fear this will be a repetition of them. I am like a parrot that has learned to talk, but only knows what it has been taught or heard and repeats the same thing over and over. If God wishes me to write anything new, He will have to speak through more or keep me from repeating myself by bringing my past writing back to my memory. I would be happy and content if He would do that, for I am very forgetful. Lest my previous writing become entirely lost, it would gladden my heart to be able to recall some of the things that people say I have written well. Still, if the Lord will not grant me this and I weary my brain and increase my headache by striving to obey—I will gain in merit even though my words may be useless to anyone.

I begin this work on the Feast of the Blessed Trinity in the year 1577, in my residence at the convent of St. Joseph of Carmel at Toledo. I submit all my writings to the judgment of the learned men by whose commands I undertake this work. If I say anything contrary to the doctrine of the Church, it may be certain the fault will be ignorance, not malice. By God's goodness I am, and will always be, faithful to the Church. May He be forever blessed and glorified. Amen.

He who bids me to write this book, tells me that the nuns of these convents of our Lady of Carmel need someone to solve their difficulties about prayer. He feels that women understand one another's language best, and that the sisters' affection for me would make them pay special attention to my words. Therefore, it is important for me to explain the subject clearly to them. I am writing this to the sisters, because the idea that anyone else could benefit by what I say would be absurd.

Our Lord will be doing me a great favor if He enables me to help just one of the nuns to praise Him more. He knows very well I have no other motivation or aim. If anything is to the point, they will understand that it does not originate from me and there is no reason to attribute it to me. My scant understanding and skill would not allow me to write anything like this, unless God, in His mercy, enabled me to do so.

St. Teresa of Avila

THE FIRST MANSION

CHAPTER 1

*This chapter explores the beauty and dignity of our
souls by comparing them to a spiritual castle formed of
transparent crystal surrounded by mansions containing
many rooms. It tells us how God grants us favor and gives
us knowledge and understanding of how prayer is the
gate of the spiritual castle.*

While I was earnestly seeking the Lord today for His
guidance and direction on how to proceed with
this work of obedience He has laid upon me, I had a vision
that I will explain, for it will serve as the foundation of this
writing.

The Interior Castle

I thought of the soul as resembling a castle, formed of
a single diamond or a very transparent crystal surrounded
by mansions containing many rooms just as in heaven there
are many mansions.

If we reflect on this, we will see that the soul of a just man
is a garden in which the Beloved takes great delight. What
do you imagine that dwelling must be like for God to delight
in it? He is our Creator, so mighty, so wise, and so pure,
containing all good in himself. Nothing can be compared to

the great beauty and capabilities of a soul. However keen our intellects may be, they are as unable to comprehend them as to comprehend God, for as He told us, He has created us in His own image and likeness.

Our Curable Self-Ignorance

This being so, we need not tire ourselves by trying to understand all the beauty of this castle, although being His creature there is as much difference between the soul and God as is between the creature and the Creator. The fact that we are made in God's image shows us how great are the dignity and loveliness of the soul. It is no small misfortune or disgrace that through our own fault we neither understand our nature nor our origin. Would it not be gross ignorance, if when a man was questioned about his name, country, or parents, he could not answer? Foolish as this would be, it is unspeakably more foolish to care to learn nothing of our nature except that we possess bodies, and only vaguely realize that we have souls, because people say so, and it is a doctrine of faith.

Rarely do we think about what gifts our souls may possess, who dwells within them, or how extremely precious they are. Therefore, we do little to preserve their beauty, all our care is concentrated on our bodies that are but the setting of the diamond, or the outer walls of the castle.

God Dwells in the Center of the Soul

Let us imagine that there are many rooms in this castle, some above and some below, some to the sides, and in the center of them all, the most important chamber, where God and the soul have their most secret conversations. Think about this comparison very carefully, and as you do, may God give you understanding of the many kinds of graces He is pleased to bestow upon the soul. No one can know all about them—much less a person so uninformed as I am—but the knowledge that such graces are possible will greatly comfort you should the Lord grant you any. Even if He does not, we should always praise Him for His great goodness in bestowing them on others.

The thoughts of Heaven and the happiness of the saints encourages and cheers us to go on in joy to the goal that is set before us. While we are still on this earthly journey, it is good for us to know that God speaks with us, and teaches us about himself, causing us to love Him for His immense goodness and infinite mercy.

Why All Souls do not Receive Certain Favors

I feel sure that displeasure at the thought of God bestowing these graces on other souls shows a lack of humility and love for one's neighbor. Why should we not feel pleasure for a brother receiving divine favors? It certainly does not deprive us of our share. Should we not rather rejoice at God manifesting His greatness wherever He chooses? Sometimes our Lord purposely does this for the sake of showing His power, as He said when the Apostles questioned whether the blind man whom He healed had been born blind because of his own or his parents' sins. God does not bestow these favors on special souls because they are more holy than others who don't receive them. He does it to manifest His greatness—as in the case of the Apostle Paul and Mary Magdalene—so that we may glorify Him in His creatures.

Reasons for Speaking of These Favors

People may say such favors are impossible and it is best not to offend the weak in faith by continuing to speak about them. It is better that they don't believe us than for us to stop telling those souls who do believe us. The souls that believe will rejoice and endeavor to love God more for His favors because He is so mighty and so great.

23

There is no danger here of shocking those for whom I write when I speak of such matters, because they know and believe that God gives even greater proofs of His love. I am certain if any of you doubt the truth of this, God will never allow you to learn it by experience, because He wants no limits to be set on His work. Therefore, never discredit them due to your unbelief.

The Entrance of the Castle

Now let us return to our beautiful and delightful castle and discover how to enter it. This may seem strange. The castle is the soul; clearly no one has to enter it because it is in the person himself. We might as well tell someone to go into a room he is already in. There are, however, different ways of dwelling in the castle. Many souls live in the courtyard outside the building where the sentries stand, neither caring to enter further, nor to know who dwells in that most delightful place or what is in the rooms it contains.

Entering Into Oneself

Some books on prayer advise the soul to enter into itself. Let me explain what that means. I was recently told by a great theologian that souls without prayer are like bodies that are paralyzed and lame, having hands and feet they cannot use. In the same way, there are souls so infirm and accustomed to thinking of nothing but earthly matters, that there seems no cure for them. It appears impossible for them to retire into their own hearts, because they have become accustomed to living outside the castle with reptiles and other creatures, and they imitate their habits. Though these souls are by their nature richly endowed and capable of communion with God himself, yet their case seems hopeless, and unless they endeavor to understand and remedy their most miserable plight, their minds will become bereft of movement—just as Lot's wife became a pillar of salt for disobeying God's command not to look back at Sodom.

Prayer

As far as I can understand, the gate by which we enter this castle is prayer and meditation. I do not allude more to mental than to vocal prayer, because if it is prayer at all, the mind must take part in it. If a person neither considers who he is, what he is asking for, or the holy God to whom he is speaking, though his lips may utter many words, I do not call it prayer. Sometimes because of practice, a person may pray devoutly without making all these considerations, if they are accustomed to entering God's presence in this manner. The custom of speaking to Almighty God as casually as we speak to another person—not caring if the words are suitable, but simply saying the first thing that comes to mind, and learned by repetition—cannot be called prayer. God grant that no Christian may address Him in this manner.

I trust God will prevent any of you from doing so. Our habit of conversing about spiritual matters is a good preventive against such evil ways.

Those Who Dwell in the First Mansion

Let us speak no more of these crippled souls who are in a most miserable and dangerous state, unless the Lord bids them rise as He did the paralyzed man who had waited more than thirty years at the pool of Bethesda.

We will now consider the others who at last have entered the area around the castle. They are still very worldly, yet they have some desire to do right, and at rare times commend themselves to God's care. They think about their souls every now and then. Although very busy, they pray a few times a month with their minds generally filled with a thousand other matters—for where their treasure is, there is their heart also. Still, they occasionally cast aside these cares, realizing for their own good the state of their souls, and that they will never reach the gate by the road they are following.

Entering the First Rooms

Finally they go through the gate and enter the first rooms in the basement of the mansion. To their dismay, they are surrounded by numerous reptiles that disturb their peace and prevent their seeing the beauty of the building. Still, it is a great gain that these persons have found their way at all.

Difficulties of the Subject

If you think that all this does not concern you, because by God's grace you are further advanced, please be patient with me; I can explain myself on some spiritual matters concerning prayer in no other way. May our Lord enable me to speak directly to the point on this most difficult-to-understand subject, because I have no personal experience of such graces. Anyone who has received them will know how impossible it is to avoid touching on subjects that, by the mercy of God, will never apply to us.

CHAPTER 2

Describes the hideous appearance of a soul in grievous sin as revealed by God. This chapter contains important points on self-knowledge and humility, etc. Provides an explanation of the mansions.

Before going further, I wish you to consider the state that grievous sin brings this magnificent and beautiful castle—this pearl of the East, this tree of life, planted beside the living waters of life that symbolize God himself. No night can be so dark, no gloom, or blackness can compare to its obscurity. Suffice it to say that the sun in the center of the soul that gave it such splendor and beauty is totally eclipsed, though the spirit is as fitted to enjoy God's presence as is the crystal to reflect the sun.

Sin Prevents the Soul from Gaining Merit

While the soul is in grievous sin nothing can profit it. None of its good works merit an eternal reward because they do not proceed from God as their foundation. By Him, and by Him alone, is our virtue real virtue. The soul separated from Him is no longer pleasing in His eyes; by committing a grievous sin instead of seeking to please God, it prefers to gratify the devil, the prince of darkness, and share his blackness. I knew a person to whom the Lord revealed in a vision the result of a grievous sin. She felt no one who realized its effects could ever commit it and would suffer unimaginable torments to avoid it. This vision gave her a great desire for all to grasp this truth. Therefore, I beg you, to pray fervently to God for sinners who live in blindness and do deeds of darkness.

The Soul Compared to a Tree

In a state of grace the soul is like a well of clear and transparent water from which flow only streams of clearest crystal, rising from the River of Life where it is planted and rooted like a tree. The waters of grace nourish it, keep it from withering from the drought, and cause it to bring forth good fruit; otherwise it would produce neither leaves nor fruit. By contrast, the soul by sinning withdraws from this stream of life, grows beside a black, foul-smelling pool that can produce nothing but disgusting and unwholesome fruit.

Notice that it is not the fountain and the brilliant sun that lose their splendor and beauty, for they are placed in the very center of the soul where they cannot lose their luster. This soul is like a crystal in the sunshine that has had a thick, black cloth thrown over it, so no matter how brightly the sun may shine the crystal can not reflect it.

Disorder of the Soul in Sin

O souls, redeemed by the blood of Jesus Christ, take these things to heart, have mercy on yourselves. If you realize your pitiable condition, how can you keep from removing the darkness from the crystal of your souls? Remember, if death should take you now, you would never again enjoy the light of this Sun. O Jesus! how sad a sight must be a soul deprived of light. What a terrible condition the chambers of this castle are in. How unruly must be the senses—the inhabitants of the castle, those blind, unrestrained magistrates, governors, and stewards, the powers controlling the soul. The soil that this tree is planted in is the devil's domain; how can it produce anything but evil? A man of great spiritual insight once told me he was not so much surprised at such a soul's wicked deeds as he was astonished that it did not commit even worse sins. May God in His mercy keep us from such great evil, for nothing in this life is as evil in comparison and if unchecked delivers us over to evil eternally.

Vision of a Sinful Soul

This is what we must fear and pray to God to deliver us from—because we are weakness itself, and unless He guards the city, in vain shall we labor to defend it.

The person I spoke of also said she learned two things from the vision given to her. The first was a great apprehension of offending God for fear of the consequences, so she earnestly pled with Him to preserve her from falling into sin. Secondly, it was a mirror to teach her humility, for she saw that nothing good in us springs from ourselves, but comes from the waters of grace where the soul abides like a tree planted beside a river, and from the Sun that gives life to our works. She understood this so vividly that on seeing any good deed performed by herself or by other people, she at once turned to God—without whose help she well knew we can do nothing—and burst forth into songs of praise to Him. After this experience when she did anything good, her only thought was of God not herself.

Profit Learned by These Lessons

The time which I have spent reading or writing on this subject will not have been lost if it has taught us these two truths; though learned clever men know them perfectly, women's reasoning power sometimes lacks clarity on this subject without spiritual help. Perhaps this is why our Lord has suggested these comparisons to me. May He give us grace to profit by them.

Prayer Required

These hard to understand spiritual matters are difficult to explain. Therefore, I may say much that is superfluous, and even alien to the subject, before coming to the point. Please be patient with me, as I must be with myself while writing what I do not fully understand. I often take a piece of paper to write, not knowing what I will say, nor how to begin to say it. No doubt I need to do my best to explain these spiritual subjects to you, for we know how beneficial prayer is for our souls. The laws of our Order require us to pray many hours a day, yet tell us nothing about how it applies to us, or about what work God has done in our souls in response to our prayers.

It will be helpful to you as I present this teaching by using various explanations, to consider this heavenly edifice within us, so little understood by men, though they often are close to comprehending it. Our Lord gave me grace to understand some of these matters when I wrote on them before, yet I believe I have more light now, especially on the more difficult questions. However, I do not understand the subject well enough to keep from saying much that is already well known.

Beauty of the Castle

Now let us turn at last to our castle with its mansions and many rooms. You must not think of a suite of rooms placed in succession, but fix your eyes on the keep [the stronghold or innermost fortified part of the castle], the court inhabited by Almighty God. Like the kernel of the palmetto fruit that has several rinds which must be removed before coming to the edible part, this most important chamber is surrounded by many others. However large, magnificent, and spacious you imagine this chamber to be, you cannot exaggerate it. The capacity of the soul is beyond all our understanding, and the Sun within this palace enlightens every part of it.

Self-Knowledge

A soul that gives itself to prayer, either much or little, should on no account be kept within narrow bounds. God has given it great dignity, so permit it to wander at will through the rooms of the castle from the lowest to the highest. Let it not force itself to remain for a very long time in the same mansion, even that of self-knowledge. Be advised, however, that self-knowledge is indispensable, even for those whom God takes to dwell in the same mansion with himself. Nothing else, however elevated, can perfect the soul like self-knowledge, because it never forgets its own nothingness.

Let humility be always at work, like the bee at the honeycomb, or all will be lost. Remember, the bee leaves its hive to fly in search of flowers, and the soul should cease thinking of itself and rise in meditation on the grandeur and majesty of its God. The soul will learn its own wickedness better this way—instead of by self-contemplation—and it will also be freer from the reptiles that enter the first room where self-knowledge is acquired. Although the practice of self-examination is a wonderful grace from God, too much is as bad as too little. Believe me; by God's help we shall advance more by contemplating His divinity, than by keeping our eyes fixed on ourselves, poor creatures of earth that we are.

Self-Knowledge Gained by Meditation

I do not know if I have put this clearly enough. Because self-knowledge is of such consequence, I would not have you careless with it, though you may be lifted to Heaven in prayer. Nothing on earth is more needful than humility. Therefore, I repeat not only a good way but the best of all ways, instead of rushing into the castle by any room, enter the castle the first time by the room where humility is practiced. If this is the right and safe way to enter, why would we choose any other? In this room of humility we will get to know God by beholding His greatness. By His purity our baseness will be revealed to us, and by His humility we will find how very far we are from being humble.

Advantages of Such Meditation

Two advantages are gained by this practice. First, it is clear that white looks far whiter when placed near something black, and on the contrary, black never looks so black as when seen beside something white.

Secondly, our understanding and our will become more noble and capable of good in every way when we turn from ourselves to God. It is harmful never to raise our minds above the mire of our own faults. I described how murky and foul the streams are that spring from the source of a soul in grievous sin. This is not the same case, it's only a comparison. When we are continually absorbed in contemplating the weakness of our earthly nature, we will never escape from weakness, timidity, and cowardly thoughts.

Thoughts such as: "I wonder if people are noticing me? If I follow this course will harm come to me? Do I dare to

31

begin this work? Would it not be presumptuous to do so? Is it right for one with all my faults to speak on sublime spiritual subjects? Will people not think too well of me if I make myself an exception? Extremes are bad, even in virtue—sinful as I am I shall only fall lower. Perhaps I shall fail and be a source of scandal to good people. A person such as I am has no need of peculiarities."

Christ Should be Our Model

Unfortunately, what loss the devil must have caused to many a soul by such thoughts as these! The soul concentrated on self thinks such ideas, and many others of the same sort arise from a lack of understanding true humility.

This comes from not understanding our own nature. Self-knowledge becomes so warped that unless we take our thoughts off ourselves, these and many worse fears will threaten us. Therefore, I maintain that we should fix our eyes on Christ, our only good. There we will learn true humility and our minds will be elevated so that self-knowledge will not make us base and cowardly.

Although only the first, this mansion contains great riches and such treasures that if the soul learns to elude the reptiles dwelling here, it cannot fail to be further advanced. Terrible are the wiles and schemes the devil uses to hinder people from realizing their weakness and detecting his snares.

The Devil Tries to Snare Beginners

From personal experience I could give you much information as to what happens in these first mansions, I will only say, however, that you must not think there are only a few, but a number of rooms for souls to enter in many different ways and always with good intentions. The devil is so angry at this that he keeps legions of evil spirits hidden in each room to try and stop the progress of Christians, who since they are ignorant of this, he hopes to trap in a thousand ways. He cannot so easily deceive souls that dwell nearer to God as he can beginners still absorbed in the world and its pleasures, who are eager for its honors and distinctions. In bondage to their souls, the senses and the powers bestowed on them by God are weak. Such souls are easily conquered even though they desire not to offend God.

Our Strength Must Come From God

Those conscious of being in this state must as often as possible have access to Almighty God and Jesus Christ who will do battle for them, for we creatures possess little strength for self-defense. In every stage of life all our help must come from God. May He in His mercy grant it to us—otherwise what a miserable life we will lead. As I have often spoken more fully in other writings on the ill that results from ignoring the need of humility and self-knowledge, I will speak not more about it here, though it is of primary importance. God grant that what I have said may be useful to you.

Sin Blinds the Soul

You will notice that the light from the King's palace hardly shines in these first mansions. Although they are not as gloomy and black as the soul in grievous sin, they are like twilight when it is difficult to see clearly. This is not the fault of the mansions themselves; it is because of the number of snakes, vipers, and venomous reptiles from outside the castle blocking the light, and preventing those souls who enter the room from seeing the light. It is like a person entering a chamber full of brilliant sunshine with their eyes clogged and half closed with dust. The room itself is light, but the person cannot see because of the condition of their eyes. In the same way, these fierce and wild beasts blind the eyes of the beginner, so that he sees nothing but the beasts.

Worldliness

It seems to me that the soul—though not in a state of grievous sin—is so worldly and preoccupied with earthly riches, honors, and affairs, that even if it wishes to enter into itself and enjoy the beauties of the castle, it is prevented by these distractions and seems unable to overcome the many obstacles. It is most important to withdraw from all unnecessary cares and business, as much as is compatible with the duties of one's life, in order to enter the second mansion. This is so essential that; unless done immediately, I think it is impossible for anyone to ever reach God's chamber or even to remain where he is without great possibility of losing what he has gained, and risk being bitten by the very venomous creatures surrounding him.

Worldly Things Invading Religious Cloisters

What about persons like us in religious convents and monasteries that have already freed ourselves from worldly things? What if we fall back into sin by our own fault and return into all this chaos? Though we are blessed by God by being free from some of the things of the world, our own inner imperfections could cause us to fall back into this wretched state. May God deliver us from them.

Assaults of the Devil

Do not trouble yourselves with cares that do not concern you. You will notice that the struggle with demons continues through nearly all the mansions of this castle. However, in some of them, the guards, the powers of the soul, have strength for the battle, but we must be keenly on the watch for the wiles of the devil lest he deceive us in the form of an angel of light. He creeps in with great subtlety in numerous ways and does much harm if we are unaware of him.

Examples of the Devil's Wiles

As I have said, the devil works like a file, secretly and silently shaping its way. For instance, say a sister has a certain longing for penance and has no peace except during penance. If she has been advised by a spiritual advisor not to continue in such austerities, but does not heed the advice, loses her health, and can not fulfill her responsibilities, the devil has gained, not the Lord.

Another person is very zealous about religious perfection and magnifies every tiny fault in others, causing them to be wary of her. Unfortunately, she does not seem to notice her own faults because she is so busy watching others. Even though her intentions were for perfection, they were turned to the perfection of others and not herself. Who gained? The devil.

Perfection is Gained by Love

The devil's chief aim is to destroy our love for God and to hamper the love we feel for each other. True perfection consists in the love of God and in our neighbor. If we strive to keep these commandments, the more perfect we will be.

Indiscreet Zeal

I have already spoken of how indiscreet zeal can adversely affect others, so I will not enlarge on it again, but I will remind you of the importance of mutual affection. Our souls may lose peace and even disturb others if we are always criticizing the trivial action of others.

Danger of Detraction

The last thing I will say on this subject is the danger of being detracted by others' actions. If you truly see someone who has a spiritual problem, pray for them. If possible speak to them about it and urge them to seek advice from their spiritual counselor. Look to your own progress and always be on guard against the enemy of our souls.

THE SECOND MANSION

CHAPTER 1

*This chapter teaches the importance of perseverance in
order to enter the last mansions, and of the fierce war the
devil wages against us. How essential it is to take the right
path from the very beginning of our journey.
Gives a method of action, that by its power,
produces the desired result.*

How let us consider who the souls are that enter the
second mansion, and what they do there. I will not
dwell on this subject, for I have taught on it fully elsewhere,
but having a bad memory I cannot avoid repeating myself. If
I could state my ideas in another form, they might not weary
you. However, as many books as there are on this subject,
we do not get tired of reading them.

The State of Their Souls
In this part of the castle we find souls that have begun
to practice prayer. They have realized the importance of not
remaining in the first mansion and have gone on to the second
mansion, yet they often lack the desire and determination to
stop sinning—a very perilous state to be in.

Their Sufferings

By God's great grace, however, they have escaped being bitten by the vipers and poisonous creatures that surround them by understanding the need of avoiding them. In some ways these souls suffer a great deal more than those in the first mansion, although they are not in as much danger. Their newly acquired understanding of their present danger has caused them to have great hope of entering further into the castle. The reason I say they suffer more is that those in the first mansion in earlier stages of understanding are like deaf-mutes, distressed at being unable to hear or speak. While these in the second mansion find it more difficult, because they can hear, but cannot speak. At the same time they do have the advantage of not being deaf.

They Cannot Rid Themselves of Imperfections

These souls hear our Lord calling them as they approach nearer to His chamber in the center of the castle. He proves to be a loving neighbor, even though they are still engaged in the amusements, business, pleasures, and vanities of this world. While in this state, these souls continually fall in and out of sin as they try to avoid being tripped up by the venomous, vicious, and dangerous, creatures living among them. Yet the pity and compassion of the Lord never ceases to call them to seek Him. His sweet voice encourages the soul to desire to do His bidding, and if unable to follow His bidding at once, the soul becomes disconsolate and suffers more than if it could not hear Him.

How God Calls These Souls

I do not mean that God's communications and inspirations received in this mansion are the same as those I will describe later. Here God speaks to souls through words from others, by sermons or good books, and in many other ways. Sometimes He calls souls by means of sickness or troubles, or by some truth He teaches during prayer. Lukewarm as these souls may be in seeking Him, God holds them very dear.

Perseverance is Essential

Do not think lightly of this first grace—God calling you closer to Him—nor be downcast if you have not responded immediately to His voice. He is gracious and willing to wait many days and many years for us, especially when He sees our perseverance and the desire to obey in our hearts. Perseverance is the first essential, for with it we are sure to profit greatly. However, because the soul can now hear, it will resist the demons, as they will assault the soul fiercely in many different ways. When the soul was in the first mansion it was mute and deaf and offered feeble resistance like one who has lost all hope of victory. Now the soul will resist the demon onslaught.

Temptations of the Devil

Now that the understanding has made the soul more vigilant and alert, it cannot avoid hearing the fighting and cannons firing around it. Now the devil has set the reptiles on the soul—the reptiles being thoughts about the world and its joys unending. They whisper thoughts reminding them of the high esteem friends, relatives, and man held them in. They tell them that trying not to sin is not necessary and may even injure their health. The evil spirits will try and place many blockages to keep them from progressing closer to God.

Delusion of Earthly Joys

What turmoil the demons cause in the poor soul. How unhappy it feels. How uncertain whether to go forward or retreat to the first mansion. On the other hand, reason shows the soul the delusion of overrating worldly things, and faith fulfills the promise of victory over all worldly things. Memory, among other things, reminds the soul of how earthly joys end, by recalling how those who lived for earthly things and wealth died suddenly and were soon forgotten. Those dead were once very prosperous, but are now buried beneath the ground—the prey of worms, as men of every circumstance, rich and poor, pass by their graves. The mind recalls many such incidents.

God Alone to be Loved

The will is inclined to love the Lord and longs to return to Him, for He continually gives so many proofs of His love. His faithful love and constant presence with the soul give it life and being. The understanding of His love shows the soul that for as many years as it may live, it could never have a better friend then God. The world is full of falseness, and the worldly pleasures pictured by the devil in the mind are nothing more than troubles, cares, anxieties, and annoyances, in disguise.

Reasons for Continuing the Journey

Reason convinces the soul not to seek outside the castle for peace, security, and riches, for it is inside the castle that the soul may enjoy at will all the innumerable blessings of the Lord. Where else can the soul have all its need supplied? Where else—but the Lord God— can it find a host who will give it all the desires of its heart? Unless it is like the prodigal son—choosing to go astray, living with, eating with, and feeding the swine.

Surely these arguments are strong enough to defeat the devil's wiles. But, oh, how the strength of worldly habits and the examples of others who practice them can ruin good intentions. Our faith is so weak that we trust more in what we see with our physical eyes, and feel with our senses, than we do the word of God. Even though we know that trusting in ourselves and the world brings us to no good end. All this is from the venomous thoughts I described. Unless we are very careful it will deform the soul as the sting of a viper poisons and swells the body.

Warfare of the Devil

When this happens, great care is needed to cure it. Only God's mercy prevents its resulting in death. The soul passes through severe trials at this time, especially when the devil perceives from a person's character and behavior that they are likely to make very great progress. He will then cause his demons to press harder to try and force the soul to retreat. At this point there is great need to call out to God to intervene and prevent the soul from being deluded into forsaking its journey to Him. The soul must look unto Christ Jesus, the author and finisher of its faith; it will then be encouraged to persevere in its journey and withdraw from the evil one.

Choice of Friends

It is of the utmost importance for the beginner to associate with those who lead a spiritual life, not only with those in the same mansion, but also with others who have gone on further into the castle. This will aid greatly and encourage the soul to go on and join them. The soul should resolve never to submit to defeat, or return to the first mansion, for the devil will retreat if he sees the soul is staunchly determined to pay no attention to all he may offer.

Vigilance Required

Let the Christian be vigilant; let him not be like those who lay down to drink from the brook before they went to battle, looking only at the cool water, not watchful for the enemy (Judges 7:6). Let him resolve to go forth to combat the host of demons, fully convinced that there is no better weapon than the cross. I have already said, and because it is of such importance, I repeat, let no one think only of the rewards to be reaped. This would be a very dishonorable way to continue

41

the journey into this large and stately castle. If the building is built on sand, it will soon fall down (Matthew 7:26). Souls who do this will continually suffer from discouragement and temptations, for in these mansions no manna rains. Further on the soul will be pleased with all that comes, because it will desire nothing but what God wills.

Strength is in the Christ of the Cross

How absurd and shameful it is that we who are newly born and have little strength and a thousand obstacles, drawbacks, and imperfections within ourselves, complain of feeling dryness and a lack of sweetness in our prayers.

Do not act this way; look instead unto Jesus Christ, His death on the cross, His resurrection, and the new life He lives within us. If we would be like Him, we must deny ourselves and pick up our cross daily (Luke 9:23). Most happy and content are we who follow after our Lord and Savior, Christ Jesus. The life that Jesus Christ gives us will empower us to endure all trials set before us; He knows what is best for us and we should not presume to advise Him in what we need. This is of vital importance: The soul allowing its will to be conformed to the will of God shall have the strength to overcome all the trials and obstacles on its journey. The soul has no need of some mysterious formula in conforming to and doing the will of God. If we start with the idea that God should follow our will and lead us in the way we think best, we will have no firm foundation for our spiritual edifice to stand on.

Falls Should Raise Us Up

Let us endeavor to do our best. Beware of the poisonous reptiles that is to say the bad thoughts and the dryness in prayer often permitted by God to teach us to trust in Him. Look instead to Him as our strong tower, giving us strength and encouragement to press on. If perchance we feel the reptiles sting, it will teach us to be more on guard; and if we occasionally lapse into sin, do not lose heart and cease trying to advance. God will turn even our falls to our good. The combat, trials, and temptations effectively teach us, as no other way can, the injury we receive from a life of dissipation. Can any evil be greater than what we find in the world? What peace can we find elsewhere, if we do not have it within us? The powers of the soul will try to convince us that they are our friends and that they will give peace. We have learned that is a lie. Christ said, "Peace I leave with you, my peace I give unto you: not as the world giveth, give I unto you. Let not your heart be troubled, neither let it be afraid" (John 14:27).

Trust and Perseverance

By the blood our Lord shed for us, I implore you who have not yet begun to enter this castle within themselves, to stop this warfare against God's call. I beg those already on the right path to persevere, and not to let the warfare turn them back from it. Let them realize that retreat is worse than the ruin of a fall. Trust in God's mercy, trusting nothing of themselves. Then they will see how God will lead them from one mansion to another, bringing them to a place where these wild beasts can no longer touch them. Then, even in this life, they will enjoy far greater happiness than they are even able to desire.

Recollection

As I said at the beginning of this work, I have explained elsewhere how you should behave when the devil disturbs you. I also told you the habit of recollection is not to be gained by force of arms, but with calmness. That will enable you to practice it for a longer period of time.

43

Why We Must Practice Prayer

The practice of prayer is highly important, but it does not require you to forsake your necessary responsibilities. Prayer is a necessity to prevent us from constantly falling into temptation. I will say no more now, except that I think it very helpful for those of you who are beginners to seek counsel with those who have already walked this journey.

Meditation Kindles Love

Some of you may even think it better not to start this journey and would rather stay outside the castle. Remember what Christ said about Himself: "I am the way, the truth, and the life: no man cometh unto the Father, but by Me" (John 14:6). If we never look to Him and reflect on His sacrifice for us how can we ever hope to know Him and understand what He did for us? What value is there in faith without works? And what are they worth if they do not spring from the goodness of Christ Jesus? How will we know our Lord if we do not meditate on Him? May He give us grace to understand Him as we pray to Him. Prayer is the constant necessity in our lives to know Him better and to live for Him all our days.

THE THIRD MANSION

CHAPTER 1

This chapter deals with the souls who have overcome the challenges in the first two mansions. The dangers of looking back on the past life. The characteristics of those in the Third Mansion. Examination of the dry prayer life. Humility. Being lukewarm. Walking in the fear of the Lord. Giving all to God.

To those souls who, by the mercy and help of God, have conquered their enemies and persevered to the third mansion, we can say nothing more appropriate than this. " I will lift up mine eyes unto the hills, from whence cometh my help. My help cometh from the LORD, which made heaven and earth" (Psalm 121: 1-2).

We may well call these souls blessed, for unless they turn back now, they are pressing on in their journey on the right path. Now we can clearly see how important it was for them to conquer their former struggles, because I am convinced that our Lord will never cease to keep them secure as they walk this path.

The Insecurity of Life

I am wrong in saying security, for there is no security in this life. Understand that in such cases I always imply, "If they do not cease to continue as they have begun." What misery to live in this world. The world is like men whose enemies are at the door; they must not lay aside their weapons even while sleeping or eating, for they are always in fear lest their foe should enter their fortress by some breach in the walls. "O my Lord, and my all, how can You wish us to prize such a wretched existence? We can not stop longing and begging You to take us from it, unless it were for the hope of losing it for Your sake or devoting it entirely to Your service. Most importantly we know it is Your will that we live. That being so, as St. Thomas said, 'Let us die with Thee!' For to be away from You is but to die again and again, haunted as we are by the dread of losing You forever."

Danger of Falling Back into Sin

That is why I say we ought to ask our Lord to grant us the gift of some day dwelling in safety with the saints. With such fears, what pleasure can we enjoy when our only pleasure is to please God? Remember, many saints have felt this as we do, and were even more zealous, yet fell into grave sin. We cannot be sure that God would stretch forth His hand to raise us from sin again, and to do such penance as they performed requires extraordinary grace.

St. Teresa Mourns Her Past Life

Truly, I feel such terror as I tell you this that I know not how to write it, nor even how to go on living when I think upon it, as I very often do. Beg the Lord with me to abide in me; otherwise, what security could I feel after a life so badly spent as mine has been?

Do not grieve at knowing this, for I have often seen you troubled when I spoke about it. You wish that my past had been a very holy one—in that you are right; I wish the same myself. But what can be done now? I wasted it entirely through my own fault. I have no right to complain that God withheld the help I needed to fulfill your wishes. It is impossible for me to write this without tears and great shame. Especially when I realize I am explaining these matters to those capable of teaching me. What a hard task obedience has laid upon me. God grant that as I obey Him it may be of some service to you. Beg Him, therefore, to pardon me for my miserable overconfidence in myself.

Reliance Upon His Mercy

God knows that I have nothing to rely upon but His mercy, for I cannot change the past. I have no other choice but to flee to Him, asking forgiveness through Jesus Christ His Son.

The Necessity of Godly Fear

Still I must give you one warning. Be not overconfident because you are nuns. King David was very holy, yet you know what Solomon became. Therefore, having left the world and the horrors it holds, do not rely on your enclosure within the convent, your life of penance, good behavior, or on your continual prayer and constant communion with God. All that is good, but it is not enough, as I have already said. To remove all fear, meditate on this text and often recall it. "Praise ye the LORD. Blessed is the man that feareth the LORD, that delighteth greatly in his commandments" (Psalm 112:1). I do not recall what I was saying, and have digressed much, for when I think of myself my mind cannot soar to higher things. It is like a bird with broken wings.

Characteristics of Those in
the Third Mansion

So, I will leave this subject for now to return to what I began to explain about the souls that have entered the third mansion. God has shown them no small favor, but a very great one in enabling them to pass through the first difficulties. Thanks to His mercy. I believe there are many such people in the world that desire not to offend the Lord, even in small unintentional sins. They love penance, spend hours in meditation, use their time well, do works of charity to their neighbors, dress and speak modestly, and govern their households well. This is greatly to be desired. There is no reason not to allow them entrance to the last mansions, nor will the Lord deny them if they desire to go on. This is the right attitude for receiving all His favors.

The Rich Young Man

O Lord Jesus, can anyone who has already passed through these main difficulties say that he does not desire this great blessing of entering the last mansions? No, no one can. We all say we desire it, but there is need of more than that for the Lord to possess entire dominion over the soul. It is not enough to say we want to go on, anymore than it was enough for the rich young man when our Lord told him what he must do to be perfect. "Jesus said unto him, If thou wilt be perfect, go and sell that thou hast, and give to the poor, and thou shalt have treasure in heaven: and come and follow me" (Matthew 19:21).

Since I began speaking on the dwelling rooms I have had that Scripture on my mind. We are exactly like the rich young man if we say we desire to go with our minds and not with our hearts.

Dryness in the Prayer Life

This, among others is cause for dryness in prayers. I am not speaking of specific interior suffering that gives intolerable pain from this trial to so many devout souls through no fault of their own, for our Lord always delivers them with great gain to themselves. I do make exception for the people who suffer from depression and other infirmities, for in these cases as in all others, we must leave judgment to God.

Reasons for Dryness in the Prayer Life

Such souls know that nothing would induce them to commit a sin, not even unknowingly; they conduct their lives and riches well. Therefore, they will not accept being excluded from the presence of our Lord. They consider themselves to be His love slaves, and that they are. An earthly king may have many subjects, yet not all of them enter his court. To these I say enter, enter your inner self, pass beyond the thought of your own petty works that are no more. Even beyond the works Christians are required to perform, find your sufficiency in being God's servants. Do not pursue so many things that you catch nothing. Look at the lives of the saints who have already entered the Divine Presence and you will see the difference between them and yourself.

Humility

Do not ask for what you do not deserve, nor should we ever think we have done so much for God that we deserve the reward of the saints, for we have offended Him. Humility, humility. I do not know why, but I am always tempted to think that persons who complain much of dryness in prayer must be wanting in virtue. However, I am not speaking of severe inner sufferings that are far worse than a desire for fruitful prayer.

Being Lukewarm

Let us try ourselves to see if we are passionate or lukewarm in our desire to go on in this journey. Perhaps I should say, let our Lord try us. He knows very well how to do so, though we often pretend to misunderstand Him. In examining those souls who have progressed to this state, let us consider what they do for God and we shall see immediately what little right we have to complain to God. If we turn our backs on Him and go away sorrowfully like the rich young man in the Gospel of Matthew, when the Lord tells us what to do to be perfect, what can God do? He must reward us in proportion to our love for Him. This love must not be the fabric of our imagination; we must prove it by works. Not that the Lord has any need of our works; He only dismisses us to manifest our willingness to do charitable works.

Give All to God

It seems to us that we who have taken the religious habit of our own will, and renounced worldly things and possessions, have already given all to God. Though they may have only been the nets of St. Peter, they seemed much to us, for they were our all. This is an excellent outlook if we continue in it and do not return even in our thoughts or desires to the company of the reptiles of the first rooms. No doubt in our persevering in this poverty and detachment of soul, we shall obtain all for which we strive. But mark this, it must be on one condition—that we think of ourselves as unprofitable servants, and that we do not think that our Lord is obligated to grant us any favors. We are deeply in His debt for all we have received and will receive from Him.

Our Debt to Him

We can do so little for our wondrous Lord. He created us, He died for us, He gives us our life being. We should be exceedingly happy for all that He has favored us with already, without asking for more mercies and favors. I do not like to use this expression, yet it is so: during all the time He was on this earth, He lived to serve us and died for us.

Consolations and Dryness

Meditate carefully on the things I have said, perhaps somewhat confusedly, though I do not know how to explain them any better. Our Lord will help you to understand them, so that you may reap humility from your dryness, instead of the anxiety that the devil strives to cause. I believe that where true humility exists—even though God may never bestow comfort—He gives a peace and resignation that make the soul happier than are others who experience a more fruitful prayer time. These comforts, as you have read, are often given by God to the weakest souls, who I am quite sure would not exchange them for the perseverance of Christians serving God in dryness of prayer. We do love comfort more than the cross. "O Lord, You know all truth; test and establish us that we may know ourselves."

CHAPTER 2

Continues on the subject of dryness in the prayer life and the results of it. How the Lord tests those who are in the mansions.

I have known some, in fact, many souls who have reached the third mansion and are in times of dryness of prayer, and are apparently living a well-ordered life, both in body and mind. They seem to have gained mastery over this world, or are at least they are detached from it; yet if the Lord sends very moderate trials to them, they become so disturbed and disheartened that I am concerned and anxious about them. Advice is useless, for having practiced virtue for so long they think themselves incapable of teaching it and prefer to believe they have abundant reasons to feel miserable.

Trials Show Us Our Weaknesses

The only way to help them is to show them compassion, for one cannot help but feel sorrow for people in such an unhappy state. You cannot reason with them, because they are fully convinced they are acting perfectly when they suffer for God's sake, and cannot be made to understand they are acting imperfectly. They may be advanced in their walk with the Lord, but this attitude pushes them further into error. It is easy to understand why they should have trials during this time; however, they should be more concerned about why they are having the trials instead of complaining about them. God wishes His elect to realize their own shortcomings, and often removes the awareness of His presence for a short time to allow us to see what we really are.

Humility Learned by Our Faults

Souls quickly learn the reason for their trials when God does this; they see their faults very clearly. Discovering how quickly they are overcome by slight earthly trials is very painful to them. I think that God shows them great mercy, for though their behavior may be faulty, they gain in humility. This is not true of the souls in the early mansions. They believe their conduct is saintly and want others to agree with them. I will give you some examples that will help us to understand and cause us to test and try ourselves instead of waiting for God to test and try us. It is far better to prepare and examine ourselves beforehand.

Love of Money

Example: A rich man without son or heir loses part of his property, but still has more than enough money for himself and his household. If this misfortune causes him so much anxiety that he feels he will have to beg for his bread, how can our Lord ask him to give up all things for His sake? This rich man may well tell you the reason he is so anxious about losing part of his property is that he wanted to give it to the poor.

I believe God would prefer this rich man to keep peace of soul, though he is unable to give the property to the poor. If this man cannot resign himself to surrender to the will of God, let him beg our Lord to grant it to him and receive God's will in an approved manner.

Example: Another person has more than sufficient means to live on, when an opportunity presents itself for acquiring more property. If it is offered to him, by all means, let him accept it. If, however, the person receives the property offered to him and it causes him to work even harder to gain more and more, however good his intention may be—for I am speaking of people who lead prayerful and good lives—he cannot possibly enter the mansions close to the Lord.

Bearing Contempt

Example: Persons who are accustomed to receiving great admiration and respect may be very upset if they feel they have not been properly and sufficiently acknowledged for their good deeds to the public. God may give them grace to bear it well, for He loves to see virtue upheld in public. God will not condemn it because these persons may have served Him faithfully, and He, our supreme God, is exceedingly good to us all. These people will still experience their self-righteous feelings for some time. Alas, have they not meditated on the pains our Lord Jesus Christ endured and how good it is for us to suffer, and have they not even longed to do so? They wish everyone was as virtuous as they think they are. God forbid that they consider the public to blame for their troubles and give credit for all good things to themselves.

Perfection Requires Detachment

You may think that I have wandered from the subject, and that all this does not apply to you. You own no property, nor do you endeavor to gain any. All the examples I have mentioned apply to all of us, because within each one of the examples there will be something that pertains to our own condition. These examples will show you whether or not you are really detached from all you own and if you can control you passions.

Virtue and Humility are the Essentials

Believe me, the question is not whether we are very religious and practice all good works, but whether we practice all goodness and submit our will in all things to the will of God. The object of our lives must be to do what He requires of us. Not our will, but His be done. If we have not yet attained to this, let us be humble. As I said before, "humility is the ointment for our wounds." God may withhold healing for a time, but God, who is our physician and healer will come and will heal us.

The penances performed by the persons I spoke of are a regular part of their lives. They valued these penances very highly because they wish to serve the Lord by doing them. I do not blame them for that wish; they are very careful in their penance, lest they should injure themselves. Never fear, they will not kill themselves; they are far too sensible. Their love is not strong enough to overcome their reason. I wish it were. Then they would not be satisfied to creep along on their journey to God at a pace that will never bring them to their journey's end.

Seek Rapid Progress

We seem to ourselves to be making progress, yet we become weary, for we are walking through a mist, and will be fortunate if we do not become lost. Do you think if we could travel from one country to another in eight days that it would be all right to spend a year on the journey—through snow, wind, a flood of water, and bad roads? Would it not be better to get it over with all at once, for it is full of dangers and serpents? There are many instances I can give you of this. God grant that I have passed beyond this state myself, for often I think I have not.

Leaving Cares and Concerns in God's Hands

All things obstruct our paths while prudence rules our actions. We are afraid of everything and therefore fear to make progress. It is impossible to reach the inner chambers by someone else making the journey for us. For the love of God, let us exert ourselves leaving our concerns and fears in His hands. We must pay no attention to the weaknesses of our nature that try and keep us from going on. Let those who look after our bodies do the caring for them. Too much concern for our health will not improve it, this I know well. Let our concern and care be to hasten our journey to His presence.

Emphasis on Humility

I know too that our bodies are not chief factors in the work we have before us. They are an accessory. Humility in extreme is the principal point. I believe the passionate desire for humility helps our progress. It may seem that we have made little progress, and that others are advancing more rapidly than we are. Well, that is the way it should be. Not only should others consider us slower to advance than they are, but we should endeavor to allow them to think so. If we act in this manner, our soul will do well. Otherwise we shall make no progress and remain the prey of a thousand troubles and miseries. The way will be difficult and wearisome without self-denial, weighed down as we are by burdens and frailties of human nature. We will suffer these no more in the mansions close to the Lord.

Comforts Increase
in the Fourth Mansion

In this third mansion the Lord never fails to repay our services. He is a just and merciful God who always bestows on us far more than we deserve and gives us greater happiness than we had in earthly pleasures and amusements. I think He grants few consolations here, except to occasionally persuade us to prepare ourselves to enter the last mansions by showing us what they contain.

Differences Between Comforts
and Sensed Devotions

There may seem to you to be no difference except in name between sensed devotions and comforts, and you may ask why I distinguish between them. I think there is a very great difference, though I may be mistaken.

This will best be explained when I write about the fourth mansion and speak of the consolations received there from our Lord. The subject may seem pointless, yet may prove useful by urging souls who know what each mansion contains to persevere in their journey through them. It will comfort those whom God has advanced to this point, and encourage others who thought they had reached the summit to go on by God's help if they are humble.

Perfection Grows in Love,
Not Rewards or Comforts

Those who do not receive these comforts may feel despondency. That is unnecessary, for perfection does not consist of comfort given, but in our greater love to God. God will reward us in proportion to this and to the justice and security of our actions. Perhaps you may wonder why I teach on these interior graces and their nature. I do not know, I only know they bade me write this. I must obey those in authority over me, not argue or question them, which I have no right to do.

Joy at Seeing Others Rewarded

I assure you that before I received these gifts from God or the understanding by experience, I didn't expect to receive them. Rightly so, for I probably would have felt reassurance and even imagined that I was pleasing to God in spite of the condition of my soul at the time. When I read of the gifts and mercies that our Lord grants to His servants, I was delighted and praised Him fervently. If someone like me acted this way, how much more would the humble and good glorify Him.

Graces are to be Desired

I think it is worthwhile to explain these things, even for the sake of moving a single soul to praise God just once. It also shows us what wondrous gifts and delights we lose out on by not continuing our journey to God.

When these joys are from God, they come laden with love and strength that not only aid the soul on its way, but also increases the good works and virtuous actions. Do not even imagine that it is unimportant for you to try and obtain these graces. If you are without blame the Lord is just, and what He may refuse in one way He will give you in another. His ways are secret and very mysterious and no doubt He will do what is best for you.

Obedience and Direction

Souls who are brought this far by the mercy of God, will benefit from their prompt obedience and will very likely climb higher. Though they may not be in a convent or monastery, it would benefit them if they would seek a spiritual advisor to guide their ways and decisions to help keep them from error. They should not choose someone who is overly prude in actions, but should choose someone who has learned how to be free from the things of the world and who can teach them by experience.

It is encouraging to see that trials that seemed to be impossible to submit to, are possible by others who bear them beautifully. Their flight makes us want to soar like baby birds taught to fly by their elders. They can not fly very far at first, but little by little they imitate their parents. I personally know the great benefit of encouragement.

No matter how determined such persons may be not to offend the Lord, they must not expose themselves to temptation, for they are still very near the first mansions that promise an easy retreat. Their strength is not yet established on a solid foundation like that of the souls more experienced in these trials. These souls whose experiences have taught them, now know how little there is to fear of the desires for the world and its pleasures. In contrast, those just beginning their journey, though they may be very zealous, might succumb to the attacks made upon them by the devil who knows well how to injure and discourage us.

Misguided Zeal for Others

We must look at our own faults, not those of others. People who are extremely proper in themselves are often shocked by everything they see. However, we might just learn a great deal from those we tend to criticize. We may think we have better manners and actions than others seem to; however, this is not of primary importance. The most important thing is that we do not insist that others must follow in our footsteps, or take it upon ourselves to give spiritual advice when we are not advanced enough in spiritual matters ourselves. Being zealous for the good of other souls without complete guidance from God may lead one's own self astray. It is sometimes better to be silent, living in prayer and hope for others. Our Lord will care for the souls belonging to Him and He may grace us by urging us to pray for them. May He be forever blessed!

THE FOURTH MANSION

CHAPTER 1

*This chapter teaches the difference between sweetness,
tenderness, and comfort in prayer. Saint Teresa explains
how advantageous it was for her to realize that the
imagination and the understanding are not the same thing.
This chapter also addresses the problem of wandering
thoughts during prayer.*

It is of primary importance that I commend myself to
the Holy Spirit and beg Him to speak for me as I begin
writing this chapter on the fourth mansion. The nature of
these matters demand that I speak with a surety of knowledge
and clarity of speech. These matters are of a supernatural
nature, and difficult to explain clearly without the help of
the Holy Spirit. When the Holy Spirit helped me with these
matters fourteen years ago I wasn't as advanced in knowledge
as I am now. I believe I now possess more light about the
gifts that God grants some souls, but having the light and
explaining it clearly is the challenge. I pray that this will be
useful to you, and that the Lord will enable me to do so with
great clarity.

consalations & spiritual delights

Supernatural Gifts

The fourth mansion is very beautiful and much closer to the center of the castle where our Lord dwells. The things that are seen and heard in the fourth mansion are mystical, and difficult to explain clearly to those inexperienced in supernatural matters. People who have received and enjoyed these gifts, especially those who have received them to any great extent, will easily understand me.

Temptations Bring Humility and Merit

Apparently souls must have dwelt for long periods of time in the former mansions before entering the fourth mansion—probably for a longer period of time in the third mansion, the last one we examined. Yet, there is no fixed rule; God gives gifts to whom He wills, and moves us on, when, where and how He wills. The choice is always His, and His choices are always right.

The poisonous reptiles very rarely come into this mansion, and if they do enter, they will do more good than harm. The reason I say that is, it may be better for the reptiles to come into this mansion to make war on a soul in this state of prayer, for if the soul is not tempted, the devil might injure it more by whispering deception about the divine gifts. The soul constantly absorbed in God would lose out on the benefits of the temptations provided by the opportunity to face the challenges of the enemy and overcome them. I am not confident that this constant absorption in God is genuine when it remains always in the same state, nor does it seem possible for the Holy Spirit to dwell constantly within us, to that extent during our time on earth.

Sweetness in Devotion and Natural Joy

I will now describe, as I promised, the difference between sweetness in prayer and spiritual comfort. It seems to me that what we receive through meditation and petitions in prayer to our Lord may be termed sweetness in devotion. It is by the grace of God that we receive this natural sweetness in devotion, for without Him we can do nothing. We receive sweetness in devotion primarily from the good works we perform, a just reward for time well spent. By contrast, many temporal matters give us the same pleasure, such as coming into a large fortune, suddenly meeting with a dearly loved friend, or succeeding in any important or influential affair that gives us worldly acclaim.

Another example would be the response of one who had been told in error their husband, brother, or son, was dead and later found they were actually alive. I have seen people weep from such happiness, as I myself have done. I consider both these joys, and those we feel in religious matters, to be natural ones. There is nothing wrong with the former ones, yet those produced by devotion spring from a more noble source; in short, they begin in ourselves and end in God. Spiritual comforts, on the contrary, come from God and our nature feels them and rejoices keenly in them, far more keenly than in worldly ones.

Sweetness in Devotion

Oh, Lord Jesus, how I wish I could explain this point more clearly. It seems to me that I can perfectly distinguish the difference between the two joys, yet I do not have the skill to make myself understood. May God grant it. I remember a verse we say at the end of one of the Psalms, "*Cum dilatasti cor meum*"—it translates to "When Thou didst dilate my heart." [Today we might say, Oh Lord, You have enlarged my heart with Your sweet love.]

To those with much experience, this sufficiently shows the difference between sweetness in prayer and spiritual comforts. Those less experienced will require more explanation. The sweetness in prayer or heartfelt devotion I mentioned does not dilate the heart, but generally appears to narrow it slightly.

A person who shows great joy at working for God, also may shed tears of sorrow produced by the passions. I know little about the passions of the soul. If I knew more I could write about them more clearly and could better define what comes from a sensitive disposition and what is natural. I passed through this state myself, but I do not clearly remember the feelings I experienced. Learning experiences that result in retained knowledge are to be greatly desired.

Saint Teresa Shares a
Personal Experience

My own experience of this delight and sweetness in meditation was when I began to weep over the Passion of Christ. I could not stop weeping until I had a severe headache. The same thing occurred when I grieved over my sins. I consider this a great grace from our Lord. I do not know if one of the states of prayer is better than the other, but I do wish I could explain the difference more clearly between the two. I believe the tears and the good desires experienced during this time are a result of one's own nature. If this is the case, the feelings experienced will bring us to God. Heartfelt devotion is very desirable if the soul is humble enough to understand that it is not more holy because of the feelings sensed, because they do not always arise from love even though they are also a gift of God.

Increasing our Love for God

These feelings of devotion are most common with souls in the first three mansions, who commonly use their understanding and reason in meditation. This is good for them, for they have not been given grace for more. However, it would be helpful to them if they meditated on the wonder of God, who He is, and what He has done for them. That will create a desire in them to honor and glorify Him. Meditation on Him and His goodness will certainly bring forth great rejoicing in them—then worship from their inner being is sure to stir their hearts and produce sweet praise pouring from their lips. The Lord loves us to worship and praise Him like this, and He will increase our desire to continue in this manner. When God increases the desire to worship Him in this manner, the soul should be obedient to the desire and not set it aside for other forms of dutiful prayer and meditation they are accustomed to. Having spoken on this subject elsewhere, I will say no more at this time.

I only wish to warn you that to make rapid progress and reach the mansions you wish to enter, it is not as essential to think much as to love much. Love is a powerful force that emanates from us, changing circumstances, others, and ourselves. Thinking and meditating cause us to grow in knowledge in our inner being. If I asked you to define love, you may not know how to describe it, and that doesn't surprise me. Love is not only great sweetness, and heartfelt devotion, but it is a fervent determination to please God in all things. Love is also avoiding anything that would offend Him, praying for the glory and honor of His Son, Christ Jesus, our Savior, and for the growth of His Church. These are the signs of love—but you should not be concerned if your thoughts wander to other things—all is not lost.

Distractions

Often when we are meditating and in prayer, our thoughts will wander. Don't despair, all is not lost. This happens to all of us. I, myself, have sometimes been troubled by this turmoil of thoughts. I learned by experience, little more than four years ago, that our thoughts or imagination are not the same as our understanding. I questioned a theologian on this subject—who told me it was true—it was a great consolation to me.

Understanding is one of the powers of the soul, so it puzzles me to see how slow the understanding is at times.

65

In comparison, when God unites us to Himself and controls the imagination, it takes flight, soaring to such great heights that we seem detached from our bodies. It is a mystery to me to see that while to all appearances the powers of the soul are occupied with God, the imagination is wandering elsewhere.

Distractions Do Not Destroy
Divine Union

O Lord, take into consideration all that we suffer through our ignorance. Our thinking is in error if we think the only thing we need to know is to keep our thoughts fixed on You. We need to understand that we have much to learn and should consult with those who can instruct us. We pass through terrible trials because we don't understand our own nature, refusing good advice because we think it is faulty. This is the cause of suffering for many people, particularly the unlearned. They complain of inner trials, become depressed, lose their health, and even give up prayer altogether because of a lack of recognition of the interior world within themselves.

We cannot stop the revolution of the heavens as they rush with great velocity on their course; neither can we control our imagination. When the imagination wanders we think that all the powers of the soul follow it. We think everything is lost, and that time spent in God's presence is wasted. Meanwhile, the soul is entirely united to Him in the innermost mansion, while the imagination is in outer areas of the castle warring with multitudes of wild and venomous creatures, and gaining victories in its warfare. The devil is working his wiles, but we do not need to be disturbed, nor give up prayer. As a rule, all our understanding and troubles come from misunderstanding our own nature.

Saint Teresa's Physical Distractions

While writing this I am thinking of the loud noise in my head that I mentioned in the introduction. That noise has made it almost impossible to obey the command given me to write this. It sounds as if there rushing waterfalls in part of my brain, and in another part—drowned by the sound of the waters—are the voices of birds singing and whistling. This tumultuous noise is not in my ears, but in the upper part of my head, where, I've heard it said, the superior part of the soul resides. I have long thought it might be true, for the flight of the spirit seems to take place from this part with great speed. This is not the proper time or place to explain the cause of these distractions. Perhaps God will remind me to explain this when we get to the latter mansions. It may be that God has sent this suffering in my head to help me understand the matter; the reason I say that is, the noises do not interfere with my prayer, nor my speaking with you. The great calm, love, and desires in my soul remain undisturbed and my mind is clear.

How to Treat Distractions

How then can the superior part of the soul remain undisturbed if it resides in the upper part of the brain? I cannot explain it, but I am sure I am speaking the truth. This noise disturbs my prayer when unaccompanied with ecstasy, but when it is ecstatic I do not feel any pain, whatever the intensity. I would suffer very much if I was forced to cease praying because of these infirmities. We should not be distressed because of our thoughts, nor allow ourselves to worry about them. If they are from the devil, pay no attention to them and he will let us alone. If they are one of the many frailties we suffer because of Adam's sin, let us be patient and suffer them for the love of God. We may wish to be where no one despises us, but for now we are earthbound creations of God on our journey to Him. I think no earthly scorn or suffering can try us so severely as these struggles within our souls. We can bear all uneasiness and conflict as long as we have peace in ourselves. If the uneasiness and conflict are because of an obstacle within ourselves, the trial will prove to be long, painful, and almost insufferable, until we are made aware of the problem within and deal with it.

Disregard Distractions

"Continue to draw us to you, O Lord; show us the reason for our miseries and deliver us from them." We know God delivers us from them when we reach the last mansion, and by His grace I will show you. Not everyone is so violently distressed and assaulted by these weaknesses as I have been for many years. Because of my wickedness it seems that I strive to take punishment on myself. Since I suffer so much in this way, you may also suffer the same way, so I will continue to explain the subject to you with more clarity. The suffering is inevitable; therefore do not let it disturb or grieve you. Just continue to work with all your intelligence and willpower.

Necessity of Self-Knowledge

I should remind you that these troubles annoy us more or less according to the state of our health or different circumstances in our lives. Remember what I have taught you about wandering thoughts while you are in prayer. God wishes us to learn by the circumstances we go through in our lives. We need to understand ourselves and recognize our part in the problems caused by our wandering imagination, our self-nature, and the devil's temptations.

CHAPTER 2

*Explanation by comparison of what divine comforts are.
How we should prepare ourselves to receive them, as
opposed to seeking to obtain them.*

I have wandered from my subject again. I forgot what I
was speaking about. My responsibilities and ill-health often
force me to stop writing for awhile. This writing may seem
somewhat disconnected, for my memory is extremely bad
and I have no time to read what I have written. I fear even
the things I understand are expressed somewhat vaguely.

I believe I said the spiritual comforts are occasionally
connected to the emotions. These feelings of devotion
may produce uncontrolled sobbing. I have also heard that
sometimes they may cause a compression of the chest,
hysteria, and uncontrollable actions violent enough to cause
bleeding from the nose and other painful effects. I have no
comment on that, never having experienced anything of the
kind myself. But there appears some cause for comfort if it
ends in the desire to please God and to enjoy His presence.

Effects of Divine Consolations

What I call divine consolations, or have termed elsewhere
"the prayer of quiet," is a very different thing, as those who
by God's mercy have experienced and attested to.

Example: The Two Fountains

To make the subject clearer, let us imagine we see two
fountains with basins that can be filled with water. I can find
no simile more appropriate than water to explain spiritual
things, for I am very unlearned and have a poor brain to
help me. I love the element of water so much that I have
studied it more attentively than many other things. God, in
His great wisdom, has no doubt hidden secrets in all things

69

He created that we will greatly benefit by knowing. Indeed, I believe that even in the tiny ant—the smallest creature He made—there are more wonders to be comprehended. The two basins are filled in different ways, the one with water from a distance flowing into the basin through many pipes and waterworks. The other basin is built near the source of the spring itself and fills quite noiselessly. If the fountain is large and the basin is full of water, it overflows in a great stream that flows continuously. No machinery is necessary to make it flow, nor does the water run through aqueducts to this fountain.

Two Kinds of Prayers Symbolized

Such is the difference between the two kinds of prayer. The water running through the aqueducts resembles prayer that is obtained by meditation. We gain it by our thoughts, by meditation on created things, and by the labor of our minds. In other words, it is the result of our own endeavors, and has the outer physical effects that I spoke of, while profiting the soul. The other fountain, like divine comforts, receives the water from the source itself, being God. When God desires to bestow on us any supernatural gifts, we experience the greatest peace, calm, and sweetness in the inmost depths of our being. I do not know how or why.

Divine Consolations Shared
by Body and Soul

This joy is not like earthly happiness immediately felt by the heart after being filled to the brim with delight. This kind of joy overflows throughout all the mansions of the soul and faculties, until it finally reaches the body. Therefore, I say it comes from God and enters us. Whoever experiences it will find that the whole physical part of our nature shares in this delight and sweetness. While writing this I have been thinking of the verse "*Dilatasti cor meum*," "Thou hast dilated my heart"; it declares that the heart is dilated. This joy does not appear to me to originate in the heart, but in some more inner part in the depths of our being. I think this must be the center of the soul, as I have since learned and will explain later.

I discover secrets within us that often fill me with wonder. How many more must there be that are unknown to me? "O my Lord and my God, how astounding is Thy grandeur! We are like so many foolish young people. We think we know something of You, yet it must be comparatively little, for there are profound secrets hidden within You. We do not even understand the profound secrets within ourselves that are but nothing compared to the secrets within You. Yet how great are Your mysteries that we do know and can learn as You reveal them by the study of Your word and Your works."

The Incense within the Soul

To return to the dilation of the heart, the dilation is begun by the celestial waters in the depths of our being. The waters appear to dilate and enlarge us internally and benefit us in an unexplainable manner. The soul itself does not even understand how it receives, but it is conscious of what may be described as a certain fragrance, as if within its innermost depths there is a brazier of hot coals sprinkled with perfume Although the soul never sees the flame, and does not know where it is, still it is penetrated by the warm scents that are sometimes even perceived by the body.

Understand me; the soul does not feel any real heat or smell any scent. It is something far more subtle—which I have used this metaphor to explain. Let those who have never experienced it believe that it does occur. The soul is conscious of it and feels it more distinctly than can be expressed. This is not an experience that we can produce from ourselves—clearly it could not come from base human nature—it comes from the pure gold of God's divine wisdom.

I may be contradicting what I wrote elsewhere—for it was done about fifteen years ago—and God may have given me clearer insight into the matter during that time. I also may be entirely mistaken on this subject, but I would never willfully say what is not true. No, by the mercy of God, I would rather die a thousand times than tell a falsehood. I speak of the matter as I understand it, and I believe in this case the will must in some way be united with the will of God. The effects on the soul and the subsequent behavior of the person is the best test to show if this prayer is genuine or not.

Graces Received in this Prayer

Our Lord bestows a very notable grace on the soul who receives this gift, and another even greater if it does not retreat from its onward journey to God. Many of you are longing to enter into this state of prayer at once, and that is good. The soul cannot understand the value of the graces given to it by God, and how they draw the soul to a closer relationship with Him, unless they have a strong desire to obtain this gift. I will tell you what I know about it, setting aside certain cases where God has given this gift for His own reasons, which we have no right to question.

Such Favors Should not be Sought After

I encourage you to practice what I have taught in the preceding mansions, especially humility, for the humble soul is very dear to God and He always hears their petitions. The first proof that you possess humility is that you do not think you deserve these graces and gifts from God, nor will you as long as you live. You ask me: "How shall we receive them if we do not try to gain them?" My answer is that there is no surer way to obtain them than the one I told you—practice the things I taught in the first mansions, dwelling long and always on humility, and do not try by your own efforts to receive them any other way for the following reasons:

1. The first is that the most important means of obtaining these gifts is to love God with pure motivations and no other reason.

2. The second is, it is somewhat a lack of humility to think our poor service to Him can win so great a reward.

3. The third is taht the real preparation for them is to desire to suffer and imitate our Lord Jesus Christ rather than receive these gifts, for we have all offended Him.

4. The fourth is that our holy God has not promised to give us these gifts in the same way He gives us eternal glory if we keep His commandments. We can all be saved without these special graces, for He knows better than we do what is best for us and all those who love Him sincerely. I know for a certainty—being acquainted with some who walk by the way of love, and seeking only to serve Jesus Christ and Him crucified—I would neither ask for, nor desire this grace for them, even begging Him not to give it to them during this life on earth. That is a fact.

5. The fifth is that we labor in vain thinking this water flows through aqueducts made by man and trying to obtain it for ourselves. If the spring does not give it, we toil in vain. We can meditate, try our very best, and even shed tears to gain it, but we cannot make the water flow. God alone gives it to whom He chooses, often when the soul is least thinking about it. We are His; let Him do what He will with us, leading us where He will. If we are really humble and die to our self-life, we shall receive all He has for us and more than we could ever imagine or desire.

CHAPTER 3

This chapter is a continuation on the gifts of prayer to the soul on its journey to God.

The effects of divine gifts are very numerous, and before describing them I will speak of another kind of prayer that usually precedes the divine gifts. I do not need to say much on the subject, having written about it in the Second Mansion. This is a kind of prayer I believe to be supernatural. There is no reason to lie down, or close the eyes, as it does not depend on anything exterior. The eyes will involuntarily close and the soul will be in solitude. Without any labor on one's own, the temple will appear for the soul in which to pray. The senses and surroundings seem to lose their hold, and the spirit gradually regains its lost sovereignty. Some souls say it enters into itself, others say it rises above itself. I can say nothing of these opinions and shall endeavor to speak on the subject as I understand it.

You will probably grasp my meaning, although I may be the only one who understands it. Let us imagine that the senses and powers of the soul— that I compared in my allegory to the inhabitants of castle— have fled and joined the enemy outside. After long days and years of absence from the castle and realizing how great has been their loss, they return to the castle but cannot manage to re-enter. They are no longer traitors, but they still have their hard-to-break evil habits, so they wander around outside the castle.

The Shepherd Recalls His Flock
into the Castle

God— who holds His court within the castle— sees their good intentions, and out of His great mercy desires them to return to Him. Like the good Shepherd, He plays sweetly on His pipe to those outside. Although they barely hear it—like the lost sheep—they recognize His call, wander no longer, and prepare to enter the castle. So strong is this Shepherd's power and care for His flock, that they immediately shed the worldly cares that misled them and re-enter the castle.

This Recollection is Supernatural

I believe I have never taught this matter so clearly before. To seek God within ourselves avails us far more than to look for Him among creatures. Saint Augustine tells us how he found Almighty God within his own soul after having long sought Him elsewhere. This recollection helps us greatly when God bestows it upon us. Remember, do not think you will gain it by thinking of God dwelling in you, or by imagining Him as present in your soul. Recollection is a good practice and an excellent kind of meditation based on the fact that God resides within us; it is not, however, the gift of prayer, because by divine help everyone can practice prayer.

Sometimes before the soul has begun to think of God, the powers of the soul find themselves within the castle. I do not know how they entered nor how they heard the Shepherd's pipe. The ears heard no sound, but the soul is keenly conscious of a sense of a memory they once experienced. I cannot describe it more clearly.

Supernatural Recollection is Preparation for Higher Favors

I think I read somewhere that the soul in that state is like a tortoise or sea urchin that retreats into itself. Those who said this, no doubt, understood what they were talking about, but these creatures can withdraw into themselves at will. But this is not within the power of the soul, unless God gives the grace. In my opinion, God only bestows this favor on those who have the desire to renounce the world, but their state of life has so far not permitted them to do so.

He calls them to devote themselves to spiritual things, and if they allow His power to act freely, He will bestow still greater graces on those He begins calling to a higher life. Those who enjoy this recollection should thank God fervently, for it is of the highest importance for them to realize the value of this gift. Their fervent gratitude prepares them to receive still more important graces. Some books advise us to keep our minds at rest, waiting to see what He will work in our souls. Unless He suspends our faculties, however, I do not understand how we are to stop our thinking faculty without doing ourselves more harm than good. This very point has been often debated by those learned in spiritual matters. I confess my need of humility in having been able to yield to their opinion.

Mind Must be Active Until God Calls It to Recollection by Love

Someone told me of a certain book written on the subject by saintly Friar Peter of Alcantara. I should have submitted to his decision, knowing that he was a competent judge. In reading his decision, I found he agreed with me that the mind must be active until called to this state of prayer, although he stated it in other words. I may be mistaken, but I rely on it for these reasons.

Firstly, he who reasons less, and does least, does most in spiritual matters. We should make our petitions like beggars before a powerful and rich Emperor. Then with downcast eyes, humbly wait. When He secretly shows us He hears our prayers, it is good to be silent. Because He has drawn us into His presence, it would be good to keep our minds at rest. If the King makes no sign of listening or of seeing us, it is no longer necessary to wait in silence with minds at rest.

In this case dryness would greatly increase, and the imagination would be made more restless than before by its very effort to think of nothing. Our Lord wishes us at such a time to offer Him our petitions and to place ourselves in His presence. He knows what is best for us.

Soul Must Abandon Itself
into God's Hands

I believe that human efforts avail nothing in these matters, for the Lord appears to reserve them to Himself by setting limits on our powers. In many other things like penances, good works, and prayers, with His help we can help ourselves, as far as human weakness allows.

Secondly, any painful effort does us more harm than good, because these interior operations are sweet and peaceful. By painful effort I mean any forcible restraint we place on ourselves, such as holding the breath. It is far better to abandon our souls into the hands of God. Let Him do as He chooses with us, forget our will and resign ourselves entirely to His will.

Thirdly, the very effort to think of nothing excites our imagination even more.

Fourthly, because we render to God the most true and acceptable service by caring only for His honor and glory. We should forget ourselves, our advantages, comforts, and happiness. How can we be self-oblivious by keeping ourselves under such strict control? How can we do this if we are afraid to move, think, or leave our minds enough liberty to desire God's greater glory, and rejoice in the glory He possesses? When the Lord wants the mind to rest from working He employs it in another way. He gives it light and knowledge far above any obtainable by its own efforts and absorbs it entirely into himself. Then, though it knows not how, it is filled with wisdom that it could never gain for itself by striving to suspend the thoughts. God gave us faculties for our use, each of them will receive its proper reward. Therefore, do not let us try to force them to sleep, but permit them to do their work until divinely called to something higher.

Recollection Prayer and
Distractions in Prayer

In my opinion when God chooses to place the soul in this mansion it is best for it to do as I advised. Endeavor without force or disturbance to keep free from wandering thoughts. However, no effort should be made to suspend the imagination entirely from arming, because it is good to remember God's presence and to consider who He is. If transported out of itself by its feelings, well and good, but do not try to understand what is passing within the imagination. This favor is bestowed on the will which should be left to enjoy it in peace. In this kind of prayer, the soul makes no effort towards it, for the mind ceases to think at all. I explained why this occurs during this spiritual state elsewhere.

When I first started teaching on the fourth mansion, I told you I had mentioned divine consolations before the prayer of recollection. The latter should have come first because it is far inferior to consolations. Recollection does not require us to give up meditation, nor to cease using our intellect. In the prayer of quiet, when the water flows from the spring itself and not through conduits, the mind ceases to act. It is forced to do so, but it does not understand what is happening, and wanders around in bewilderment finding no place to rest. Meanwhile the will—entirely united to God—is much disturbed by the tumult of thoughts. No notice should be taken of them or they will cause the loss of a great part of the favor the soul is enjoying. Let the spirit ignore these distractions and abandon itself in the arms of divine love. His Majesty will teach it how to best act, which consists in its recognizing its unworthiness of so great a good, and occupying itself in thanking Him for it.

Liberty of Spirit Gained by Consolations

In order to teach the prayer of recollection, I passed in silence over the effects and symptoms to be found in souls thus favored by God. Divine consolations evidently cause a dilation or enlargement of the soul that may be compared to water flowing from a spring into a basin that has no outlet. It is constructed to increase in size and proportion to the quantity poured into it. God seems to work the same effect by this prayer—besides giving many other marvelous graces— to prepare the soul to contain all He intends to give it. After interior sweetness and dilation the soul is less restrained in God's service and possesses much more liberty of spirit. It is also no longer distressed by the terror of hell. It is more anxious than ever not to offend God, but it has lost servile fear and feels sure that one day it will possess its Lord. It does not dread the loss of health by austerities, because it believes there is nothing it can not do by His grace. It is more desirous than ever to do penance. Greater indifference is felt toward sufferings because faith is stronger and it trusts that if born for God, He will give the grace to endure them patiently. Indeed, such a one at times even longs for trials, because of a most ardent desire to do something for His sake. As the soul better understands the divine Lord, it realizes more vividly its own baseness. Divine consolations show it the vileness of earthly pleasures. By gradually withdrawing from them it gains greater self-control. In short, the soul's virtues are increased and it will not cease to advance in perfection unless it turns back and offends God. If the soul did this, it would lose everything, no matter how far it had progressed.

The Soul Must Be Watchful

It should not be thought that all these effects are produced merely by God's having shown these favors once or twice. They must be received continually, because it is on their frequent reception that the whole welfare of the soul depends.

I strongly urge those who have reached this state to most carefully avoid all occasion of offending God. The soul is not yet fully established in virtue, but is like a new-born babe first feeding at its mother's breast. If it leaves her will it not die? I greatly fear that when a soul that God has granted this favor discontinues prayer—except under urgent need—that soul will go from bad to worse.

The Devil Especially Tempts Such Souls

I realize the danger of such a case because I had the grief of witnessing the fall of persons I knew because they withdrew from God. The Lord who sought them with so much love made himself their friend, as He proved by the way He treated them. I urgently warn such persons not to run the risk of sinning, because the devil would rather gain one of these souls than many our Lord has not granted such graces. Satan tries to destroy the work of God by putting grievous temptations on souls who serve God, because they are a desired conquest. The loss is even greater, because the souls who fall often take others along with them.

False Trances and Raptures

Pray that God will keep you from falling away and from all forms of pride. The devil sometimes offers counterfeits of these gifts, but they are easily detected, as the effects are exactly contrary to those of God's genuine gifts. Although I have spoken of it elsewhere, I wish to warn you of a special danger those who practice prayer are subject to, particularly women who are the weaker vessels and more liable to error. Some people cannot receive these gifts from God merely because they will be spiritually overcome by them; when feeling any inner joy, their bodies—if not accustomed to the physical manifestations—may fall into slumber or spiritual sleep, abandoning themselves to this state as if intoxicated.

The more they lose self-control, the faster they slip into this state. Some feel that this is a trance and call it one, but I call it nonsense; it does nothing but waste their time and injure their health.

Treating Those Suffering
from this Delusion

This state has lasted with certain people for eight hours, during which time they were neither conscious nor had any thought of God. They are cured by being made to eat and securing a restful sleep. They owe their recovery to those who understand this state and know how to bring someone out of it. Prior to this help, people—though not intentionally—would deceive themselves and others by thinking this was a spiritual state. I feel quite sure the devil is hard at work in these cases to serve his own ends.

It should be known that when God bestows such favors on the soul—though there may be seeming unawareness and relaxation of the body and mind—it is not shared by the soul, which at the time feels great delight when sensing its nearness to God. The soul continues in this state for a very short time and experiences no exhaustion or pain. I advise any of you who experience the possibility of slipping into a trance to control the mind by diverting the attention elsewhere. The length of time in prayer should not be more than a few hours as the body needs food and rest to restore its strength. Great care must be taken to keep the body rested and nourished during long times of prayer, otherwise it may become a detriment to the health. The soul should not be concerned about not spending extended periods of time in prayer; love for the Lord grows also by constant awareness of His presence. The Lord, according to His will, may give additional grace for longer periods of prayer.

Risks of Delusion in this Mansion

There are some people whose minds and imaginations are so active that they say they see whatever they think about. That is very dangerous. Perhaps I may teach more on this later on. I have dwelt at length on this mansion, for I believe it to be a very important one that most souls enter. When the natural is combined with the supernatural, the devil has more opportunities to do harm, even more so in this mansion than in the later ones, for God does not allow him many opportunities in those. May God be forever praised! Amen.

THE FIFTH MANSION

CHAPTER 1

*The union of the soul with God in prayer. How to be sure
we are not deceived in this matter.*

Oh, my friends, how shall I describe the riches, treasures,
and joys contained in the fifth mansion! It would
probably be better if I did not try for they are impossible
to depict. The mind can not conceive them, nor is there any
comparison to portray them, because all earthly things are
too vile to serve the purpose. O Lord, I pray you will send
me light from heaven that I may give it to Your servants. By
Your grace, some will often enjoy these delights, their only
desire being to please You. Let not the devil, in the disguise
of an angel of light, deceive them in any way.

Strive for Contemplation
I said some would enjoy these delights, but in reality
there are very few who never enter this mansion. Some of
them come in often, and some seldom come in, but almost
all of them at least gain admittance into these rooms. I
think certain gifts I am about to describe are bestowed on a
few. However, all who arrive at the portal of this mansion
will receive a great blessing from God, for many are called,

but few are chosen. All we who wear the holy habit of the Carmelites are called to prayer and contemplation. This is the primary objective of the Order we belong to. The Lord Jesus Christ and His Apostles taught us to seek first the kingdom of God—the most precious pearl—and all these blessings would be added unto us.

It often pains me how little we care to prepare our souls so that our Lord may reveal the precious jewel of contemplation to us. Outwardly we may appear to desire the blessing of contemplation, but inwardly we have far more to be done before we attain it. Rouse yourselves—and since some foretaste of Heaven may be had on earth—beg our Lord to give us grace not to miss it by our lack of preparation and desire to receive it. Ask Him to show us where in our heart it resides. Ask Him for strength of soul to dig until we find this hidden treasure that lies buried in our hearts. Oh Lord, enable me to show it to them. I said "strength of soul" that you might understand that strength of body is not essential when our Lord chooses to withhold it. The Lord does not make it impossible for anyone to obtain these riches but is content that each of us should do our very best to do so. Blessed is our just and holy God.

Physical Effects of the Prayer of Union

If you seek this treasure, hold back nothing from God. Give Him your all, for in proportion to what you give, the same proportion your blessing will be. Do not imagine that the prayer of union with God is like the prayer of quiet, in which a sort of drowsiness occurs. I call it drowsiness because the soul seems to slumber, being neither quite asleep nor wholly awake. In the prayer of union the soul is asleep, fast asleep to itself and the physical world. In fact, during the short time this state lasts, it is deprived of all feeling whatsoever, unable to think on any subject no matter how much it may want to. No effort is needed to suspend the thoughts. The soul may know it can love, but not how, or whom it may love, not what it desires. In essence it has died entirely to the world, to live more truly than ever to God. This is a delightful death, for the soul is deprived of the faculties it uses in the body. It also seems to have left its mortal covering to abide more entirely in God. So completely does this take place that I do not know how the body retains sufficient life to continue breathing. If it is breathing, it does so unconsciously.

Amazement of the Intellect

The mind entirely concentrates itself on trying to understand what is happening, which is beyond its power. The mind is so astounded that unless consciousness is lost or no movement is sensed, the person may be compared to one who faints from shock.

Prayer of Union and
of Quiet Contrasted

Oh, the mighty secrets of God. Never should we become weary of trying to explain them. I would write a thousand foolish things if only one would be to the point and cause us to praise God more. I said this prayer caused no drowsiness in the mind; on the other hand, in the prayer of quiet described in mansion four, until the soul has gained much experience, it doubts what really happened to it. Was it imagination, or was it asleep? Did it come from God, or the devil as an angel of light? The mind feels very wary of what happened, and from what source—as well it should, for we are easily deceived in this state.

There is little chance of poisonous reptiles entering during this state. However, agile little lizards will try to slip in, but they can do no harm, especially if they remain unnoticed. They are trivial little fancies of the imagination—irksome as they may be—they cannot enter the fifth mansion. Neither the imagination, the understanding, or the memory, have the

85

power to hinder this gift. I would even venture to say, that if this is a genuine union with God, the devil cannot interfere or do harm. God is so joined and united with the essence of the soul, that the devil dares not approach, nor does he even understand the mystery.

This is certain, for it is said the devil does not know our thoughts, much less can he penetrate a secret so profound that has not even been revealed to the family of God. Oh, blessed state, in which the cursed one cannot injure us. What riches we receive while God works His works in us—neither we ourselves nor anyone else can impede Him. Is there any gift He cannot give? He is so eager to give us all He desires. You may have been puzzled at my saying "if this is a genuine union with God," as if there might be other unions. There are—not with God, but with varying forms of pride. However, when the devil transports the passionately addicted soul in his deception, the mind senses no delight, satisfaction, peace, or happiness as in God's divine union.

These heavenly comforts are above all earthly joys, pleasure, and satisfaction. The difference can only be compared to all that is good, as opposed to all that is evil. I said somewhere, that the one seems only to touch the surface of the body, the other penetrates to the very marrow: I do not believe I can express it more clearly.

Seek Competent Spiritual Advisors When in Doubt

Be wary of deception that may cause you not to be satisfied with the explanation of this subject, for spiritual matters are very hard to explain. Enough said for those who have received this grace, as the difference between divine union and any other is easy to detect. However, I will give you a clear proof that will erase your fear of deception, and your doubt of the origin of the gift. The Lord brought it back to my memory this very day; it is an unmistakable sign: In difficult questions, I always say, "It appears to me," for if I am wrong, I am most willing to submit to the judgment of theologians. Though they may not have experienced such matters, God gives them light on the subject, enabling them to recognize truth presented to them. If they are spiritually sensitive servants of God, they will never be dismayed at His mighty works, knowing perfectly well that it is in His power to perform far greater wonders.

Even if some of the marvels are new to them they will not be surprised, for having seen or read of many they know they are possible. I have had much experience dealing with spiritually sensitive people, and at a dear cost to me, I have also met with timid, half-instructed, spiritually ignorant people. I am convinced that God closes the hearts of those who do not believe the wonders He performs. Do not imitate the unbelievers: be believers, fully convinced that it is possible for God to perform even greater wonders.

Do not be concerned whether those who receive these gifts are good or wicked. As I said, He knows best and it is not your judgment. Your obligation is to serve Him single-heartedly, with humility and praise, in all His works and wonders.

Proof of Union

Let us now speak of the sign that proves the prayer of union to be genuine. As you have seen, God deprives the soul of all its senses to better imprint within it true wisdom. In this brief period of time the soul does not see, hear, or understand anything; and brief as the time is, the soul perceives it to be a much shorter time than it really is. God visits the soul in a manner that prevents all doubt when it returns from this state. The soul knows it was in Him and He was within the soul, and even though many years may pass before the soul experiences this gift again, the soul will never forget, nor doubt the experience. The prayer of union leaves definite effects on those who experience it, effects that I will refer to later on. The main point here is the conviction felt by the soul.

The Soul's Assurance of this Experience

You may ask, how can a person who is incapable of sight and hearing , know these things? I do not say that at the time it happened they saw or heard it; but they clearly perceive it afterwards—not by a vision, but by a clear certainty in their heart that only God can give. I know of someone who was unaware of God's being in all things by His presence, power, and essence, yet was firmly convinced of it by a divine experience like this. She asked a priest—who was spiritually ignorant in this area—to explain in what way God dwells within us, having no knowledge on the subject. The only thing he could tell her was God is only present in us by grace. Yet so strong was her conviction of the truth learned during the prayer, she did not believe him. She continued questioning other spiritual persons on the subject, who—to her great joy—confirmed the truth of the doctrine.

Do not mistake or imagine that this certainty of God's having visited the soul concerns any physical presence. If we do not see it, how can we feel so sure of it? I cannot answer that, except to say it is the work of Almighty God. Of that I am certain. I maintain that a soul that does not feel this assurance has not been united to God entirely, but may have received another of God's many gifts. In matters such as these, we must not seek to know how things happen. Our understanding could not grasp them; therefore, why trouble ourselves on the subject? It is enough to know that it is the all-powerful God who has performed the work. We can do nothing on our own to receive this gift, nor is our understanding of it fruitful. It is sufficient for us to know it comes from our loving God.

Divine Union is Beyond Our
Power to Attain

Concerning my words "We can do nothing on our own," I was struck by the remembrance of the words of the Bride in the Canticles: "The King brought me (or placed me) into the cellar of wine." She does not say she went of her own accord. She goes on to tell how she wandered up and down seeking her Beloved. I think the prayer of union is the "cellar" in which our Lord places us when and how He chooses, but we cannot enter it through any effort of our own. God alone brings us there and comes into the center of our souls.

In order to declare His wondrous works more clearly, He will give us no share in them, except complete abandonment of all things to Him and conformity of our wills to His. He does not need our faculties or senses to open the door to Him; they are useless and asleep. He enters the innermost depths of our soul in the same way as He entered the room where the disciples were sitting after His Resurrection and said, "*Pax Vobis*" ["Peace be unto you"], and in the same way He emerged from the sepulcher without removing the stone that closed the entrance. You will understand this more clearly when God brings the soul into the very center of His presence in the seventh mansion. Humility will keep human frailties and weaknesses before our eyes and allow us to see extreme wonders and marvels beyond our comprehension. May God be forever praised! Amen.

CHAPTER 2

*Explains the Prayer of Union using a delicate comparison.
Speaks of the effects upon the soul. Emphasis on
explanations in this chapter require careful attention.*

You may imagine there are no contents left to describe in this mansion, but a great deal remains to be told, for as I said, it contains favors of various degrees. I think there is nothing to add about the prayer of union. However, I could tell you much about the marvels the Lord works on the souls who have prepared themselves to receive them, and I will describe some of them in my own way, also the effects they have upon the soul. I will use an appropriate comparison to clarify this matter. We have no active part in this work of God within us, yet we should do much to prepare ourselves to receive this gift.

No doubt you have heard of the wonderful process only God could plan of silk-making from an egg resembling a tiny peppercorn. I have only heard of and not seen the process myself, so if the facts are inaccurate the fault will be mine. In the warm weather the mulberry trees burst forth with leaves, and a little egg that was lifeless before its food was ready, comes to life. The caterpillar nourishes itself upon the mulberry leaves until it is full grown. The caterpillar is then placed near or on small twigs where it begins to spin silk from its tiny mouth until it has made a narrow little cocoon in which it buries itself. After some time has passed, this large, ugly caterpillar leaves the cocoon in the form of a lovely white butterfly.

The Grandeur of Creation

If this process had not been seen—and only heard of as an old legend—who would believe it? Could we persuade ourselves that insects so utterly without the use of reason—

such as a silkworm or a bee—would work so industriously, and with such skill in our service, that the poor little silkworm loses its life over the task? This provides reason for meditation for all of us, for from it we learn the wonders and wisdom of God. What a blessing it would be if we knew the reason for and the characteristics of all things. It is most profitable to ponder the grandeur of creation and to rejoice in being the bride of such a wise and mighty Lord.

The Silkworm as a Symbol of the Soul

Let us return to the subject at hand. The silkworm symbolizes the soul that begins to live when it is kindled by the Holy Spirit. The soul uses the ordinary helps given by God to all and applies the remedies left by Him to His Church: such as the Bible; confession and repentance; pastors, preachers and teachers of His Word; prayer; meditation; and religious books that encourage by example from those who have walked this journey of faith. These are cures for a soul dead in sin, and for those liable to fall into temptation because of their own negligence. The soul comes to life and continues nourishing itself on this food and on devout meditation. It feeds on this nourishment during this growth process until it has reached a degree of maturity that is essential for continuing on its journey and in serving God. When the silkworm is full-grown, it begins to spin silk and build the house where it will die. In contrast, the house for the soul is Christ Jesus. I think I read or heard somewhere that our life is hid with Christ in God, and that Christ is our life.

Preparation of the Soul for God's Indwelling

By the grace of God, this shows us what we can do in preparation for the prayer of union, in making our souls a home and a dwelling place with Him. You may think I mean that we can add to or take away something from God, when I say that He is our home, and that we can help make this home and dwell in it by our own power. We can add to or take away only from ourselves, like the silkworm. The little we can do in preparation of ourselves to receive the Lord indwelt within us, is insignificant—especially in relation to what God does in us when we are united to Him and His greatness. The Lord himself is the reward for our toil. Although He has had the greatest share in it, He will join our trifling pains to the bitter sufferings He endured for us and make them one.

Mystical Death of the Silkworm

Desire this with all your heart and hasten to help build the little cocoon. Renounce self-love and self-will; have no desire for earthly things; do penance, pray, mortify self, and be obedient to perform all good works according to your understanding and the light of knowledge you have been given by God. Die, die, die to self, just as the silkworm does when it has fulfilled it purpose in creation. Then you will see God and be immersed in His greatness, just like the little silkworm is enveloped in its cocoon. When I say you will see God, I mean in the manner He manifests Himself in this kind of union.

Effects of Divine Union

Keep in mind what I said happens to the silkworm when it dies and breaks forth from the cocoon, because all I have been saying leads to this point. By means of this prayer, the soul has become entirely dead to the world, and it comes forth as a lovely little white butterfly. Oh, how great is our God! How beautiful is the soul after being immersed in God's grandeur and united closely to Him for just this short time. Indeed, I do not think it is ever as long as one half hour. Truly, the soul does not recognize itself, for it is as different from what it was as the white butterfly is from the repulsive caterpillar. It does not know how it could have deserved so great a gift, for it deserves nothing, nor does it know where the gift came from. What it does know is that it has a deepening desire to praise our Lord God and longs to sacrifice itself and die a thousand deaths for Him. It feels an insurmountable desire for great crosses to bear and would like to perform the severest penances. It sighs for solitude, longs to have all men know God, and suffers grief at seeing them offend Him.

These matters will be described more fully in the next mansion. Although they are of the same nature, they are in a more advanced state and the effects are far stronger. This causes the soul to strive for even more progress, for it will experience great things. Oh, to see the fluttering about of this charming little butterfly, although never in its life has it been more tranquil and at peace. May God be praised! It does not know where to land and rest, for everything on earth is new and not at all like what it experienced as God nourished it with the sweet wine of His grace in every sip.

Increase of Fervor and Detachment

If the butterfly—with its beautiful wings of flight—now thinks back of the work it did while it was a caterpillar—that slow weaving of the cocoon, silken thread by silken thread— could it be content to crawl as the caterpillar? Likewise, the soul in thinking of what it can do for God, seems like nothing compared to what it desires to do. The soul no longer wonders how the saints now gone on, could withstand things they suffered. The soul has learned by experience how our Lord helps transform it until it no longer seems the same in character or appearance. While formerly it feared penance, now it is strong. It needed courage before it could forsake relationships, friends, or possessions. Even though it tried to detach itself by actions and resolutions, they only served to increase the fondness for them. Now it finds any claims from them on its time a burden, fearing contact with them lest it should offend God. The world and the things of it are now tiresome to the soul, for it now realizes there is no true rest to be found in the world or in its creatures.

Trials after the Prayer of Union

I seem to have enlarged on this subject greatly, yet far more could be said. Some, on the other hand, who have received this teaching may think I have treated it too briefly. It is no wonder this pretty butterfly, estranged from earthly things, seeks rest elsewhere. Where can the poor little creature go? It cannot return to its former state of being. The same with the soul, it cannot return to from where it came—for as I told you—that is not in the soul's power to do; it is totally dependent upon God's pleasure. Alas, what fresh trials begin to afflict the mind. Who would expect this after such a sublime gift of grace? It is a fact, in one way or another, we must carry our cross all our lives. If people tell me that since they received the gift of the prayer of union they have enjoyed constant peace and consolation, I would tell them they could not have received the gift of the prayer of union. I would tell them they could never have reached that state, and at the most, if they arrived as far as the last mansion, their emotion must have been some spiritual satisfaction joined to physical debility. It might even be a false emotion caused by the devil, who gives peace for a time, only to wage fiercer war later on. I do not mean that those who reach this stage possess no peace; they do have peace to a high degree. Their sorrows—though extremely severe—are so beneficial and proceed from so good a source as to give them both peace and happiness.

Longing for Death and Zeal for God's Honor

Discontent with this world produces a painful longing of the soul to be free from it, and if the heart does find comfort, it is solely from the knowledge that God wishes the soul to remain here until He calls it home. Yet even this is sometimes not enough to reconcile the soul to its fate, for after all the gifts are received it still may not be entirely surrendered to the will of God. The comfort is that it will be fully surrendered as it continues on in its journey. Although conformed to His will at this stage, the soul feels an unconquerable reluctance to submit, for the Lord has not given it higher grace. During prayer this grief breaks forth in floods of tears, probably from the great pain it feels at seeing God offended by the soul's reluctance to submit to His will. Also, the soul may be thinking of how many souls, both heretics and heathens are lost eternally—and the worst grief of all—Christians who have turned away from God and Christ Jesus. The soul realizes the greatness of God's mercy and knows that no matter how wicked men are, they may still repent and be saved—although many seal themselves to the fate of hell by their own rashness, ignoring or not caring about the danger their souls are in.

Supernatural Zeal

Oh, infinite greatness of God! A few years ago, or maybe only a few days ago, this soul thought of nothing but itself. Who has made it feel such tormenting cares? If we tried for many years to obtain this much sorrow by means of meditation, we would not succeed.

God Alone Works this Grace

God help me! For if I considered how great a wrong it is that for long days and years God should be offended by my lack of concern for my fellow man. The lost souls are His children and my brethren. If I pondered over the dangers of this world and how blessed it would be to leave this wretched life, would that be sufficient pain to suffer? No, the pain would not be the same at all, for pain like this we can obtain through meditation. But the pain derived by meditation does not penetrate the very depths of our being.

The pain from the depths of our being feels like it cuts the soul to pieces and grinds it into powder, with no action or wish of its own. What is this sorrow? Where does it come from? I will tell you. Now is the time to apply the words of the bride I mentioned earlier in this chapter. Remember the bride said that God "brought her into the cellar of wine and set impartial love within her"? This is exactly what happens here. The soul has yielded itself into His hands and is so subdued by love for Him, that it knows or cares for nothing but God's will.

I believe He bestows this grace only on those He takes entirely for His own. He desires the soul to go forth stamped with His seal, like the wax when pressed by the signet ring. It does not mold itself; its only need is to be in a fit condition—soft and pliable by no action of its own—but merely by remaining still and quietly submitting to the impression of the seal.

The Zeal of Christ Jesus

"How good You are, O God. All that You do is for us, and You ask only that we give our wills to You so that we may be like clay in Your hands to mold and shape according to your will." God does all this so that the soul will know His love for it—the same gift Christ Jesus possessed when here on earth—God could give us no greater gift. Who could ever have longed more eagerly to do the will of His Father than Christ did? He said at the Last Supper, "With desire have I desired this." O Lord, does not that bitter death You are to suffer present itself before Your eyes in all its pain and horror? "No, for My ardent love and desire to do My Father's will and save souls is immeasurably stronger than any torments. This deeper sorrow I have suffered and still suffer, while here on earth, makes other pain seem as nothing in comparison."

Intense Suffering of Christ

I have often meditated on this, and I know the torture a friend of mind has felt, and still feels, when seeing our Lord sinned against—a torture so unbearable she would rather die than continue in such anguish. Then I thought if a soul experiences this insufferable grief from seeing our Lord sinned against, this soul's love, if compared to His love, would barely exit. What were Christ's feelings and what must His life have been like? For all things were present before His eyes and He was a constant witness of the great offences committed against His Father. I believe without a doubt this pained Him far more than His most sacred Passion. There, at least, He found the end of all His trials, and His agony was relieved by the consolation of gaining our salvation through His death and Resurrection.

Thus, people who are urged by fervent love perform great penances and hardly feel them, but want to do even more and count even that as little. What then must God have felt when Christ publicly manifested His perfect obedience to His Father and His love for His brethren? What joy it is to suffer in doing God's will. Yet I think the constant sight of the many sins committed against God and the numberless souls on their way to hell must have caused the Lord much sorrow.

CHAPTER 3

Chapter 3 describes another kind of union that the soul can receive from God. The importance of love of one's neighbor. Deals also with works, feelings, and how they effect our union with God. Defects that hinder this union. Real and imaginary good qualities.

Let us return to our little soul and see what grace God gives in this state. This implies that the soul endeavors to advance in self-knowledge and in the service of the Lord. However, if it receives the gift of union and then does no more because it believes itself safe, but instead of advancing in the things of God, it goes backward to leading a careless life, it will remain at this level until God gives grace to go on.

Soul May Fall from this State

I knew a person this happened to. Although she erred greatly, she longed for others to profit from the gift God had bestowed on her and taught the way of prayer to others, thus helping them immensely. After this, God gave fresh light to her, bringing her to a new understanding of the gift He had given her.

There must be many people the Lord has given this gift of union to who lose this gift through their own error, like Judas, called to be an Apostle, or Saul, anointed to be King. We should learn from this that if we desire more gifts we should be good stewards of those we already possess. Our only safety is in obedience to and following the law of God. This is true for those who have received these gifts and those who have not.

How Divine Union May
Always be Obtained

In spite of all I have written, there still seems to be some difficulty in understanding things within this mansion. The experience of even entering it is so wonderful, that no one should be discouraged if they do not receive the supernatural gifts described above. With the help of God's grace, true union can always be attained by forcing ourselves to renounce our own will and being obedient to the will of God in all things.

Basis of Supernatural Union is
Union with the Will of God

Many of us affirm that we do this already, believing we seek for nothing else but His will—indeed we would die for the truth of what we say. In this case, I can only say—as I did before and shall over and again—that we have already received this gift from God. Therefore, we do not need to wish for that other delightful union described above, for its chief value lies in the resignation of our will to the will of God, without which it cannot be reached. Oh, how desirable is this union. The happy soul who has received it will live in this world and in the next without cares of any kind. No earthly events will trouble it, unless it sees itself in danger of losing God, or if it witnessed a serious offence against Him. Neither sickness, poverty, or death can affect it, except perhaps the death of persons God uses to do much for His Church. However, the soul is well aware that God's ways are above our ways and desires.

Advantage of Union Gained by Self-Mortification

You certainly know there are different kinds of sorrow. Both grief and joy rise from an urge of human behavior or from love that makes us pity our neighbor, like that felt by our Lord Jesus Christ when He raised Lazarus from the dead.

These feelings do not destroy our union with the will of God, nor do they disturb the soul with a restless, turbulent, and lasting passion. As I said of the sweetness of prayer, they soon pass away. They do not affect the depths of the soul, only the senses and faculties. These feelings are found in the former mansions and do no enter the last at all. In order to gain this kind of divine union, is it necessary for the powers of the soul to be suspended? No, God has many ways of enriching the soul and bringing it through these mansions without what some call a "short cut." However, you can be sure of this, self must die and it is much easier to die to self with God leading the way, than to die by trying to force oneself and making it a long and weary battle.

In the former manner this death is facilitated by finding ourselves introduced into a new life; in the latter, we must give ourselves the deathblow. Granted the work will be much harder for the soul, but it will be of higher value and gain a greater reward if you are victorious. There is no doubt it is possible to receive this true union with the will of God.

Defects that Hinder this Union

This is the union I have longed for all my life and that I beg God to grant to me. It is unfortunate so few of us obtain it. Those who are careful not to offend God, and even those who enter convents or monasteries, think there is nothing more to do to gain these gifts of grace from God. How many maggots remain in hiding until, like the worms that gnawed at Jonas' ivy, they have destroyed our good works. These pests are evils such as: self-love, self-esteem, a critical spirit, and loving ourselves more than our neighbor. Although we may satisfy our obligations sufficiently to avoid sin, we fall far short of what must be done to obtain perfect union with the will of God.

Divine Union Obtained by Perfect Love of God and Neighbor

What do you think is His will? Is it not that we should seek perfection and become one with Him and with the Father as He prayed? What then do we need to do to obtain this? I assure you it is most painful for me to write on this subject, for I see by my own fault, how far I am from attaining perfection. Do we need to ask for more comfort and grace from God in order to conform to His will? Has He not given us all we need in Christ Jesus, who is the way, the truth, and the life?

This does not mean that we must forsake feeling sorrow at the death of a loved one or that we must bear our crosses and sicknesses with joy. However, Christ said, "And he that taketh not his cross, and followeth after me, is not worthy of me" (Matthew 10:38). Our joy is in our obedience. Our Lord asks but two things from us: love for Him and love for our neighbor; we must strive to obtain both. If we practice both of these virtues, we shall be doing His will and shall be united to Him. We may be far from obeying and serving our Lord perfectly, but He sees our desire, and hears the prayer of the righteous, and He will give us the grace and power necessary to be perfect.

"The important thing is not to think much but to love much and so do that which best stirs you to love. Love is not great delight but desire to please God in everything." (Saint Teresa of Avila)

Love for God and Neighbor Are Proportionate

I think the most certain sign that we are keeping these two commandments is that we have a genuine love for others. We may not know if we love God with all our heart, but we do know that is our desire. However, we do know if we love our neighbor or not. You can be certain that as you grow in love for others, you are also growing in your love for God.

101

You can also be certain that He will repay our love toward others by increasing in a thousand different ways our love for Him. We must watch over ourselves in this matter of love most carefully, because if we are without fault on this point we have done well. I believe that human nature is so evil that love for our neighbor could not be perfect unless it is rooted in the love of God.

Real and Imaginary Virtues

In this most important matter of love, we should be most vigilant in little things, taking no thought at present of greater works, for we must be faithful and obedient in the small things first. When we have learned vigilance in the small things, He will then trust us with larger things. It is the same with humility and other virtues. The devil's wiles are many and he will try in thousands of ways and multiplied times to make us think we are better than we really are. He has good reason to do it, for such lies are very injurious. False virtues springing from this root are always accompanied by a self-pride never found in those from God.

Illusions of Grandeur

It is unfortunate to hear souls at prayer saying they are willing to be despised and publicly insulted for the love of God, then when someone unjustly accuses them of something, they do all they can to hide their hurt and animosity. God deliver us from their outcries. Let those who cannot bear such things, make no great plans that have no genuine determination of the will to carry out. Self can imagine many things it would like to do, but the actual doing of those things is a matter of the will. The devil assaults and deceives people in this way, often doing great harm to those who are ignorant of his ways and do not understand the difference between the powers of the soul and the imagination. It is easy to know which of you have attained a sincere love for your neighbor and those of you who are far from it. If you knew the importance of this virtue, you would do all you could to gain it.

Works, not Feelings Bring Union

When I see people acting very anxious over what kind of prayer they pray, or how they pray, covering their faces and being afraid to move or even think lest they lose any tenderness and devotion they may feel, I know they are thinking by their actions they can attain union with God in prayer. They need to be taught the correct way and to practice it until a deep desire for this union in prayer with God is the most important gift for them to attain. Sitting, standing, laying prostrate, kneeling—it makes no difference to God what position we assume to pray. The most important thing is seeking relationship with Him. As for things we do, God does expect good works from us; for example, if you see someone who is ill, have compassion on them and comfort them when they are in pain. You may also feel the urge to fast for them. That urging comes from the Holy Spirit, so fast and pray for that person to be relieved from the pain and to take nourishment from food to strengthen their body. When a person fasts, the benefit is received not only by the person(s) you are fasting for, but also by the one who is fasting and praying in obedience to God. This is the true union of our will with the will of God.

When others are spoken well of and praised for something, be more pleased for them than you would be if the praise was for you; if you are really humble it would be distressful to you to be praised. It is good to rejoice for someone else when their good works are being praised. Likewise if you see a fault in someone and they are being careful to hide it from others, feel sorry for the fault in that someone as if it were your very own. God will deal with the person and the fault according to His will and way.

Charity Will Gain this Union

I have often spoken on having lack of love for others, for if we fail in this, it takes away from our love relationship with the Lord. Pray that this may never be the case for you. If you possess brotherly love, I assure you that you will obtain the union I have described. However, if you know that you lack love, yet you feel devotion and sweetness in your time of quiet prayer—making you assume you have been given union with God—believe me you have not yet obtained it. Humbly petition our Lord to grant you perfect love for your neighbor and leave the rest to Him. He will give you more than you could ever ask or think to ask, if you will strive with all your power to gain it, and you force your will to comply with all He asks of you. Forget you own self-interests and needs and pray for others and their needs no matter how much your old nature may rebel. If the opportunity presents itself, take upon yourself the burdens of your neighbors so they may be relieved and comforted. Do not think it will cost you nothing or that helping bear the burdens of others is easy; but keep your eyes on the Lord Jesus Christ and the burden He bore for us, to free us from death by suffering the most painful death of all—the Cross.

CHAPTER 4

Further explanation of prayer. The importance of being on guard, for the devil eagerly desires to turn back souls from the path to God. Spiritual progress.

At this point, you may be wondering when the soul obtains rest, since obviously it is not found in spiritual comforts nor in earthly pleasures. This I will tell you, the soul takes a higher path, but I cannot tell you more until we come to the last mansion. I pray that God will help me to remember and have the time to write it. It is nearly five months since I began this work, and because my head is too weak to read it again, it may seem very disconnected and repetitious. Yet I would like to express myself more fully on this matter of the prayer of union by using a comparison.

Later on we will speak again of the little butterfly that is never still, for it can find no true rest, but is always busy and doing good both for itself and others. You have often heard that God spiritually espouses souls: may He be praised for His mercy in humbling Himself. Though but a poor comparison, yet I can think of nothing better to express my meaning than the Sacrament of Matrimony, though the two are quite different. In divine union, everything is spiritual and far removed from anything corporeal. All the joys our Lord gives, and the mutual delight felt in it being a spiritual union, far excels human marriage. In the spiritual union love is united to love. It is very pure, more refined, and the felt awareness of these delights cannot be expressed in mere words.

Prayer of Union Resembles a Betrothal

I think the prayer of union does not attain the depth of spiritual union, but resembles the preliminaries that take place when two people are contemplating marriage. Their suitability and willingness for this union are discussed first, then they may be allowed to see each other at varying times to enable them to come to a decision about each other. It is the same in the spiritual unions; when the preliminary agreement to the union has been made and the bride completely understands the advantages to be gained from this union, she resolves to fulfill the will of the Bridegroom in all things and to do all she can to please Him. The Bridegroom, knowing the truthfulness of the bride, wishes also to gratify His bride. He therefore bestows great favor upon her, visits her, and draws her into His presence that she might know

Him better. We might compare the prayer of union to a visit, for it lasts only a brief time. There is no longer any question of deliberation for the bride. In a spiritual manner she gains knowledge and sees the wonders of the Bridegroom to whom she is betrothed. This brief visit brings about a spiritual deepening of love the bride feels for the Bridegroom, bringing an even deeper resolve not to be neglectful or set her affections on anything but her Lord, the Bridegroom. For if she neglected Him or set her affection on anything else, she would forfeit everything. The loss would be as great to her as the gifts she has continually received which are precious beyond description.

Danger of Temptations Before
Spiritual Nuptials

O Christian souls, you whom God has brought this far, I implore you for His dear sake not to grow careless, but to avoid all occasions of sin for you are not yet beyond temptation. Be encouraged. You will be beyond temptation after the marriage take place in the next mansion. In this mansion the betrothed are, as is said, only acquainted by sight, and the devil will spare no pains to oppose and prevent the nuptials. After the marriage when he sees that the bride is wholly given to her Bridegroom, he will be afraid to interfere, having learned by experience that if he molests her, he will lose everything.

Great Good of Soul's Faithfulness
to these Graces

I can assure you that I have known people far advanced in the spiritual life who have reached this state of prayer, yet the devil reclaimed them by his subtlety and wiles. As I have often said, all hell gathers together against such souls because the loss of one gives perdition many more—as Satan is well aware. If we consider how many men God draws to

Himself by means of only one person who has prayed for their salvation—or the prayers of mothers and fathers interceding for their children, loved ones, friends and neighbors—we should fervently praise Him. Think of the multitudes converted by the martyrs, or by one young maiden like Saint Ursula, or how many victims the evil one was deprived of by Saint Dominic, or Saint Francis, and other founders of religious orders. Even now, he loses more because of the work of Father Ignatius Loyola, who founded the Company of Jesus. As we read about their lives, we learn they received these same graces in prayer from God. They determined not to forfeit by any weakness or error on their part, the many divine graces they received in order to accomplish their good works. Oh, how willing our Lord is to grant us the same graces! In fact, the need is even more urgent now for persons to prepare themselves to receive these favors, because there are far fewer now who care for His honor. We love ourselves too much and we are too selfish to give up any of our rights. What a deception! May God in His mercy give us light, lest we sink into darkness.

The Soul is Constantly Subject to the Devil's Deceptions

You may question, or be in doubt on two points. First, if the soul is entirely united with the will of God, how can it be deceived, since it always seeks to follow His pleasure? Second, how can the devil enter and wreak such havoc as to destroy your soul while you are so completely withdrawn from the world and constantly in prayer? At the same time you enjoy the fellowship of other Christians, by the mercy of God how can you be deceived when you desire nothing but to serve and please Him in all things? We are not at all surprised that people in the world would take such risks for they are unaware of the dangers. I admit, I can understand why you have the right to ask these questions, sisters, for God has shown us notable mercy. However, as I said above, knowing as I do that Judas was amongst the Apostles, and that he had constant conversation with Christ himself, listened to His words, and yet fell away into betrayal of Christ Jesus, God's Holy Son, tells me that no matter how advanced one may be in religious knowledge, it is no guarantee of safety.

Satan's Strategies

To your first question I reply that doubtless if such a soul is always faithful to the will of God, it cannot be lost. However, the evil one comes with his keen subtlety and under the pretext of good, leads the soul astray in some trivial matter, causing it to commit small sins that he makes the soul believe are harmless. Thus, little by little, the reason is obscured and the will is weakened as the devil builds up his victim's self-love, until he succeeds in withdrawing the soul from union with the will of God and back to following its own will.

Why They are Permitted

The answer to your first question will also serve for the second and any others. No enclosure can be too difficult for satan to enter, nor any desert too remote for him to visit. Remember, God may permit satan to tempt the soul to prove its virtue, for if the soul is going to teach others, it is better that it fall in the beginning rather than when it might do others great harm.

Petition God to Earnestly
Uphold Us by His Hand

We must beg God constantly in our prayers to uphold us by His hand, and we should keep our minds on the truth He gave us and not on our own understanding. For we must never trust in ourselves alone, or we will most certainly fall into error or worse. I think the greatest safeguard is to be very careful and to make sure we advance in virtue. Ask yourself, am I advancing or am I falling back, especially in the area of love of my neighbor? We must also desire to be thought the least important of all and take great care in performing our everyday duties. If we do this, and beg our Lord to enlighten us, we will be able to perceive our gain or loss.

God Never Abandons the Soul

Do not suppose that after advancing the soul to this state that God abandons it, thereby making it easy prey for the devil to regain it. When the Lord sees the soul drifting away from Him, He feels the loss so dearly that He gives the soul many secret warnings that reveal the hidden danger to it.

Strive for Constant Progress

In conclusion, work diligently to make constant progress. We should feel great concern if we do not find ourselves advancing daily, for without a doubt the evil one is watching and planning to injure in some way those who are not constantly aware of their relationship to God. Truly, it is impossible for the soul attaining this state not to advance, for love is never idle, but always seeking to please the object of its affection. Therefore, it is a bad sign when one comes to a stand-still in doing good. Those who aspire to become the bride of the Lord and have a close understanding of Him through the relationship of the union with Him in prayer, must always be on guard against the enemy of their souls.

How Little We Suffer in Comparison
to what We Gain

To show you how Christ treats the souls He takes for His bride, I will now speak of the sixth mansion. You will better understand how little is the comparison of the things we suffer in His service and in preparing ourselves to receive such immense gifts.

St. Teresa's Prays for Guidance
of the Holy Spirit

I pray that God will enable me to explain some of these difficult matters by the power of His Holy Spirit, for without His guidance the task will prove impossible. I pray not to say anything that will not profit you. The Lord knows I have no other wish but that His Name may be glorified and that we may strive to serve Him who recompenses us even in this world.

Perhaps our Lord decreed that I should write this to make known the knowledge of the great rewards to come, and of His infinite mercy in seeking to give and manifest himself to such worms as we are. This should make us forget our complaining, our petty, earthly pleasures, and become inflamed with love for Him, fixing our eyes on Him, the Author and Finisher of our faith. Amen.

THE SIXTH MANSION

CHAPTER 1

This chapter explains the reason more severe afflictions are suffered when God bestows greater gifts on the soul. Love is kindled by divine gifts. Trials that accompany divine gifts. Some of the afflictions are described and directions on how to bear them for those who have attained this mansion. This chapter is especially directed to those who are suffering from inner trials. Preparation for entering the seventh mansion.

By the aid of the Holy Spirit, I will now describe the sixth mansion. The soul, filled with love for its Spouse, withdraws as far as duties permit from all interruption and seeks solitude to be with the Bridegroom continually. The sight of Him is so deeply imprinted on the bride that her only desire is to behold Him again. I have already mentioned that even by imagination nothing that can be called seeing is visibly seen in this prayer. I use the word *sight* because of the comparison I used, but this could be described as an *awareness* of His presence. I have also heard that there may be a delightful and indescribable fragrance when He is present.

The Lord Increases the Soul's Longing for Him

The soul is now determined to take no other Bridegroom than our Lord. Though the soul wishes for immediate marriage, the Bridegroom wants to wait, thereby increasing even more and stronger longings of the soul. Though at some cost to the soul, the longer wait will increase the desire and longing for the marriage. This is a most excellent benefit for the soul and in reality a very tiny sacrifice when compared to the wondrous promises of the Bridegroom. I assure you those promises inspire the soul with courage to daily bear its cross.

Courage Needed to Reach the Last Mansion

My blessed God, how many troubles both interior and exterior must one suffer before entering the seventh mansion? Sometimes while I ponder this question I fear that if we knew beforehand, human infirmity—in spite of the gain—could scarcely bear the thought nor have the courage to encounter them. However, if the soul has already reached the seventh mansion, it will fear nothing. It will boldly undertake and suffer all things for God, for it gathers strength from its time of uninterrupted union with Him.

Trials Accompany Divine Favors

I think it would be good to tell you of some of the trials certain to occur in this mansion. It is possible that not all souls will be led in this way, but I think those who enjoy truly heavenly gifts cannot be altogether free from some sort of earthly troubles. Therefore, although I did not intend to speak on this subject, I think it might greatly comfort the soul in this condition if it knew what may happen to it when God bestows this grace upon it, because it might experience a feeling of having lost everything.

Outcry Against Souls
Striving for Perfection

I will not describe these trials in their proper order, but will tell them as they come to my memory, beginning with the least severe. One of them is an outcry against the soul by those whom the soul lives among. They say the soul wants to be a saint, goes to extremes in piety in hopes of calling attention to itself, and deceptively decries others more qualified to be saints. However, the soul does not respond to them, but carries on its normal duties and responsibilities with more perfection. Many whom the soul thought were friends, desert the soul and make the worst accusations and bitterest remarks of all. They believe the soul is suffering delusions of grandeur, and that it is all the devil's work. They may go so far as to say the soul will no doubt share the same fate as so-and-so, who led others astray and was lost due to the wiles of the devil. They continually make scoffing remarks to the soul and accuse it of deceiving people. They tell others about it also, citing examples of others who were ruined in the same way.

Saint Teresa's Description of
Someone's Experience

I know of one soul who feared she would never find a priest who would hear her confession. She was right, but it is a long story and I will not stop to tell it now. The sad part is that these troubles do not go away but last all through life, for one person tells another, and another, and so on it goes. You may say some people speak in the her favor; that is true, but they are very few in comparison to the many that despise her.

Praise Can Cause Pain Until the Soul Matures

Not only that, but those who favor and praise the soul may cause more pain for it than blame, for it clearly realizes that a short time ago it was weak in virtue and involved in grave sins, so any good it possesses is a gift of God and not of itself. Therefore, commending words cause the soul great suffering in the beginning until it matures and becomes comparatively indifferent to criticism or praise. It has learned some things from the experience.

First, some people are more than willing to speak well or badly of others, as the occasion demands, so the soul attaches no more importance to one than the other.

Secondly, the soul having been granted greater light by the Lord, perceives that no good thing in it is of itself, but a gift of God, so it becomes oblivious to self, giving God all the praise.

Thirdly, the soul wants to be sure others profit from discovering that the graces the soul received from God were not due to any virtues of its own.

Fourthly, souls seeking God's honor and glory more than their own are safe from the temptation (that usually besets beginners) of thinking that human praise will hinder them as it has others. The souls at this stage are far more oblivious to man's contempt.

Perfect and Final Indifference
to Blame or Praise

To a certain extent, these and other reasons alleviate the great distress formerly caused by praise from man. However, unless the soul completely disregards the praises of men, it could still be bothered. It is more grieved by undeserved praise by men than by slanderous remarks, and when it nears complete indifference to praise it cares even less about criticism.

Love of Enemies

This is true because the soul is strengthened by trials rather than depressed by them. Experience has taught it the great advantages to be gained by trials. The soul does not think men offend God when they persecute it, because the soul knows that God permits the persecution to strengthen the soul for its greater gain. The soul has a strong belief that those who persecute it are closer friends and greater benefactors to it than those who speak well of it.

Bodily Sufferings

Our Lord may now send severe bodily infirmity. This is a far heavier cross, especially if acute pain is suffered. I think this is the hardest of earthly trials. I am speaking of exterior trials. This affects both spirit and body, and in its anguish the soul does not know what to do and would rather suffer quick martyrdom than suffer this. However, this sudden onset of extreme pain does not last long, for the Lord never sends us more than we can bear and always gives us patience and grace first.

Saint Teresa's Speaks of Her
Own Physical Ills

Now I will speak of other trials and illnesses of many kinds that may occur to people in this state. I knew someone about forty years ago whom God began to bestow this favor of suffering upon. So much so that she could not remember a single day without pain and other kinds of suffering. I am speaking of physical infirmities and heavy crosses to bear. True, she had led a wicked life, and because of her past wickedness she felt these trials were very light in comparison with the hell she deserved. Our Lord may lead others who have offended Him in fewer sins in some other way. However, I would always choose this way of suffering—if only for the sake of imitating the Lord Jesus Christ—for it profits us in many other ways. Yet the other trials would seem trifling in comparison if I could relate the interior torments met with here, but they are impossible to describe.

A Timid Confessor

Let us first speak of the trial of meeting for confession with a priest who is so timid and inexperienced as a confessor that nothing seems safe and right to him. He dreads and suspects the very worst of any commonplace sin, especially in a soul in which he detects any imperfection, for he thinks people on whom God bestows such favors must be angelic and free of sin, which, of course, is impossible while we are still in these bodies. He at once blames the devil or depression. As to blaming the devil, I am not surprised, as there is so much in the world the evil one has done, and he loves to work this kind of deception to cause the confessors to have the strong reasons for anxiety and vigilance in this area.

Anxiety Over Past Sins

The poor soul who fears the same fears, and seeks the priest in confession as a judge, feels the kind of torture and dismay at his condemnation that can only be described by one who has experienced it. One of the severest trials, especially for those who have lived wicked lives, is their belief that God permits them to be deceived as punishment for their sins. In actually receiving this punishment they feel secure and believe it is from the Spirit of God. The time of punishment is short, but the remembrance of their sins is ever before them, and when they discover another fault in themselves, the torturing thoughts return again to punish them.

Fear and Spiritual Dryness

The soul is quieted for a time when the priest assures it that it has been forgiven, though it may return to its former anxieties and apprehensions. However, if he does not assure it, but increases and strengthens the fears, they will become almost unbearable. This is especially true if the soul is suffering such spiritual dryness that in its mind it feels it has never touched God in its thoughts or prayers and will never be able to. When others speak of God, the soul cannot sense any relationship to Him or the wonders He has done.

Scruples and Fears Raised by the Devil

This lack of understanding by the priest adds further pain, because the soul cannot make him understand, so the priest is certain the soul is deceiving him. Although such a person may examine their conscience with the greatest care, determining to reveal any misdeed to the priest, it does not help. The soul is now becoming confused, and its understanding is being obscured by the lies suggested by the devil, who may have been given permission by the Lord to tempt it. The evil spirit even tries to make the soul think that God has rejected it. Many are the trials that assault this soul, causing an internal anguish so painful nothing can compare, except being lost in hell. It seems to the soul that no comfort can be found in this tempest of trouble.

Bewilderment of the Soul

If the soul seeks consolation from the priest during confession, demons suddenly appear to help the priest torment it more. A priest who dealt with a person suffering in this manner thought that her state must be very dangerous because so many things were troubling her. After she had recovered from her trials, he asked her to tell him if they recurred, but this only made matters worse because it caused her so much anxiety that she lost all control of herself. She was in such a state of anxiety and apprehension that, though she had learned to read, she could no longer understand a book nor the alphabet. Her mind was incapable of this function.

God Alone Relieves These Troubles

There is no remedy in such a trial as this except to wait for the mercy of God's will and timing to intervene. God's intervention will dispel all the clouds of trouble and sorrows from the mind, flooding it with light, and enabling the soul to be far happier than before. The soul will then praise God like one who has been victorious in a dangerous battle, for it was God Himself that won the victory. The defenseless soul then fully realizes its weakness and how little man can help himself if God forsakes him, for before the victory the enemy appeared to have all the weapons.

Human Weakness

The truth needs no demonstration, for past experience has taught the soul its incapacities. It also realizes the nothingness of human nature and what miserable creatures we are. Though the soul did not fall from a state of grace during this experience it suffered, it still doubts and believes that neither now nor in the past has it ever possessed the faintest spark of love for God. If at any time the soul has done good, or if the Lord has bestowed any favors upon it, they seem to have been a dream of imagination, for its sins still stand clearly before it.

Earthly Comfort of No Avail

O Lord Jesus, how sad to see a soul in such a state, and how little does earthly comfort avail. If you are ever in this state, do not ever think that others who may be rich or influential have any more sources for help than you do. No, never, for to offer such comforts would be like setting all joy in the world before those who are condemned to death, and rather than excuse their sin it would increase the torture. So it is with the souls I spoke of; nothing of earth can help them, their help must come from above. Our great God wishes us to acknowledge His sovereignty and our own misery—an important point for those who want to advance farther.

Mental Prayer is Impossible
to the Distraught Mind

What can the poor soul in this state of mind do if such a trial lasts for many days? Prayer makes no difference as far as comforting the heart because no consolation can enter. The mind cannot even grasp the meaning of the words of vocal prayer, and mental prayer is out of the question at a time like this because the faculties are not up to it. Solitude is harmful to the soul, yet having people around or conversation brings fresh torment. Strive as the suffering soul may to hide its condition, it cannot, for it is weary and impatient with all around it.

Remedies for the Inner Trials

How can the soul possibly tell anyone what is wrong with it? Its pains are indescribable, for it is filled with anguish and spiritual suffering. The best remedy for these trials (I do not mean deliverance from them, but how to bear them) is to perform external works of love and to trust in the mercy of God who never fails those who hope in Him. May He be forever blessed! Amen.

Trials Caused by the Devil

The devil also brings about unusual exterior trials that we will not take the time to describe. Sufficient to say they are less painful, for no matter what demons may do, they will never succeed in paralyzing the faculties of the mind, or disturb the soul as described before. In fact, the mind is able to discern that the evil spirits can do no more harm than God permits, and because the mind has not lost its capabilities, the sufferings are comparatively insignificant.

Other Afflictions

I will speak of other internal afflictions to be dealt with in this mansion when describing different kinds of prayer and

119

gifts given here by our Lord. Although some of these latter pains are harder to endure, as evidenced by the effects on the body, they do not deserve being called that, nor do we have the right to do so. Indeed, they are great graces from God because the soul recognizes in the midst of the pains how far it is from deserving such graces.

Sufferings Experienced Before Entrance to the Seventh Mansion

This severe torture felt by souls at the entrance of the seventh mansion is accompanied by many other sufferings, some of which I will mention. But to speak of them all would be impossible, nor could I describe them for they come from a far higher source than the rest. If I have not been successful in teaching the lesser trials, how much less successful will I be in teaching the higher ones? May God assist me in all things through the goodness of His Son, Christ Jesus. Amen.

CHAPTER 2

Chapter 2 teaches several of the ways that our Lord quickens the soul. The effect on the soul. Gifts of an exalted nature. No reason to fear deception here.

It may seem we have deserted the bride for a long time, but this is not the case, for the past trials have caused her to travel a higher road. I will describe the way the Bridegroom treats her before uniting her entirely to Himself. He increases her longing for Him in ways so imperceptible the soul itself cannot discern them. These desires are like delicate and subtle impulses springing from the innermost depths of the soul. I know of nothing they can be compared to.

The Wound of Love

These graces differ entirely from anything we ourselves can gain, and even from the spiritual comfort I described before. In the present case, when the mind is not meditating or even thinking of God, the Lord arouses it suddenly as if by a flashing comet or clap of thunder, though not a sound is heard. Yet the soul, having been called by God, hears Him well; so well that sometimes, and especially at first, it trembles and even cries out, although it feels no pain. It is conscious of having received a delightful wound, but doesn't know how, or from whom. Yet it recognizes it as a most precious grace and hopes the hurt will never heal.

The Pain Caused

The bride speaks passionate statements to her Bridegroom. She is unable to stop herself, although knowing full well the Bridegroom will not come to her so she may enjoy Him. This causes a pain so deep, so sweet, and so delicate, that the soul cannot escape from it, nor will it try, for this is what it desires. This gift is more delightful than the pleasure of the mind totally absorbed in the prayer of quiet, which is unaccompanied by suffering.

The Call of the Bridegroom

Though I have tried to think of how I might teach this for better understanding of this process of love, I can think of no other way to do so. I know it seems contradictory to say the Beloved clearly shows He dwells in the soul and calls by so unmistakable a sign and summons so penetrating that the soul cannot help but hear it; yet He appears to reside in the seventh mansion. He speaks in this manner which is not a known language; but the soul understands it, though the senses, the imagination, the faculties dare not move.

Effect on the Soul

O Almighty God, how profound are Your secrets and how different are spiritual matters from anything seen or heard in this world. I can find nothing to liken these graces to, insignificant as they are compared to many others You give. This gift acts so strongly upon the soul that it is consumed by desires, yet knows not what to ask, for it realizes clearly that God is with it. You may say, if it realizes this so clearly, what more does it desire and why is it pained? What greater good can it seek? I do not know. I do know this suffering seems to pierce the very heart, and when He who wounded it draws out the dart, He seems to draw the heart out also, for the depth, height, and breadth of this love cannot be fully comprehended.

A Spark of the Fire of Love

I have been thinking that God might be compared to a burning furnace from which a small spark escapes and flies into the soul; it feels the heat of the fire, but the spark is insufficient to consume it. The sensation is so delightful that the soul lingers in the pain produced by its contact. This seems to me the best comparison I can find, for the pain is pleasant and not really pain at all, nor does it always continue in the same degree of intensity. Sometimes it lasts for a long time and other times it passes quickly. This is as God chooses, for no human means can obtain it, and though felt at times for a long while, it is also sporadic.

The Spark Dies

In fact, it is never permanent; therefore, it does not completely inflame the soul. When the soul longs for more fire, the little spark dies out suddenly, leaving the heart longing to suffer again these loving pangs. No grounds exist for thinking this comes from any natural cause, depression, an illusion of the devil, or the imagination. Undoubtedly this movement of the heart comes from our unchangeable God. The effects this movement leaves do not resemble those of other devotions in which the heart felt delight which makes us doubt its reality.

This Grace Evidently Divine

There is no interruption of the senses or other faculties. In fact, they are filled with wonder at what is happening, but they do not impede it, for the senses or faculties cannot increase or decrease this delightful pain. Anyone who has received this gift from the Lord will understand my meaning, let them praise the Lord fervently for it. There is no need to fear deception. If there is to be any fear, it should be for lack of gratefulness for this wonderful sign of grace. Let us strive to serve Him and discipline our lives in every respect in hope of obtaining higher and higher gifts.

The Wound of Love Repays Many Trials

A person I know who received this gift was very happy and perfectly satisfied, even though she went several years without receiving any other gifts. She felt that even if she served God for many years in the midst of severe trials, she had already been abundantly rewarded. May He be forever blessed. Amen.

First Cause of Immunity
from Deception

Perhaps you wonder why we may feel more secure from the devil's deceptions after receiving this gift, as opposed to others? There are several reasons. First, the devil cannot give delightful pain. He may cause pleasure or delight that appears spiritual, but is unable to add suffering, especially intense suffering wrapped in peace and joy of the soul. His power is limited to the external things. Suffering produced by him causes anxieties and struggles, never peace.

Second and Third Causes for
Immunity from Deception

Secondly, because this welcome storm comes from a region over which Satan has no control.

Thirdly, because of the great benefits derived, the soul who receives this gift is more determined than ever to suffer for God and longs to bear even more crosses. It is also more determined to withdraw from worldly pleasures, relationships, and other things the world may offer.

Imagination Plays No Role

It is very clear that this is a true gift of God. The imagination may try to counterfeit some gifts, but not this, for it is too clearly manifested to doubt. If anyone still remains uncertain whether they really experienced this or it was imaginary, know this: these things are perceived by the soul just as a loud voice is by the ears. It is impossible for these experiences to come to someone experiencing the ups and downs of depression that exist only in the imagination. This emotion comes from the interior of the soul.

No Alarm Felt by this State of Prayer

I may be mistaken, but I will not change my opinion until I hear reason contrary from those with better understanding. I know some who have greatly dreaded any form of deception, yet, they received this gift and felt no alarm about this state of prayer.

Fragrance of the Lord

Our Lord also uses other means of rousing the soul. For instance, when reciting vocal prayer, with no intention of stirring the senses, a person may be filled with a delightful feeling of being suddenly surrounded by a fragrance so powerful it diffuses itself through all the senses. I do not mean that there is actually a fragrant perfume, but I'm using this as a comparison because it resembles the manner the Spouse uses to make His presence understood, This moves the soul to a delightful desire of enjoying Him, causing the soul to fervently praise Him.

No Reason to Fear Deception

This gift comes from God just as the former one did, but it causes no suffering, nor is it a painful longing for the soul. It offers the same experience and benefits of the former one. For reasons already given there is no cause for fear of deception, only enjoyment and thanksgiving for receiving it.

INTRODUCTORY NOTE TO CHAPTER 3

Written in 1921 by Fr. Benedict Zimmerman

The readers, especially those not well acquainted with Scholastic philosophy, will, perhaps, be glad to find here a short explanation of the visions of various kinds, such as Locution, Corporal, Imaginary, and Intellectual. The senses of taste, touch, and smell are not so often affected by mystical phenomena, but what we are about to say in respect to sight and hearing applies to these also.

A Corporal Vision is when one sees a bodily object. A Corporal Locution is when one hears words uttered by a human tongue. In both cases the respective senses are exercising their normal function. The phenomenon differs from ordinary seeing or hearing merely by the fact that in the latter, the object is either only apparent, or at any rate is not such as it seems to be.

Thus, when young Tobias set out on a journey, his companion, Azarias, was not a real human being, but an archangel in human form. Tobias did really see and hear him, and felt the grip of this hand. Sara and her parents, as well as Tobias's parents, saw and heard him, too. However, the archangel made himself visible and audible by means of an assumed body, or perhaps of an apparent body. It would be more correct to describe such a phenomenon as an apparition rather than a vision. In fact, the apparitions of our risen Lord to the holy women and the apostles belong to this category. For, though His was a real body, it was glorified and therefore no longer subject to the same laws which govern human beings. St. Teresa tells us more than once that she never beheld a Corporal Vision, nor heard a Corporal Locution.

An imaginary Vision or Locution is one where nothing is seen or heard by the senses of seeing or hearing. However, the same impression is received that would be produced upon the imagination by the senses if some real object were perceived by them. For, according to the Scholastics, the imagination stands half-way between the senses and the intellect, receiving impressions from the former and transmitting them to the latter. This is the reason why Imaginary Visions and Locution are so dangerous. According to St Teresa, St. John of the Cross, and other spiritual writers, these visions should not be sought after. As much as possible they should be shunned, and under all circumstances discountenanced.

The reason for this is that the imagination is closely connected to the memory and that very frequently makes it impossible to ascertain whether a vision might be a semi-conscious or an unconscious reproduction of scenes witnessed. It is here also that deception, willful or unknowingly, self-deception or deception by a higher agency, is to be feared. Therefore, the general rule is that such Visions or Locutions should only be trusted upon the strongest grounds. According to St. Thomas Aquinas, the visions of Isaiah and of St. John in the Apocalypse were Imaginary Visions.

An example of Imaginary Visions we may mention would be St. Stephen, who saw "the heavens opened and the Son of Man standing on the right hand of God," and St. Peter, who saw "the heavens opened and a certain vessel descending, as it were a great linen sheet, let down by the four corners from heaven to the earth ... and there came a voice to him, 'Arise, Peter, kill and eat'" (Acts 7:55, 11:5-9).

These Visions, Locutions, etc., are not hallucinations. Hallucinations are due to a physical disorder that affects the memory and causes it to represent impressions formerly received by it in a disorderly and often grotesque manner. The Imaginary Vision takes place independently of a morbid state. It is caused by an extraneous power, good or evil, and has for its object, things of which the memory neither has, nor ever has had cognizance.

An Intellectual Vision or Locution is one where nothing is seen or heard by the eyes and ears; there is also no sensation received by the imagination. However, the impression that would be delivered by the imagination to the intellect—if it had come through the senses and been relayed to the imagination—is directly imprinted upon the intellect. To understand this it is necessary to bear in mind that the impressions we receive through the senses must undergo a transformation—must be spiritualized—before they reach the intellect. This is one of the most difficult problems of psychology, for none of the solutions offered by various schools of philosophy seem to render it entirely free from obscurity.

According to St. Thomas Aquinas, the impression received by the eye is spiritualized by a faculty called *intellectus agens* by means of abstraction and is treasured up in the memory like lantern slides, available by demand. The mind, identifying itself with the abstraction, produces the word of the mind, wherein consists the act of understanding or mental conception.

In the Intellectual Vision or Locution, God, without cooperation on the part of the senses, the imagination, or the memory, produces directly on the mind the impression

127

received by the eyes. As this is supernatural with regard to its origin, and also with respect to its object, it stands to reason that it is too exalted for the memory to receive it. So as St. Teresa mentions, Visions and Locution like this are often not clearly remembered and sometimes forgotten altogether. On the other hand, they are far less dangerous than Corporal or Imaginary Visions and Locutions, because the senses and imagination have nothing to do with them, while evil spirits are unable to act directly upon the mind, and self-deception is altogether excluded, for the reasons stated by St. Teresa.

An example of such a vision is mentioned by St. Paul, "I know a man in Christ above fourteen years ago (whether in the body I know not, or out of the body I know not: God knoweth) such an one caught up the third heaven" (2 Corinthians 12:1-3).

CHAPTER 3

Describes how God sometimes speaks to the soul.
Discusses what signs to look for regarding deception.
Resisting false doctrine.

God stirs the soul in another manner, which in some ways seems to be a greater gift, but it may prove to be more dangerous. Therefore, I will give some description of it. God does this by means of words spoken to the soul in many different ways. Sometimes they appear to come from outside the soul, and other times from the inner depths of the soul from its highest part. Other words are like a real voice spoken and heard outside the body by the ears.

Words from a Dream

Very often this may be only a dream. This is especially true for persons with a lively imagination who are afflicted with depression to any marked extent. I think no attention should be paid to either class of people when they say they see, hear, or learn anything supernaturally. Do not disturb them by saying that it comes from the devil; just listen to them as if they were sick persons. When they tell the priest their story, he will tell them to think no more about it, for such matters are not essential when serving God. The devil has deceived many Christians in this way. Although this may not be so in their case, they do not need to trouble themselves about it. In this way we humor them, rather than tell them their imaginations are from their depressed state. Otherwise, they will persist in saying they have seen or heard these things, because this is what they believe.

Caution Required

The truth is, care should be taken to keep such people from too much prayer, and if possible to take no notice of their imaginations. The devil uses these weak souls to injure others, even though the weak soul itself seems to be unhurt. There is an initial need for caution with both feeble and strong souls at first, until there is absolute certainty from what spirit these things came from. I believe that in the beginning it's always wise to resist these communications. If they are from God they will receive more, for they increase when one is discouraged. At the same time, care should be taken that the soul is not too strictly controlled or disquieted, for it cannot help itself in this matter.

Words Heard During Prayer

Returning to the discussion on words addressed to the soul. The kind I mentioned may come from God, the devil, or the imagination. By the help of God I will try to describe these signs by distinguishing one from the other. I will also discuss when they may be dangerous, for many persons praise during their prayers. There is no harm in either believing in them, or in disregarding them, because if they speak only words of consolation or warn you of your faults, it does not matter where they came from or if they are only imaginations

Resist False Doctrine

I caution you on one point, however; although they may come from God, you must not become puffed up. Remember, He also spoke to the Pharisees, and all good comes from profiting by His words. Take no more notice of any words you hear that disagree with the Holy Scriptures than you would if you hear from Satan himself. Though they may only come from a vivid imagination, treat them as a temptation against your faith. Always resist them, then they will cease and leave you, for they have little strength of their own.

First Sign:
Words Originating from God

Returning to the first point—whether these communications come from the inferior or superior part of the soul, or from outside the soul, does not affect their originating from God.

Effect of Divine Words: "Be Not Troubled"

In my opinion these following things are the most certain signs of their being divine: The first and truest is the power and authority they carry with them, for these words are significant. For example; a soul is suffering all the sorrow and disquiet I have described and the mind is dark and dry, but it is set at peace, freed from all trouble and filled with light by merely hearing the words, "Be not troubled" (Matthew 24:6). These words deliver the soul from all its pains, though it had been feeling all the world and its theologians had united in trying to persuade it that there was no reason for grief. In spite of all their efforts, the soul would never have been delivered from its affliction.

"It is I, be Not Afraid"

Another example: a person is told by the priest and other people that their soul is under the influence of the evil one, then they hear a single sentence that says, 'It is I, be not afraid" (Mark 6:50). And at once they are freed from all fears, filled with comfort, and believing it would be impossible for anyone to disturb their new found confidence and assurance.

"Be at Peace"

Another person in the throes of anxiety over an important business problem, and not knowing if the solution will be successful, hears these words, "Be at peace, all will go well." Immediately that person feels reassured and free from all care in the matter. I could mention many other instances of the same sort.

Second Sign

The second sign is a great calm and a devout and peaceful recollection that dwells in the soul along with a desire to praise God. They say communications, in this mansion, are not spoken directly by God, but are transmitted by an angel. Then, O my God, if a word sent to us by You through Your messenger has such force, what wondrous effects will You leave in the soul united to You in a mutual bond of love?

Third Sign

The third sign is that these words do not pass from the memory; they remain there for a very long time and perhaps are never forgotten. This is not the case with words men say—

no matter how serious and learned they may be, the words will not be impressed in this way upon the memory. Even if they prophesy of things to come, we are not to believe them as we do divine words that leave us convinced of their truth. For there remains in the soul a certainty of their truthfulness that cannot be destroyed. Even though everything may seem to war against what was heard, and though years pass by, the soul never loses its belief that God will use means unknown to men to bring forth what was foretold. Indeed, His words never return to Him void; they always accomplish what He sent them to do.

Devil Suggests Doubts

As I said, however, the soul is troubled at seeing many obstacles in the way of the fulfillment of the prophecy. The words, their effects, and the assurance they carry with them, convinces the soul at first that they came from God. Later, doubts may arise as to whether the words heard came from the devil or the imagination, although while hearing them the person would have died defending their truth. But, as I said, these misgivings are suggested by the evil one to afflict and intimidate. We know the evil one will do all he can to cause doubt in the person who received the words by trying in whatever way to hinder. However, knowing his wiles and ways, there can be great growth in faith for the person who believes the word of God. God receives honor through it all, when with His help the soul overcomes any difficulties the enemy may cause.

Satan will continue to whisper doubts and work his wiles on those who have received a word from God. Does he ever stop? His goal is to weaken the faith, and it is a terrible evil to doubt or not believe that God has the power to work in ways far beyond our understanding.

Confidence Rewarded

Despite all these difficulties causing an unfavorable turn in the possibility of these predictions coming true, and though the priests who were consulted on these matters say the words are birthed in the imagination, there remains a spark of certainty that no doubts will quench. At last, when the Lord's words are fulfilled, the soul is so satisfied and joyful that it can do nothing but praise and glorify Him.

Joy in the Truth of God's Word

I do not know why the soul attaches such importance to these communications it has received being proven true. I think if a person was accused of lying, the person should not be so grieved at the accusation, but they should be more grieved if the word was not received and believed to be of God.

Zeal for God's Honor

In fact, because these words come from the Spirit of God, it is right to trust and believe them, and to desire that He who is supreme truth should not be thought of as a deceiver. Justly, therefore, the hearer rejoices when after many difficulties and delays, the prophecy is accepted and fulfilled. Although this success may have caused much suffering, the soul considers it nothing in comparison to the fulfillment of God's foretold words.

Words from the Imagination

If these prophecies proceed from the imagination they show no such signs, bringing neither conviction, peace, nor inner joy. But in some cases I have noticed, because of a physical weakness, a vivid imagination, or some other cause, persons absorbed in the prayer of quiet, or in a spiritual trance, are so entirely unaware of their deep state that it is as if they were unconscious of anything external. All their senses are dormant, as if asleep—as indeed at times they really are—and they will, in a sort of dream, think they are spoken to or see things they imagine come from God. However, only the dreams seem affected.

Imaginary Answers to Prayer

Again, one who very lovingly asks something of our Lord may imagine the answer comes from Him. This often occurs, but I think no one accustomed to receiving divine communications could be deceived on this point by their imagination.

Spiritual Advisor Should Be Consulted

The devil's deceptions are more dangerous, but if the two preceding signs are present, we may feel fairly confident they are from God. If not certain, and there is an action to be taken or some other very important matter, one should seek counsel from a third person, or from a priest who is both learned and a servant of God. No action should be taken until this is done, even though the message may be repeated several times and we are convinced of the divine origin. The Lord wishes us to take this course, and it is not disobedience to His commands, for He has told us to consider His priests as His representatives even when there is no doubt that the communication comes from Him. This is especially helpful if the matter is a difficult one. Our Lord will reassure the priest, and inspire him with faith that these words are from the Holy Spirit. If not, we are free from all further obligations in the matter. I think it would be very dangerous to act against the priest's advice and to prefer our own opinions in such a matter. Therefore, I admonish you in name of our Lord never to do that.

Interior Words

God speaks to the soul in another way—I call it an intellectual vision. I think this undoubtedly comes from God, and I will describe it later on. It takes place far within the innermost depths of the soul, which appears to hear distinctly in a most mysterious manner by spiritually hearing the words spoken to it by the Lord Himself. The way the soul understands these words, and the results produced by them convince us they cannot in any way come from the devil. Their powerful aftereffects force us to admit this and plainly show they do not come from the imagination.

First Signs of Genuine Inner Words

Carefully consider the following reasons:

First Sign

First, the clearness of the language varies in the different kinds of messages. Those that are divine are so distinct that the hearer will remember everything, including a missing syllable, and what words were used, even though a whole sentence was spoken. However, if the message was a product of the imagination, it would not be so distinctly heard, nor would it be heard in its full length.

Second Sign

Secondly, often the person is not thinking of what is heard. The message may come unexpectedly during a conversation. At times it refers to some thought that may have passed quickly through the mind, or to a subject being discussed. Frequently it concerns things the hearer knows nothing about, or events the person never imagined could come to pass. Therefore, it is impossible for the imagination to conceive such messages and deceive the mind into thinking what it has never known, sought, or even thought about.

135

Third Sign

Thirdly, in the case of a soul who hears a genuine message from the Holy Spirit, the soul listens to the words intently and the imagination is not fruitful, but when the message is from the imagination, it composes what the person wants to hear.

Fourth Sign

Fourthly, because divine messages differ immensely from others, sometimes they consist of a single word comprising a depth of meaning. The imagination could not quickly turn that into a phrase.

Fifth Sign

Fifthly, in a way I cannot explain, these communications frequently give us far more understanding than is implied by the words alone.

I shall speak further on this way of understanding the hidden things of God, which is very subtle. We should thank God for this divine favor. Some people are exceedingly suspicious about these and other communications. I speak particularly of one who experienced them herself. She considered the event very carefully by the grace of God, for He often bestowed His grace upon her. Her principal difficulty was to find out if the messages were from His Holy Spirit or a fancy of her imagination. It is easier to know if they come from the devil, for one of his wiles is to imitate an angel of light. The Holy Spirit, however, would give this message using very distinctly pronounced words, so there would be no doubt as to the source, but those from the imagination leave one uncertain if the words were even heard. Satan could never counterfeit the effects I spoke of, for he leaves neither peace nor light in the soul, only anxiety and confusion. In any case, he can do little, or no harm, to one who is humble and does not act rashly on what is heard.

Results of True Words

Let us carefully examine the soul who has received gifts and loving words from our Lord to see if it has become highly puffed up as a consequence, for unless self-abasement increases with God's expressions of love, they are not from the Holy Spirit. When they are of divine origin, the greater the favors, gifts, or words of love, the less the soul esteems itself, and more keenly remembers its sins. It becomes more oblivious to self-interest as the will and memory grow more fervent in seeking only God's honor. It also becomes increasingly careful not to deviate from the will of God, feeling a keener conviction that instead of deserving favor and gifts, it deserves hell.

No Alarm to the Soul

When these results follow, no graces or gifts received during prayer need alarm the soul. Rather it should trust in the mercy of God, who is faithful and will not allow the devil to deceive it. This does not mean we should let down our guard; one must always be on guard, for we have an enemy who roams about seeking whom he may devour.

Answer to an Objection

Those our Lord does not lead on this path may think the soul can avoid listening to these messages; and even though they are interior, it could at least turn its attention away from them so it could escape the danger of hearing them. This cannot be done with messages from the Holy Spirit; when He speaks all other thoughts are stopped, and the mind is compelled to listen. Messages from the imagination, however, can be stopped in their tracks by turning away from them and ceasing to think of them.

Mark this: I believe it would be easier for a person with very keen hearing to avoid listening to a loud voice, because he could occupy the thoughts and mind with other things.

Not so here. The soul can do nothing, for it has no ears to hear, or power to think of anything but what is said to it. Only God, who can stop the sun on its course, can so quiet the faculties and the interior of the soul. He causes the soul to listen, making it absolutely certain that He, who is stronger and wiser governs it, thereby filling it with profound devotion and humility. May our divine Lord cause us to forget ourselves and grant our only desire, which is to please Him. Amen. God also grant that I have succeeded in explaining this, and that it may be a guide to those who may experience such gifts.

CHAPTER 4

Explains how God suspends the soul in prayer by a trance, a feeling of ecstasy, or rapture. Saint Teresa believes these to be one and the same. Great courage is required to receive extraordinary gifts from God.

How can the soul find any rest from the trials I have told you of and many more? They serve only to increase her desire for the Bridegroom. The Bridegroom, well aware of her weakness, fortifies her by these and other means to help her obtain courage for union with Him and receive Him as her Spouse. Perhaps you will laugh and think I am speaking foolishly, after all there is no need for courage here. For there is no woman, however low her class, who would not dare to wed a king. I agree if this was an earthly monarch, but there is a far greater need for fortitude than you may suppose to be the bride of Lord and King of heaven.

Our nature is too timid, inferior, and lacking in morals for anything so high. Unless God gives the grace, it would be impossible for us, no matter how much we might desire it. You will learn how the Lord ratifies these espousals. This probably occurs when He ravishes the soul with ecstasies, depriving it of its faculties, for if they were retained, the sight of its physical closeness to so mighty a Sovereign would probably deprive the body of life. I am speaking of genuine raptures—not imaginations from women's weakness that so often occur these days, making them feel everything to be a rapture or ecstasy. As I said, some are of such a feeble constitution they feel they will die from a single prayer of quiet.

Raptures

I would like to describe several kinds of raptures that I have learned of from spiritual persons during discussions of this subject. I am not sure, however, that I will be successful in explaining them. I think it will not be considered amiss to repeat what I said about these and other things that happen in this state and teach on all the mansions in their proper order.

Raptures Caused by the Spark of Love

In one kind of rapture, the soul—although not praying at the time—is struck by a word of God that it either remembers or hears. The Lord, touched with pity for the long suffering of the soul in longing for Him, appears to increase the spark of desire described in the interior of the soul until it is entirely inflamed and rises with new life like a phoenix from the flames. Such a one may piously believe their sins are now forgiven, supposing they are in this disposition, and have made use of all means required by the Church. The soul being now purified, God unites it to Himself in a way known only to Him and the soul, though the soul does not understand enough to be able to explain it to others afterwards. Yet the mind did not lose the use of its faculties, for this ecstasy does not resemble a swoon or a fit in which nothing interior or exterior is felt.

Powers and Senses Absorbed

What I do understand is that the soul has never been more alive to spiritual things, nor so full of light and knowledge of our Lord God as it is now. This might seem impossible if the powers and senses were so absorbed that we might call them dead. How does the soul understand this mystery? I cannot tell, and perhaps no one but our Creator himself can say what occurs in these mansions. I mean this mansion and the following mansions being treated as one, for the door leading from one to the other is wide open. However, because some things in the rooms of the last mansion are only shown to those who get this far, I thought it better to speak of the mansions separately.

Mysteries Revealed During Ecstasies

When the soul is in this suspension, our Lord favors it by revealing secrets to it. Secrets such as heavenly mysteries and imaginary visions that are easily described afterwards, because they remain so imprinted upon the memory they are never forgotten. But when the visions are intellectual they are not so easily described, for some of them are so awe-inspiring that it is not right for man while living in this world to understand and describe them. However, when the faculties are once again operating much can be described from an intellectual vision. Possibly you do not know what a vision is, especially an intellectual one. Since I have been told to explain this, I will at the proper time. Although some may feel this is not important information, it may prove useful to some.

These Mysteries are Unspeakable

But, you ask. "If the very awe-inspiring gifts the Lord bestows on souls in this mansion cannot be remembered, what profit are they?" Oh, their value cannot be overrated, for though the recipient is incapable of describing them, they are deeply imprinted in the center of the soul and never forgotten. How can they be remembered if no image is seen and the powers of the soul do not understand them? Well, I too do not understand this, but I know that certain truths of the greatness of God remain deeply impressed on the spirit by this gift. Many things do not teach who God is, but that does not change our belief that God is who He says He is. We do not praise God because we see Him, we praise Him for who He is, and the soul experiencing this gift will worship Him as such, just as Jacob did when he saw the ladder. No doubt the patriarch learned other secrets he was unable to reveal, for if he had not received more inner light, he never would have discovered such sublime mysteries merely by watching angels ascending and descending the steps of the ladder (Genesis 28:12).

Moses and the Burning Bush

In Exodus 3:2-5, Moses was not able to tell more than God willed of what he had seen in the burning bush. Moses could never have undertaken such great things God commanded him to do if Almighty God had not clearly revealed certain mysteries to his soul, causing him to see and know God was present. Such awe-inspiring revelations were shown to him amidst the thorns of the bush that they created within him needful courage for his great deeds on behalf of the children of Israel. We must not search for reasons to understand the hidden things of God, but believing Him to be Almighty, we should be convinced that such worms as ourselves, with our limited power of intelligence, are unable to comprehend His wonders. Let us praise Him forever for allowing us to understand what He wills.

Simile of the Museum and a Visit to the Duchess of Alva

I wish I could find some comparison for my subject, but none seem to suit the purpose. However, I will try the following: Imagine you are in a private museum belonging to a king or great nobleman, and there are numberless kinds of articles of glass, porcelain, and other things arranged so that most of them are seen when you enter the room.

While on a visit to the house of the Duchess of Alva where I was staying during a journey, I was taken into such a room as described. I stood amazed on entering it and wondered what could be the use of such a jumble of knick-knacks— then I thought that the sight of so many different things should lead one to praise God. It is fortunate I saw them, for they offer me a suitable comparison in this case. Although I was in the room for some time, there were so many objects that I forgot what I had seen and could not remember each object, or what it was made of. It was like I had never seen it, though I recalled the sight of the whole collection.

Joy of the Soul During Raptures

Something like this occurs when the soul is very closely united to God. It is introduced into this mansion of the most heavenly part of the soul, which must be in the center of the soul since God resides there. While the soul is in ecstasy, our Lord does not appear to wish it to understand these mysteries, for its extreme joy in Him is sufficient. Sometimes it is His will to withdraw the soul from this rapture when it once perceives what the mansion contains. On returning to itself, the mind can recall what has been seen, but is unable to describe it, and has no natural abilities by which to see more of the supernatural than God has chosen to show it.

Not and Imaginary Vision

Do I seem to say that the soul really sees something and that this is an imaginary vision? I mean nothing of the sort. I am speaking of an intellectual vision. But being so ignorant and dull, I can explain nothing and am well aware that if anything is rightly stated, it does not come from me.

True and False Raptures

I think if the soul learns no mysteries at any time during raptures, they are not true raptures. I think they are natural weaknesses that may occur to people of delicate constitutions, such as women, when by its strenuous efforts the soul overpowers the physical nature and produces a stupor, as I explained in connection with the prayer of quiet.

Future Bliss Revealed

This is not so in genuine raptures, for in those I believe the Lord ravishes the soul wholly to himself as being His very own bride and shows her some small part of the kingdom she has won. However little this may be, everything is great that is in our Lord. He will allow no obstacle from the powers or the senses, but commands the doors of all the mansions to be closed at once, leaving only the one He is in open so we may enter. Blessed be such mercy—well may men be accursed who do not seek to profit by it, but who forfeit it!

Preparation of the Soul

Oh, what nothingness is all that we have given up, or that we do or ever could do, for a God who wills to communicate Himself to a worm! If we hope to enjoy this favor during our mortal life, what are we doing? Why do we delay? What can repay the loss of the time of such short duration in searching for the Lord, like the bride through the streets and squares? Oh, what mockery is everything in this world that does not lead toward and help us to attain to this state! Even though all the earthly pleasures, riches, and happiness that can be imagined could last for eternity, they would be disappointing and base contrasted with the treasures that are to be enjoyed forever—and yet even these are nothing compared with the possession of our Lord.

Soul Blinded by Its Faults

Oh, human blindness! When shall this dust be taken from our eyes? Although we think it insufficient to blind us, I see some little motes or grains of dust that, if left to spread, will harm us greatly. At least let these faults convince us of our misery, serving to clear our sight as the clay did the eyes of the blind man who was healed by Christ Jesus. Then realizing our imperfections, we shall ask Him more fervently to let us benefit by submitting to His judgment, thereby pleasing Him in all things.

God Has These Graces Ready for All

Forgive me, I have wandered away from my subject. Believe me when I speak of these wonders of God's greatness, I cannot but feel very grieved when I see what we lose by our own fault. It is true the Lord grants such favors to whom He chooses, yet, if we sought Him as He seeks us, He would give them to all of us. He longs for souls He can give them to, because His gifts in no way diminish His riches.

Faculties Lost During Ecstasy

Back to what I was describing. By the commands of the Bridegroom, the doors of the mansions, those of the innermost part of the castle and all other castle doors are closed, for when He intends ravishing the soul, He takes away the power of speech, and though the rest of the faculties may be active longer, no word can be uttered. Sometimes the person is totally deprived of all faculties. The hands and body become cold as if the soul has left, and no breathing can be detected. This condition lasts for only a short while, but when this profound suspension leaves, the body seems to come to itself again with a great gain in strength that gives more life to the soul.

Spiritual Inebriation

This supreme state of ecstasy never lasts long. When it stops it leaves the will so intoxicated with ecstasy, and the mind so transported out of itself, that for a day or sometimes more, the person is incapable of attending to anything except to that which excites the will to love God. Though wide awake enough to function in this manner, the person seems asleep regarding all earthly things.

Desire for and Love of
Suffering Enhanced

When the soul finally returns to itself, human words cannot express or describe the wonder of what it has experienced. Also, it is left with a more passionate desire to serve God in any way He asks. If the former states of prayer caused the powerful effects described, what effects will such a notable grace as this cause? Such a person wishes they had a thousand lives to spend living for God. In their passionate enthusiasm they would have all earthly creatures praising Him in a thousand tongues. The soul longs to perform severe penances, which are not even felt to be costly, for the power of love almost prevents their being felt. The soul realizes how little the martyrs suffered during their torture, for pain is bearable with the Lord's help. Therefore, such a soul may even complain when He gives it nothing to suffer.

Rash Judgment Caused by
Lack of Understanding

The person who experienced this grace feels it a great favor when God sends this rapture in secret. The thought of others witnessing this experience causes the soul to suffer confusion and the fear that those who witness it may diminish

145

its experience. Knowing the evil of the world, the soul fears the ecstasy will not be attributed to its proper cause, thus giving rise to rash judgment instead of the praise due God. Although this pain and distress are unavoidable, they seem to show a certain need of humility, for if the soul truly wished to be despised, what would it care?

The Lord's Preference for This Soul

The Lord once said to someone who was troubled by such thoughts "Do not be disturbed; people will either praise Me or condemn you. In either case you will gain." I learned afterwards that the person was greatly encouraged and comforted by these words. I mentioned it in case others may suffer in the same way. Apparently the Lord would have all men know that this soul is His own and that none may molest it, for it is all His. Men are welcome to attack the body, honor, and possessions of such a person, for glory will be accrued to the Lord from all they do. But the soul they may not touch, unless by an irresponsible act they cause it to withdraw from the protection of the Spouse, for the Lord will defend it against the whole world and hell.

Illusionary Raptures

I do not know if I have succeeded in teaching you what a rapture is, for as I said to explain it fully is impossible. Still I do not think time has been lost in describing a genuine rapture. The effects in false raptures are very different. I do not call them false because the people who experience them are trying to deceive others, for they themselves are unwittingly deceived. As the signs and effects do not correspond to this great grace, the favor itself becomes so discredited that when the soul experiences it, no one believes in it. May God be ever blessed and praised. Amen.

CHAPTER 5

Describes the flight of the human spirit. The loss of self-control. Obligations following these favors. Humility produced by them. How the Lord comforts such a soul. Mysteries learned.

There is another form of rapture; though essentially the same as the last, it produces very different feelings in the soul. I call it "flight of the spirit," for the soul suddenly feels a rapid sense of motion and the spirit appears to hurry it away with a speed that is very alarming when first experienced. Therefore, I said the soul on whom God bestows this favor requires strong courage, great faith, absolute trust, and total resignation, so that God may do what He chooses with it.

Loss of Self-Control

Do you suppose a person in perfect possession of their senses feels only slight dismay at their soul being drawn above them? The person doesn't know where the soul is going, who is raising it, nor how it happens, for at the first sudden movement one does not feel sure it is caused by God. Can it possibly be resisted? No, I am told resistance accelerates the motion. God now appears to be teaching the soul which has placed itself in His hands and offered itself entirely to Him, that if it resists it will be snatched away more strongly as consequence of its resistance.

Therefore, the soul will resist no more, but will yield itself into the hands of Almighty God, for it is always best to make a virtue of necessity. Incidentally, God lifts our spirit to flight as easily as a strong man lifts a piece of straw to the wind.

Symbol of the Two Cisterns

It seems that the cistern of water I spoke of in the fourth mansion was formerly filled gently and quietly with no movement, but now God lets loose a stream with a powerful rushing flow into the cistern. A mighty wave rises with enough strength to lift on high the little vessel of the spirit. Neither the ship herself nor the pilot and sailors can control the fury of the sea or prevent it from carrying the boat where it will. Far less can the interior of the soul now stay where it chooses, nor act contrary to His dominion, for the exterior powers of the body are quite useless in this situation.

Obligations Following These Favors

Indeed, I am amazed even as I am writing of this manifestation of the immense power of this great King and Lord. What do you suppose must be felt by those who actually experience it? I am convinced that if God were to reveal himself to the greatest sinners on earth, they would never dare to offend Him again—if not through love, then by fear of Him. What obligations bind those taught in so sublime a manner to strive with all their might not to displease God? In His Name, I beg you who have received these or similar gifts, do not rest content with merely receiving them, but remember that those who receive much, have much to give.

Humility Produced by These Favors

This thought terrifies the soul, and unless great courage is given by our Lord, the soul would suffer great and constant grief. Why? When it looks at all the Lord has done for it, and then upon itself, it sees how little good it has performed in comparison with what it is required to do. The paltry service so far rendered is full of faults, failures, and a lukewarm attitude. To erase the memory of its many imperfections, it thinks it best to forget them altogether. The soul that always remembers its sins casts itself on the mercy of God, knowing it can never repay its debt to Him, and begs for the mercy and compassion He always shows sinners.

How the Crucified Lord
Comforted Such a Soul

Perhaps He will answer as He did to someone who was kneeling before a crucifix in great affliction on this account, and feeling sure she had never had anything to offer to God or to sacrifice for His sake. The Crucified One consoled her by saying that He gave her for herself all the pains and labors He had borne in His passion, that she might offer them as her own to His Father. I learned from her that she at once felt comforted and enriched by these words, and that she never forgets to recall them whenever she realizes her own wretchedness. I could relate several other incidents of the same kind from conversations with many holy people who pray much, but I will not recount them lest you think I may be relating to myself.

A Humble Soul Fears These Favors

This example is very instructive, for it shows that we please our Lord by self-knowledge, by the constant recollection of our poverty and miseries, and by realizing we posses nothing that we have not received from Him. Therefore, courage is needed in order to receive this and many other gifts that come to a soul elevated to this state by our Lord. I think that if the soul is humble it requires more courage than ever for this gift. May God grant us humility for His name's sake.

Mysteries Learned by the
Flight of the Spirit

To return to this sudden rapture of the spirit, the soul really appears to have left the body. Though not lifeless, the person is certainly not dead, but cannot for a brief period of time tell whether the spirit remains within the body or not. The person may feel they have been transported into another world where a light so unlike earthly light shines.

All the rest of their life on earth, they may try to picture and tell about all the wonders they have seen, but they cannot possibly succeed. In an instant the mind learns many things that the imagination and intellect would spend years trying to remember, yet they would not remember even a thousandth part of them.

Imaginary Visions Sometime Accompany Intellectual Ones

This vision is not intellectual but imaginary, and it's seen by the eyes of the soul more clearly than earthly things are seen by the physical eyes. Although no words are spoken, the spirit is taught many truths. For instance, if it sees any of the saints, it recognizes them at once as if intimately acquainted with them for years. Occasionally, in addition to what the eyes of the soul perceive in intellectual visions, other things may be shown it. In an imaginary vision it usually sees our Lord accompanied by a host of angels, yet neither the physical eyes nor the eyes of the soul see anything, for these visions are revealed by some wonderful intuition that I cannot explain. Perhaps those who have experienced this gift may possess more ability to describe it, though it seems to me a most difficult task.

How the Flight of the Spirit Takes Place

I do not know if the soul is still dwelling in the body at this time or not; I would not say it does, nor it doesn't. I have often thought that though the sun does not leave its place in heaven, its rays have power to reach the earth instantaneously. Likewise, the soul and spirit may remain in the body due to the strength and love coming to them from the Son of God. I do not understand what I am talking about, but the truth is like the swiftness of an arrow from the taut string of the bow, an upward flight takes place in the interior of the soul. Although noiseless, it is too manifest a movement to be an illusion, for the soul is quite outside itself—at least that is the impression felt by it. Great mysteries are revealed to it during this time, and when the person returns to consciousness they are so greatly changed and benefited that they hold all earthly goods as filth in comparison to what they have seen. Henceforth earthly life is grievous to the soul, for what once pleased it, now remains uncared for and unnoticed.

The Soul is Fortified

Those children of Israel who were sent to spy out the Promised Land brought back fruit from it, so here our Lord seems to want to show the soul something of the land to which it is traveling. He gives it courage to pass through the trials of this painful journey, for the soul has learned to go to Him to supply all it needs. You may think that such profit could not be so quickly attained, but only those who have experienced this wondrous gift can know its value.

Three Great Graces Left in the Soul

This clearly shows it is not the work of the devil. For neither the imagination, or the devil could leave peace, calm, and good fruits in the soul. The enemy and the imagination certainly could not imitate gifts of such divine order as mentioned next.

First Grace

The first is the gift of perception of the greatness of God that becomes clearer to us as we witness more of it.

Second Grace

The second is the gain of self-knowledge and humility when we see how inferior we are in comparison to God our Creator. We wonder at how we even dared to offend Him in the past or even desire to gaze upon Him now.

Third Grace

The third is a constantly growing contempt for all earthly things, unless they are consecrated to the service of our wondrous God. The Bridegroom begins to adorn His bride with gifts such as these. Their value to her is beyond measure and she keeps them with great care. These visions are so deeply engraved in her memory that I believe she could never forget them, and to do so would be a great loss. Praise God, the Bridegroom who gave her these gifts also has power to give her the grace not to lose them.

Fear Caused by This Favor

I told you that courage is required by the soul, for do you think it is a small matter for the spirit to feel literally separated from the body, as it does when it no longer has use of the senses, and does not understand the reason? There is specific need that He who gives rest should also give fortitude. You may say this fear is well rewarded, and so do I. May He who bestows such graces be forever praised, and may our Lord grant that we may be worthy to serve Him. Amen.

CHAPTER 6

In this chapter, the soul longs for death. Saint Teresa bewails her inability to serve God as He deserves. The jubilee of the soul. Fervent praises to God.

These sublime gifts leave the soul filled with desire to enjoy Him who has given them so intensely that life becomes a painful though delicious torture, and death is longed for. Such a person often implores God with tears to take them from this earth where everything seems so wearisome. Solitude alone brings some relief for awhile, but soon the yearning grief returns and the soul almost welcomes it. In short, this soul like the poor little butterfly can find no lasting rest. So tender is its love that at the slightest provocation it flames forth and the soul takes flight again. In this mansion raptures occur frequently, and also in public where people observe them. Persecutions and slanderous remarks often ensue, and no matter how the soul may try, it cannot keep free of the fears suggested to it by so many people, especially the Clergy.

Soul Cannot Help Desiring These Favors

Great confidence is felt within the soul when it is alone with God, but it becomes troubled with fear at the thought of being deceived by the devil, thereby offending Him who she so deeply loves. The person is not concerned about blame, except when the priests may find some fault even though the person may not be able to help what happened. The soul will ask everyone to pray for it since it has been told to do so, and begs the Lord to direct it by some other way less dangerous. Nevertheless, the benefits left by these gifts that the soul easily saw, heard, and learned in the law of God, are so great that they will lead it on the way to Heaven. Strive though it may, the soul cannot resist desiring these gifts, and so it resigns itself into God's hands. The soul is still uncomfortable about being disobedient to the priest by desiring these gifts; however, it feels that being obedient to God and not offending Him is its safeguard against deception. For the soul would rather be cut in pieces than willfully commit the smallest sin, yet it often feels grieved for falling into a great number of them. God has bestowed upon souls like this a deep desire not to displease Him, however small the matter. This causes the soul to greatly envy those who live away from everything and everybody in the deserts. However, they still seek to live among society in hopes of helping but one soul to praise God better. In the case of women, they grieve over the fact they cannot proclaim aloud in the sanctuaries or other places the mighty God of hosts.

Saint Teresa Bewails Her Inability
to Serve God

Oh, poor little butterfly chained by so many fetters that stop you from flying where you desire! "Have pity on her, O God, and change her ways that she may be able to accomplish her desires for Your honor and glory! Take no notice that she deserves little, nor of the vileness of her nature, O Lord, You have the power to command the vast ocean to cease, and opened a path in the river Jordan for the children of Israel to pass through. Take notice of her, yet like the butterfly do not spare her these trials, for by Your strength she can endure—she is resolved to do so, and desires to suffer them. Stretch forth Your arm, O Lord, to help her not waste her life on trifles. Let Your greatness appear in this Your creature, weak as she is, so that men, seeing the good in her though not her own, may praise You for it. Cost what it may, she is willing to pay the price, because it is her dearest desire to lose a thousand of her lives to lead one to praise You. If a thousand lives were hers to give, she would count them well spent in such a cause, yet knowing well that she is unworthy and unable on her own to bear even the lightest cross, much less die for You."

Fervor Resulting From Ecstasies

I do not know why I have said this, nor what caused me to do so, indeed I never intended it. It is important for you to know that these effects are bound to follow from such trances or ecstasies. They are not fleeting, but permanent desires, and when opportunity occurs to act on them, they prove genuine. How can I say they are permanent even though at times the soul hesitates and feels cowardly and fears to do any work for God, even the most trivial work?

Restraining Increased Desire
to See God

I believe it is because our Lord leaves the soul to its natural weakness for its own good, thereby convincing it thoroughly that any strength it may possess came from Him, and to destroy its self-love and endue it with greater knowledge of His mercy and grace. Beware of the strong desires to behold our Lord; they can be very distressing and need to be discouraged, for in another kind of prayer I shall speak of later it is not possible to behold Him.

Care Should Be Taken to Not
Endanger Health

In this current state of prayer these longings can sometimes be stopped. The reasoning power of the mind is free to conform to the will of God, and should these desires become very oppressive, the thoughts may be turned to some other matter. Such longings are generally found in persons far advanced in perfection. The devil may use this to make us think we are in advanced perfection, so it is well to be cautious. For me, I do not believe he can cause the calm and peace given by this pain to the soul, but would more likely disturb it with much uneasiness and afflict it with worldly cares. A person inexperienced in both kinds of sorrow cannot understand the difference, and thinking such grief to be good, may cause injury to their health—for these longings are incessant or at the very least frequent.

Tears Often Result from Physical Causes

You should also know that bodily weakness may cause such pain, especially to sensitive people who cry over every trifling trouble. Numberless times they imagine they are mourning for God's sake when they are not. If for a considerable amount of time a person of this nature weeps uncontrollably at hearing the mention of God or thinks about

Him, the cause may be an accumulation of body fluid around the heart that has a great deal more to do with the tears, more so than with the love of God. Such persons seem as if they never stop crying. Believing their tears are beneficial, they do not try to stop them, but encourage them as much as possible. The devil seizes the opportunity of weakening persons like this to keep them from praying.

St. Teresa's Own Experience

I think you must be puzzling over this and perhaps thinking I see danger in everything. If so, you would like to know what you should do. You may also think that if I am afraid of delusions in so good a thing as tears, perhaps I myself am deluded, and maybe I am. But believe me, I do not say this without having witnessed it in other people. Not in me, for there is nothing tender about me, and my heart is so hard it grieves me. However, when the fire burns fiercely within, stony as my heart may be, it becomes liquid. It is easy to know when tears come from this source, for they are soothing and gentle rather than stormy and rarely do harm. This delusion, when it is one, has the advantage with a humble person of injuring the body and not the soul. But to one who is not humble, it is well to be ever on guard.

Excessive Crying

If we think that by crying a great deal we have done all that is needed, we are mistaken. It is essential for us to work hard and do good, and let the tears fall when God sends them, not by forcing oneself to shed them. If we do not take too much notice of them, they will leave the parched soil of the souls well watered and fertile for producing good fruit. This is the water that falls from heaven, and though we may tire in digging to reach it, we will never get any water like it, for this is a well springing up in the soul.

Confide Entirely in God

Therefore, I think it is best for us to place ourselves in the presence of God, contemplating His mercy and grandeur and our own vileness. Allow Him to give us what He wills, whether water or drought, for only He knows what is best for us. When we make His will our will, we will enjoy peace, and the devil will have far fewer opportunities to deceive us.

Jubilee of the Soul

Among these favors, our Lord sometimes causes a jubilation in the soul, and a strange and mysterious kind of prayer. If He bestows this grace on you, praise Him much; I describe it so you may know it is real. I believe that the faculties of the soul are closely united to God, but He allows them liberty to rejoice in their happiness together with the senses, though they don't know what they are enjoying, nor how they do so. This may sound like nonsense but it really happens. So excessive is the jubilee that the soul will not enjoy it by itself, but spreads it to all around so they may help to praise God, which is its one desire.

Joy Impossible to Conceal

Oh, such rejoicings this person would utter, and what demonstrations of joy so that all might know its happiness! The person seems to have found itself again as though lost like the prodigal son, and wants all to share in the celebration feast with it, because at least for the time being it does not doubt its security. I believe this is valid, for the devil could not possibly infuse so much joy and peace into the center of a being whose whole delight consists of urging others to praise God. It requires a painful effort to keep silent and not join in the celebration of such happiness. St. Francis must have experienced this when robbers met him rushing through the fields; they asked him who he was, and he replied that he was the "herald of the great King." Other saints who felt the same way retired into the deserts so that, like St. Francis, they could proclaim the praises of God.

The World Judges This Jubilee

I knew St. Peter of Alcantara did this. I believe he was a saint because of the life he led, though people often called him a fool when they heard him proclaim the praises of God. Oh, happy folly, would that God let us all share in it! What mercy and grace He has shown us by placing us where we are, that we may proclaim Him and not be concerned for the contempt of the world. What a wretched life and miserable times are spent in the world. How blessed are those who are free from it.

Joy at Seeing Others Praise the Lord

I am often delighted in the company of others to see the joy in their hearts as they praise the Lord for His goodness to them. It is so evident that their praises come from the very depth of their souls. I would like everyone to do this often, for when one begins to praise it causes others to join in. How can your tongues be better employed than in praising God who has given us so much to praise Him for?

The Saints Delight in This Jubilee

May God often grant this kind of prayer that is most safe and beneficial. We cannot acquire it ourselves, as it is quite supernatural. Sometimes it lasts for a whole day and the soul is like one intoxicated. It is not deprived of its senses, nor with depression, in which reasoning power is still there, but the imagination continually dwells on some subject that possesses it, and it is unable to free itself. These are very basic comparisons I am using in connection with such a precious gift, yet nothing else occurs to my mind. In this state of prayer a person experiences such joy and happiness that they become very forgetful of self and everything else, oftentimes to the point of not thinking or speaking of anything, except giving praise to God. We should all be so affected, for why would we wish to be wiser than they? What can make us happier? May all creatures unite their praises with ours forever and ever. Amen, amen, and amen!

CHAPTER 7

Describes the grief felt because of sins by souls on whom God has bestowed these gifts. How this sorrow is felt.
Saint Teresa's grief for her past sins.
Reasoning and mental prayer. Souls in every state of prayer should think of the passion of Christ.

It may seem to you that souls to whom God has communicated Himself in such a special manner may feel certain of enjoying Him forever, and are no longer required to fear or mourn over their past sins. Those of you who have never received these gifts are most apt to have this opinion, but those who have received the gifts will understand what I am talking about. This is a great mistake, because sorrow for sin increases in proportion to the divine grace received, and I believe will never cease until we are in Heaven. No doubt we feel this pain more at one time than another, and it may be a different kind of pain. A soul so advanced as that does not think of threatened punishment for its offences, but rather of its ingratitude toward Him to whom it owes so much. This is as it should be, for He justly deserves the gratitude for the sublime mysteries revealed to us about the greatness of God.

How This Sorrow Manifests
The soul wonders at its former timidity and weeps over its irreverence. It deeply regrets its foolishness in the past,

for such foolishness seems like a madness never ceasing to cause pain as the soul remembers the vile things that caused it to forsake our great sovereign Lord. The thoughts dwell on this more than on the gifts received, thoughts so powerful they seem to rush through the soul like a strong, swift, river. Yet the sins remain like the mire in the river bed and dwell constantly in the memory, making a heavy cross to bear.

Saint Teresa's Grief Over Past Sins

I know someone who, though she had ceased to wish for death in order to see God, desired it so that she might be free from her continual regret for past ingratitude toward Him, to whom she owed so much. She thought no one's guilt could be compared to hers, for she felt there could be no one whom God had been so patient with and had given such wondrous graces to.

Souls Centered in God Decrease
in Self-Interest

Souls who have reached the state I speak of have ceased to fear hell. At times they grieve over the possibility of losing God, but their only dread is that He might withdraw His hand from them and allow them to offend Him, thus returning them to their former miserable condition. They dread anything that keeps them from the presence of God. Whatever grace and gifts God may give a soul, I think it is dangerous for it to forget its former unhappy state; painful as it may be, it is most beneficial.

Remembrance of Past Sins
Increases Contrition

Perhaps I think so because I have been so wicked. That may be the reason why I never forget my sins. People who have led good lives have no cause for grief, yet we all fall at some time while in these mortal bodies. This pain is not relieved by reflecting upon the Lord, nor noting that He has already forgiven us for our sins and faults. Our grief is increased because of His kindness and the favors bestowed on us, for we deserve nothing but hell. I think the Apostle Paul and Mary Magdalene must have suffered a cruel martyrdom—their love of the Lord was so intense. They had received many mercies and realized the greatness and the majesty of God. They must have found it very hard to bear the remembrance of their sins, and regretted them with a most tender sorrow.

Meditation on the Mysteries
of Jesus Christ

You may think that one who has enjoyed such high favors need not meditate on the mysteries of our Lord Jesus Christ, but will be wholly absorbed in love for Him. I have written fully about this before, and I have been contradicted and told that I was wrong and did not understand the matter. I was further advised that it is best for me to concern myself with matters of the Godhead, and not what is physical. However, nothing will make me admit that as a better way.

Continued Meditation on the Mysteries
of our Lord Jesus Encouraged

I may be mistaken, for we may all really mean the same thing, but I found the devil was trying to lead me astray in this manner. Having been warned by experience in this respect, I have decided to speak about it again, as I have very often done elsewhere. Be most cautious on the subject, and attend to what I say about it. Do not believe anyone who tells you contrary. I will endeavor to explain myself more clearly than I did before. If the person who undertook to write on the matter had treated it more explicitly, he would have done well, for it may do much harm to speak of it in general terms to the uneducated.

Jesus the Christ is Our Example

Some souls imagine they cannot even meditate on the Passion of Christ, and even less on the Virgin Mary or the saints whose lives greatly benefit and strengthen us. I cannot think what such persons are to meditate on. To withdraw all thoughts from material or physical things like the angelic spirits, who are always inflamed with love, is not possible for us while in this mortal flesh. We need to study, meditate on, and imitate those mortals like ourselves, who performed such heroic deeds for God. How much less should we willfully endeavor not to think of our most holy Lord Jesus Christ? If anyone does this, they will be doing themselves much harm. I assure them they will never enter the last two mansions of the castle, for if they lose their guide, our Lord Jesus Christ, our holy Jesus, they will never find the way. Our Lord Himself tells us that He is the Way, the Truth, and the Life, and that He is the Light, and no man comes to the Father but by Him, and that the Father sees Him, and He sees the Father.

Meditation and Contemplation

Such persons tell us that these words have some other meaning. I know of no other meaning but this one which my soul has ever recognized as the truth, and that has always blessed me. Some people—many who have spoken to me on this subject—after our Lord has once raised then to perfect contemplation, wish to enjoy it continually. This is impossible, still the grace of this state remains in their souls in such a way that they cannot reason as before on the mysteries of the Passion and the life of Christ. I cannot account for it, but it happens often that the mind is less apt to meditate. I think it must be because the purpose of meditation is to seek God, and after He has once been found the soul is accustomed to seek Him again by means of the will. It no longer wearies itself searching for Him by the intellect.

Meditation During Dryness

It also appears to me that as the will is already inflamed with love, this generous faculty would if possible cease to make use of the power of reason. This would be good, but impossible, especially before the soul has reached the last two mansions. Time spent in prayer would thus be lost, since the will often needs the use of the understanding to rekindle its love. Notice this important point; I will explain it more fully. Such a soul desires to spend all its time in loving God and wishes to do nothing else, but it cannot succeed, for though the will is not dead, the flame that kindled it is dying out, and the spark needs fanning into a flame. Should the soul patiently wait for the fire, like Elias, who waited for fire to descend from Heaven to consume the sacrifice to God? Certainly not, it has no right to expect miracles—God will work miracles for the soul when He chooses. As I have already told you, and will do again, God wants us to hold ourselves unworthy of miracles being wrought on our account. He wants us to help ourselves to the best of our abilities. Then what we cannot do, He will do according to His will.

Not Sensing God's Presence

In my opinion, we should act this way all our lives, no matter how sublime our prayer may be. True, those whom our Lord admits into the seventh mansion rarely or never need help in their fervor. Such souls are kept in a wonderful manner, and are constantly in the presence of Christ our Lord. Therefore, when the fire in our hearts does not burn in the will, or we do not feel the presence of God, we must search for Him like the bride in the Song of Solomon. Then we will not stand like unintelligent beings, wasting our time in waiting for what we previously enjoyed. At first, it may be that our Lord will not renew His gift again for a year or even many years—the Lord knows the reason, and we should not try to find out what it is, for there is no need for us to understand it.

Reasoning and Mental Prayer

Most certainly, the way to please God is to keep His commandments and His counsels diligently, all the while meditating on His life and death and all we owe Him. Then let everything else be as God chooses. Some may say their mind refuses to dwell on these subjects, for the above reasons—to a certain extent that is true. You know that it is one thing to reason and another thing for the memory to bring certain truths to your mind. Perhaps you may not understand me, as I fail to express myself well, but I will do my best. Using the understanding in this manner is what I call meditation.

Meditation on the Lord's Life
and Passion

Let us begin by considering the mercy God showed us by giving us His only Son—don't stop there, but go on to think of all the mysteries of His glorious life. Let us turn our thoughts to His prayer in the Garden of Gethsemane, then allow your thoughts to continue through all the events that took place until they reach the crucifixion. Or you may take some part of the Passion, such as Christ's apprehension, and meditate on that mystery. Consider in detail the points to be pondered and thought over, such as the treachery of Judas, the flight of the Apostles, and all the events that followed. This is an admirable and very meritorious kind of meditation.

Simplicity of Contemplative Meditation

Souls led by God in supernatural ways and raised to perfect contemplation are right in declaring they cannot practice this kind of meditation. I cannot explain it, but I believe they are unable to do so. Yet they would be wrong in saying that they cannot dwell on these mysteries, or think about them often, especially when these events are being celebrated by the Church. It is impossible for the souls who have received so much from God to forget these precious proofs of His love. They are like living sparks that inflame the heart with a greater love for the Lord—which the mind cannot fail to understand. Such a soul comprehends these mysteries that are brought to the mind and stamped on the memory in a more perfect way than others. Even the mere sight of our Lord prostrate in the Garden of Gethsemane, covered with great drops of sweat, is enough to keep these thoughts in mind—not merely for an hour, but for several days. The soul looks with a simple gaze upon who He is, and how ungratefully we treat Him in return for His terrible sufferings. When considering all He has done for us, the will, in all tenderness, desires to render Him service for His sublime mercies, and longs to suffer for Him in a similar manner.

Souls Should Always Meditate on the Passion of Christ

I think this is why these souls think they cannot meditate on the Passion. Those who do not meditate on it had better begin to do so, for I know it will not impede the most sublime prayer. Not only that, it is not good to stop praising the Lord. If God sees fit to enrapture them, even though they may be reluctant, He will make them cease meditating.

I am certain this way of thinking is most helpful to the soul, and not the hindrance it could become if great effort was made to use the intellect. This, I believe, cannot be done when a higher state of prayer is attained. It may not be true in all cases, for God leads souls in many different ways. However, we should not place any blame on those who are unable to pray in this manner, nor should they be judged as incapable of enjoying the great graces contained in the mysteries of Jesus Christ. No one, no matter how spiritual they may be, could ever persuade me that it is not necessary to give much thought, praise, and thanks to Christ Jesus.

Jesus is the Way, the Truth, and the Life

There are souls just beginning, or advanced half-way, who—when they begin to experience the prayer of quiet and taste the sweetness and comforts God gives—desire to enjoy these spiritual pleasures continually. I feel they are wrong, and I have told them not to concentrate on this one aspect of God's gifts. Life is long and full of crosses to bear, and we need to look to Christ and imitate Him. We need to follow the examples He gave when He bore His trials, as did the Apostles. In that way we will learn to bear our own trials more perfectly. Our Lord Jesus is pleased when we grieve at His pains, though sometimes at the cost of our own comforts and joys. However, comforts in prayer are not so frequent that we have no time to meditate on Christ and His trials. If anyone would tell me they have comforts continually, and that they are one of those who cannot meditate on divine mysteries, I would feel very doubtful and concerned for them.

Never Give Up Meditation on the Lord Jesus Christ

Be convinced of this, keep yourself free from this deception and do all in your power to stop yourself from being constantly immersed in intoxicating prayer. If you cannot do so, tell your spiritual advisors, and they will help you to keep so busy you will not have time to think of the matter. Then you will be free from this danger that can greatly injure your physical and mental health when prolonged. I have said enough to those who require proof, however spiritual their state. It is as much an error to stop thinking of physical things as it is to think that meditation on Christ

Jesus can injure the soul. I am certain of this because I made this mistake myself.

I did not spend much time meditating on our Lord Jesus Christ, preferring to remain absorbed in, and waiting for more spiritual comforts. I quickly realized I was wrong when I could not stay in a state of spiritual comfort very long. My thoughts wandered and my soul seemed like a bird, always flying and finding no place to rest. Consequently, I lost much time and did not advance in virtue, or make any progress in prayer. I did not understand the reason, for I believed I was acting wisely. I would probably never have learned the truth if it had not been for the advice of a spiritual servant of God about my mode of prayer. Then I understood how very mistaken I had been, and I have never ceased praising God for that person. God had him show me the error of my ways. May He be praised forever. Amen.

CHAPTER 8

Describes how God communicates with the soul by intellectual visions. Gives advice on this vision and speaks of the effects when the vision is genuine.

The more the soul advances, the more it is aware of the Lord's closeness, and that it cannot withdraw from His presence. This is clearly shown by the manner and ways in which the Lord shows himself to us, by manifesting His love in wonderful visions, which by His help I will describe to you. I tell you this so that you will not be alarmed if this favor is granted to you. We should praise Him much for communing with us, even if we do not receive this favor for ourselves, for His majesty and power are sovereign.

Saint Teresa's Experience of the Awareness of Christ

For example, a person not expecting this favor or ever having imagined themselves worthy of receiving it, becomes aware that Jesus Christ is standing by their side, though they do not see Him with the physical eyes, or the eyes of the soul. This is called an intellectual vision—I do not know why. I knew a person to whom God granted this grace, and others I will describe later on. At first it distressed her, for she could not understand it. She could see nothing, yet was convinced that Jesus Christ was manifesting Himself to her in some kind of vision. The powerful effects of this vision were a strong argument that it was from God, still she was alarmed, never having heard of an intellectual vision nor being aware that such a thing could be. She felt certain of the Lord's presence, and He spoke to her several times. Now, before she received this grace, she had heard words spoken to her, but never knew who spoke them.

Confidence Resulting From This Vision

She was frightened by this vision, which unlike imaginary ones, does not pass away quickly, but lasts for several days and even a year or more. In a great state of anxiety she went to a priest, who asked her how, if she saw nothing, she knew it was the Lord near her, and asked her to describe His appearance. She said she was unable to do so, for she could not see His face. So, she could not tell the priest any more than she had already, except that she was sure it was Christ who spoke to her, and it was no trick of her imagination. Although people constantly cautioned her about this vision, she found it impossible to believe them, especially when she heard the words: "It is I; be not afraid."

Effects of the Words

The effect of these words was so powerful that for the time being she could not doubt its truth. She felt very encouraged and rejoiced at being in His company. This favor greatly helped her gain constant recollection of the Lord, and caused her to exercise great care not to displease Him in any way, for He was always by her side watching her. Whenever she desired to speak to Him in prayer, He seemed so close that He could not fail to hear her. Nevertheless, He did not speak to her when she wished Him to, only when the necessity arose. She was conscious of His being at her right hand—not in the ordinary way we know a person is standing beside us, but in a more subtle way that cannot be described. Yet this presence is quite as evident and certain, perhaps more so, than the ordinary presence of people—about which we can be deceived. Not so in this, for this presence brings with it graces and spiritual effects that could not possibly come from a mental disorder. This is not the devil either, for he cannot fill the soul with peace and a constant desire to please the Lord, nor cause the soul to have no interest in anything that does not lead to Him. As time went on, my friend recognized this was not a work of the evil one; our Lord showed her that more and more clearly.

Awareness of Christ Produces Humility

However, I know that she often felt great alarm and was at times overcome with confusion, because she was unable to account for so high a favor being granted to her. She and I were very close, and I knew all that happened in her soul, so my account of this is absolutely true and reliable. This favor brings with it an overwhelming sense of self-abasement and humility; the reverse would be the case if it came from satan. It is also evident that no human effort could produce such feelings; only the Lord could give such a divine gift.

Prepares Soul to Receive Other Graces

Although I believe some of the other graces are more sublime, this one brings a special knowledge of God. A most tender love for Him results from being constantly in His company, and a most fervent desire to devote one's whole being to His service is greatly expanded. The conscience is greatly purified by the knowledge of His constant and near presence, for although we know that God sees all we do, nature inclines us to grow careless and forgetful of it. This is impossible here, because the Lord makes the soul conscious that He is close at hand. This prepares the soul to receive other graces mentioned as it constantly makes acts of love to Him whom it sees or feels at its side. In short, the benefits caused by this grace prove how great and how valuable it is. The soul thanks our Lord for bestowing it on one so unworthy, but would not exchange it for any earthly riches or delight.

The Lord Withdraws the Awareness of His Presence

When the Lord withdraws the awareness His presence, the soul in its loneliness makes every possible effort to induce Him to return. This avails little, for He comes at His will, and not by our endeavors.

Obligations Resulting From This Grace

There are other spiritual matters that cannot be explained, and our inability to grasp them should teach us how incapable we are of understanding the sublime mysteries of God. Those on whom these favors and graces are bestowed should be in awe and praise God for His mercy and grace. These particular graces are not granted to everyone, and any who receive them should hold them in high esteem and strive to serve God more zealously. Such a person should not think more highly of his or herself for receiving this grace, but rather should serve Him more, feeling themselves to be under greater obligation to Him than others. Any faults committed pierce to the heart, as indeed they should under the circumstances.

Signs That This Grace is Genuine

When the effects described are felt, any of you whom our Lord leads this way may be certain it is neither deception, nor imagination. I believe it to be impossible for the devil to produce an illusion lasting so long, benefit the soul so remarkably, and cause such inner peace. It is not his customary way, and an evil creature could not bring so much good, for the soul would soon become clouded by self-esteem, and a feeling of superiority above others. The soul's continual awareness of the Lord's presence, and the concentration of its thoughts on the Lord, would so enrage satan that, even if he tried, he would never succeed. God would never permit the evil one so much power over one whose only desire is to please Him and lay down their life for His honor and glory.

Seeking Advice From a Spiritual Advisor

I contend, as I always shall, that if the soul reaps the effects described from these divine graces, the Lord will turn all things to its good. Therefore, as I said before, any of you who receive this grace need feel no alarm. Fear is good and we should be cautious and not overconfident. Overconfidence would prove not to be of God, for this is not one of the effects of this grace. If this does occur, you should speak with a well qualified spiritual advisor who can give light and spiritual advice. Best of all, speak to the Lord, and ask Him not to allow you to be misled, for I know that the same Lord beside you will comfort and guide you.

Cautions Regarding this Vision

If you choose to go to someone who is not spiritually enlightened, the matter, which should have been in strict confidence, usually becomes public This causes much grief and increased torment to one who already fears they have been deceived. Remember, our Lord guides every one in the way He knows is best; seek Him and His grace. This gift prepares the one who receives it to become a great servant of God, and sometimes the Lord chooses to bestow it on the weakest souls; therefore, it should not be esteemed or condemned. We must look to the virtues; for the soul who is most weak, humble, and single-minded in serving God is the most holy. God is the judge of all such matters. At the time of the great Judgment, we may be very surprised how different His judgment is from that of this world. May He be forever praised. Amen.

CHAPTER 9

This chapter discusses the way that God communicates with the soul by visions. Explanation of various effects of this communication. False and true visions.

We begin this chapter by discussing visions. The first we will discuss is imaginary visions {visions in the mind}. Imaginary visions are ones the devil is most likely to use to deceive people. Yet, when imaginary visions are divine, they seem more profitable to us than others, for they are more suited to our nature—with the exception of the visions sent by our Lord in the seventh mansion that surpass all others. An example of this is the presence of our Lord described in the last chapter. Let us suppose we have in our possession a gold locket containing a precious stone of the highest value and power, which, though we have not seen it, we are certain has virtues which will benefit us when we wear it. We value it highly, knowing by experience that it is remedial for maladies it has already cured us of. However, we dare not look at it, nor open it, for the owner of the jewel alone knows the secret of unfastening its lock. Although he lent it to us, he kept the key for himself. He will open the locket when he chooses to show us its contents, and He will close it again as He sees fit.

Explanation of the Simile

Our Lord treats us in the same way. Suppose the owner of the locket suddenly opened it at times for the benefit of the person to whom he has entrusted it. No doubt that person would value the diamond inside the locket more highly by remembering its beautiful luster. This may be compared to what happens when our Lord is pleased to caress the soul; He shows it a vision using any form He chooses. The vision passes as quickly as a flash of lightning—yet this most glorious picture makes an impression on the imagination that I believe can never be erased until the soul sees Christ in eternity. Although I call it a picture, you must not imagine that it looks like a painting. Christ appears as a living Person who sometimes speaks and reveals deep mysteries. You must understand that though the soul sees this for a certain space of time, it is no more possible to continue looking at it than to gaze for a very long time on the sun. Therefore, the vision passes quickly, but the brightness does not pain the inner sight as the sun's glare injures the physical eyes.

The Apparition Explained

The image is seen by the inner eyes alone. In the case of bodily apparitions I can say nothing—for a person I know very well never experienced anything of the kind herself, and could not speak about them with any certainty. The splendor of Him who is revealed in the vision resembles an infused light, like the sun covered with a veil as transparent as a diamond, and His raiment looks like fine linen. The soul to whom God grants this vision almost always falls into an intense sense of bliss or rapture, for the physical body is too weak to bear so wondrous a sight. This apparition is more lovely and delightful than anything that could be imagined. We could live a thousand years spending all that time trying to recapture the image to no avail, for it far surpasses our limited imagination and understanding. The presence of such surpassing majesty inspires the soul with great fear.

Great Awe Produced by this Vision

There is no need to ask the soul how it knew who He was, or why the certainty that it was the Lord of Heaven and earth. This is not so with earthly kings—unless we were told their names and saw their entourage of courtiers, they would attract little notice. "O Lord, how little do we Christians know You. What will that day be like when You come as our Judge, for we have known You as a friend who is closer than a brother. Will the sight of You strike us with much awe?" Let us always keep the thought of the Judgment day before our eyes, caring nothing what sufferings we endure, nor how long they last, for time is but a moment when compared to an eternity of pain. When I think of sinful lost souls looking upon a most holy God, now fully aware of their fate, it is almost more than my heart can bear.

False and Genuine Visions

Back to the vision. The soul who experiences this vision of our Lord must experience great fear when being overcome with such strong feelings and emotions that they produce unconsciousness. This must be the reason that the soul remains in this state of rapturous unconsciousness, to enable the Lord to strengthen weaknesses and unite it to

His greatness in this sublime communion with Him. When anyone can contemplate this sight of our Lord for a long period of time, I do not believe it is a vision, but rather an overwhelming idea that causes the imagination to think it sees something. But this illusion is only like a dead image in comparison with the living reality of a vision of the Lord.

Illusive Visions

Quite a number of people have spoken to me on this subject, and I know by experience that there are souls that either possess vivid imaginations or active minds, or for some reason are so absorbed in their own ideas that they feel certain what they imagine is real. If they had ever beheld a genuine vision, they would have unmistakably recognized a deception. They fabricate what they see and describe it in great detail, but no other effects are produced on the mind, which has no increased devotion for the Lord. It is clear that no attention should be paid to such imaginings that pass quickly like dreams from the memory.

Effects of a Genuine Vision

The vision we are discussing is very different, for a person who experiences this is far from thinking of seeing anything, nor has it ever crossed the mind, but when the vision is revealed in its entirety the person experiences a blissful peace. When Paul was thrown to the ground, a great light and noise came from heaven sounding like thunder to those around him. But a true voice was heard by Paul, who was now blind for a time as God worked His miraculous will in him. Then Paul's confusion was replaced by perfect calm for He had seen the Lord. It is the same for those who experience the effects of this vision. Certain sublime truths have been impressed on the mind during this time, and God's wisdom enlightens the former ignorance, producing peace and calm.

175

Vision Leaves Conviction

The soul sometimes possesses such a certainty that this grace comes from God that whatever people may say to the contrary, the soul fears no delusion. Their words only affect the soul in the same way as the temptations of the devil against faith—they disturb the mind, but do not shake the firmness of belief. In fact, the more severe the assault from unbelievers, the more certain the soul is that the devil could not produce the benefits received from the vision. He can produce a false apparition, but it does not possess truth, majesty, and value to the soul.

Conviction Effects Conduct

It is good to allow time to pass to see what effect develops from these visions, for day by day the soul should progress in humility and in all virtues. If Satan is suspected, he will soon show signs of himself and will be detected in one of his thousands of lies. If the person goes to a priest who has experienced these favors himself, he will not take long in discovering the truth. In fact, he will know immediately after being told about the vision whether it is divine, from the imagination, or from a demon, especially if he has received the gift of discernment of spirits.

Spiritual Advisor Should be Consulted

The point is, you should be perfectly candid and straightforward with the priest or spiritual advisor, not just in declaring your sins but also in giving an account of your prayer life and actions. Unless you do this, you cannot be assured you are being led by God. Our Lord wants us to be truthful and open with those in spiritual authority over us, just as we are with Him. Then you will feel no anxieties or uncertainties, because even if the vision was not from God, in your humbleness you have sought verification and you possess a good conscience regarding the whole matter.

What the devil intends for harm will turn out to your good. If the vision is from God, praise Him for granting you such a significant favor; then strive to serve Him even better and keep His image ever in your memory.

How to Deal with Visions

A great theologian once said that he would not be troubled by the devil, who is a clever artist, even if he presented before his eyes the living image of Christ, for it would only serve to kindle his devotion, thereby defeating Satan's scheme. If a sinner paints a picture of Christ, though it is only a product of the mind, it may be a tool God will use to draw sinners to himself; therefore, when we look at it, and we are stirred in love and devotion to Him, it may be serving God's plan. This great scholar also said it would be very wrong to be rude and scornful to one who comes to a spiritual advisor or priest seeking advice or verification of a vision of the Lord. How much more should we always show respect to a crucifix or a picture of the Lord whenever it meets our gaze. I have written about this elsewhere, and I am glad of the opportunity to say it again. I know someone who was deeply pained at being bidden to behave in this way. I do not know who invented such a torture for her, but she felt bound to obey the counsel given by her spiritual advisor. She thought her soul was at stake if she did not obey him. My advice is, if you are given such an order, you should not obey it. I am perfectly satisfied with the advice given by my counselor on this subject.

Effects of a Vision of Christ

A great benefit gained by the person who receives this vision is when she thinks of the Lord, or when she is praying, the remembrance of the vision will be great consolation. In the same way, we feel happier when we finally meet someone who has been a benefactor to us than we would if we had never met them personally. I can assure you the remembrance of this joy caused by this vision gives great comfort.

Seek to Edify the Church

But I most earnestly advise you, when you know or hear of God bestowing these graces on others, never desire or pray to be led this way yourself. It may appear to you to be very good; and indeed it should be highly esteemed and reverenced, yet no one should seek it for the following reasons:

First: It is a lack of humility to desire what you have never deserved. I do not think anyone who longs for these graces is really humble. A common laborer never dreams of wishing to be a king—it seems impossible and he is unfit for it. A lowly mind has the same feeling about these divine favors. I do not believe God will ever bestow these gifts on such a person until He gives the person a thorough self-knowledge first. How else can that soul filled with lofty imaginations, realize the truth and the mercy God has shown it in not casting it into hell?

Second: Such a person is certain to be deceived or at least in great danger of delusion, because an entrance is left open to the devil—who only needs to see the door ajar to slip in and play a thousand deceptions.

Third: When people strongly desire a thing, the imagination makes them fancy they see or hear it. It is just like when a man's mind thinks on a subject all day, he dreams of it at night.

Fourth: It would be very presumptuous of me to choose a way for myself without knowing what is good for me. I should allow our Lord, who knows my soul, to guide me. In that way His will is done in all things in my life.

Fifth: Do you think people on whom the Lord bestows these favors have little to suffer? No, indeed! Their trials are most severe and of many kinds. How do you know if you could bear them?

Sixth: Perhaps what you think may be a gain may prove to be a loss. Remember what happened to Saul when he was made king. In short, sisters, there are other reasons besides these. Believe me, it is safer to wish only what God wishes. He loves us and knows us better than we know ourselves. Let us place ourselves entirely in His hands so that His will may be done in us—we will never go astray if our will is abandoned to Him.

Additional Benefits

Many other benefits result from this that I will discuss later on. I earnestly advise you, as the Apostle Paul said in 1 Corinthians 14:12, " Even so ye, forasmuch as ye are zealous of spiritual gifts, seek that ye may excel to the edifying of the church." Know that for having received many favors of this kind, you will not merit more glory but will be more stringently obliged to serve Him, because to one whom much is given, much is expected. (See Luke 12:48.)

Virtues More Meritorious Than Consolations

True, such a grace is a powerful help in practicing virtues in their highest perfection. But it is far more meritorious to gain them at the cost of one's own toil. I was acquainted with some one, indeed two people, on whom our Lord had bestowed some of these gifts. They were both so desirous of serving the Lord at their own cost without these great consolations, that they argued with the Lord for giving them these favors, because they wanted to suffer for His sake. If it had been possible they would have refused to receive them. When I say "consolations" I do not mean these visions which greatly benefit the soul, and are highly esteemed. I am referring to delights given by God during contemplation.

Fervent Souls Desire to
Serve God for Himself Alone

I believe that these desires are supernatural and proper to very fervent souls who wish to prove to God that they do not serve Him for pay. A fervent desire to serve the Lord for His glory, and not for the thought of any glory the soul might receive, is to satisfy the love felt for Him. Such souls would count it gain to be annihilated forever if it would be to His glory. May He be ever praised for His manifest greatness. Amen.

CHAPTER 10

This chapter deals with supernatural favors. Intellectual visions. God is compared to a palace in which His creatures dwell. Forgiveness. Why God reveals truth.

Our Lord communicates with the soul by means of these visions on many occasions, sometimes during affliction, at other times when the soul is about to receive a heavy cross to bear, and as a means to a closer relationship with Him. There is no need for me to specify each different case. I only wish to teach you (as far as I myself am acquainted with them) what the different favors are that God shows a soul in this gift, so that you may understand their characteristics and the effects they produce. Then you will not mistake every idle fancy of your mind for a vision, and if you do have one, you will not be disturbed or unhappy. The devil gains greatly if he can cause distress and trouble for the soul who does not understand these things, because he knows how it hinders the soul from totally loving and serving God.

An Intellectual Vision

Our majestic God has higher ways of communicating himself to the soul; they are less dangerous for the devil cannot imitate them. They are more difficult to describe, because they are more difficult to understand, that is why imaginary visions are easier to describe. God is sometimes pleased to suspend the senses while someone is praying so He can help the soul discover sublime mysteries the soul sees within God Himself. This is not a vision, nor can I rightly say the soul "sees," since it sees nothing. This is not an imaginary vision but a highly intellectual one, in which the knowledge is given to the soul of how all things are beheld in God, and how He contains all things within Him. It is of great value, and though it passes quickly, it remains deeply engraved in the memory and produces a greater perception of sin and its offense to God. I will try to explain this truth to you by a comparison. Although it has often been taught us, we either never think about it or do not wish to understand it. If we realized what it actually means we would not behave with such audacity.

God Compared to a Palace in Which
His Creatures Dwell

Let us compare God to a very spacious and magnificent mansion or palace and remember that this edifice is God himself. Can the sinner withdraw to some far off place to commit sins? No, certainly not, for God is omniscient—it makes no difference where the sinner goes, God is there. God sees all the abominations, impurities, and evil deeds that sinners commit. Oh, awful thought, well worthy to be pondered over. What profit it would bring to us who know so little, to understand these truths only partially. If our understanding was truly fruitful, how could we possibly be so reckless in our daring? Let us praise God in His infinite

181

mercy and patience for not casting us all down to hell at once when we were sinners. We should be ashamed of being resentful when derogatory things are said about us, especially when we compare them to the outrages done before God. Yet we are easily wounded whenever we hear of an unkind word spoken about us in our absence, though perhaps not spoken with evil intent.

Forgive as We are Forgiven

Oh misery of mankind. Oh, let us not think we are doing great things if we suffer injuries patiently, rather let us bear them with eagerness, and love our enemies, for our Lord has not ceased to love us in spite of our many sins. This is indeed the chief reason that all should forgive any harm done to them. I assure you that though this vision passes quickly, our Lord has bestowed a notable grace on those to whom He grants it. The soul will profit greatly by keeping this vision constantly in mind.

The Vision Shows God is Truth

Short as this vision is; in a manner indescribable God also manifests that in Him there is a reality that makes all truth in creatures seem obscure. He convinces the soul that He alone is that Truth that cannot lie, thus demonstrating the meaning of Paul's words in Romans, "Let God be true, but every man a liar" (Romans 3:4). As I recall Pilate and how he asked the Lord to answer his question: "What is truth?" I realize how little mortals know of the sublime truth of God.

We are Commanded to be Truthful

I wish I could explain this more clearly, but I do not know how. Let us learn that if we want to bear any resemblance to our God and His Son Christ Jesus, we must strive to walk ever in truth. I do not only mean we should not lie, but I mean we should be truthful before God and man. Above all, we should not wish to be thought of better than we are, for in all our good deeds we should give the glory to God. Thus we shall care little for this world, its deceptions, and falsehoods.

Once when I was wondering why our Lord so dearly loves the virtue of humility, the thought suddenly struck me that it is because God is the supreme Truth and humility is the truth, for it is most true that we have nothing good of ourselves. Whoever ignores this, lives a life of falsehood. Those who realize this fact most deeply, are the most pleasing to God, the supreme Truth, for they walk in truth. God grant that we may have the grace to never lose this self-knowledge. Amen.

Why God Reveals these Truths

Our Lord shows the soul these favors because the soul is His bride, resolute to do His will in all things; therefore, He wishes to help the bride in all things and manifest some of His divine attributes within her. This should lead us to praise God for bestowing all these graces. Neither the devil nor our imagination have any part in them, therefore the soul may rest in perfect peace.

CHAPTER 11

Favors increase the soul's desire for God. The dart of love. Spiritual sufferings. Courage needed and given by God.

Will all these graces bestowed by the Bridegroom upon the soul be sufficient contentment for our little butterfly (you see I have not forgotten her after all), so that she may settle down and rest? No indeed, her state is worse than ever; although the soul has been receiving these favors it still sighs and weeps, because each grace intensifies the pain of wanting to be with the Bridegroom. The soul sees itself still far away from God. Even with the increased knowledge of His attributes, the soul longs for Him and its love for Him grows stronger as it learns more fully how this great God and Sovereign deserves to be loved. As year by year the yearning after Him gradually becomes keener, the soul experiences the bitter suffering I am about to describe. I speak of years because of what happened to the person I mentioned, and though I know that God does not exist in time, I also know that He can raise a soul to this sublime state I have described in a single moment. Our Lord has the power to do all He wishes, and He wishes to do much for us. These longings, tears, sighs, impetuous desires, and feelings, that seem to come from our powerfully strong love, are as nothing compared with what I am about to describe. In fact, they seem but a smoldering fire, the heat of which, though painful, is tolerable.

The Dart of Love

While the soul is inflamed with love, it often happens that a passing thought or spoken word of death, though still a long time away, will delay fulfillment of the desire to be with the Lord. The heart receives this as a blow from a fiery dart. I do not mean this is an actual dart, but whatever it may be, it does not come from any part of *our* being. Neither is it really a blow, though I call it one. It wounds us severely—not in that part of our nature subject to pain—but in the very depths and center of our soul. This thunderbolt on its rapid course reduces the earthly part of our nature to powder. We may not even be able to remember our own existence, because in an instant the faculties of the soul are so fettered as to be incapable of any action, except the power they retain of increasing torture. Do not think I am exaggerating. Indeed, I fall short of explaining that which can not be described.

Spiritual Sufferings Produced

In this trance the senses and faculties seem to be suspended as the agony of desire increases. The understanding, however, realizes acutely what cause there is for grief in continual separation from the Lord. This increases the anguish to such a degree that the sufferer gives vent to loud cries that cannot be stifled. No matter how patient and accustomed to pain the soul may be, this torture attacks the innermost recesses of the soul.

Physical Effects of This Trance

I saw someone in this condition that I really thought was going to die from the agony of this desire. Though it lasts for only a short time, it leaves the soul feeling like the limbs are disjointed and the pulse is feeble—the soul feels weak and unable to function well for several days.

The health can become feeble as a consequence. At the time this is not felt, probably because the spiritual torments are so much more keen and the bodily ones remain unnoticed, just like when there is severe pain in one part, slight aches elsewhere are unnoticed. I know this by experience. During this favor there is no physical suffering either great or small. If there were, I am not sure the person would even feel it.

Intense Desire for God

Perhaps you will say this is imperfection, and why does the soul not conform itself to the will of God in this matter? Because up to this time the soul has been able to control this desire, but now the desire has caused our reason to be reduced. The soul can think of nothing else except that which brings torment. Why should it seek to live apart from the only Good? The desire to be with the Bridegroom is so overwhelming that the soul feels a strange loneliness. It finds no satisfying companionship in any earthy creature and desires only the heavenly relationship with the Bridegroom.

The soul is like one suspended in mid-air, touching neither earth or Heaven. It is unable to reach water to slake the parched thirst, because this is a thirst that cannot be quenched by earthly water. It must be the water the Lord spoke of to the Samaritan woman at the well. (See John 4:13-14.)

Indescribable Sufferings

"Alas, O Lord, to what a state do You bring those who love You? Yet these sufferings are as nothing in comparison to the reward You will give." It is right that great riches are dearly bought. Moreover, the pains cleanse and purify the soul so that it may enter the seventh mansion, for then indeed these trials will seem like a drop of water compared to the sea. Though this torment and grief could not be surpassed by any earthly cross, (so this person said who had endured much both in body and mind), yet they appeared as nothing in comparison to their recompense. The soul realizes that it does not deserve mental anguish of such measureless value. This conviction, although bringing no relief, enables the sufferer to bear the trials willingly, for an entire lifetime if God so wills. Although instead of dying once for all, this would be only a living death, for truly it is nothing else.

Torments of Hell

Let us remember how those who are destined for hell lack this submission to the divine will of God. God also gives the submissive and resigned soul the consolation and solace of knowing that their pains benefit them—for the damned will continually suffer more and more if they continue in their evil actions in hell. The soul feels far more deeply than the body, and the torments I have just described are incomparably less severe than those endured by the lost, who also know that their anguish will last forever. What will become of these miserable souls? What can we do or suffer during our short lives that is worth reckoning if it will free us from such terrible and endless torments? I assure you, unless you have learned by experience, it would be impossible to make you realize what gratitude we owe Him for having called us to a state where we may have hope, for by His mercy He has freed us and forgiven our sins.

Saint Teresa's Painful Desire for God

Let us return to the soul we left in such cruel torment. This agony does not continue for long in its full violence, never longer than three or four hours. If it were prolonged, the weakness of our nature could not endure it except by a miracle. In one case where it lasted only a quarter of an hour, the sufferer was left utterly exhausted; indeed, so violent was the attack the soul completely lost consciousness. This occurred on Easter when the soul unexpectedly heard some verses to the effect that life seemed unending. All through the period of time around Easter, the soul had suffered such dryness, that it could hardly realize what day was being celebrated.

Impossible to Resist this Suffering

It is as impossible to resist this suffering as it would be to prevent a flame having heat enough to burn us if we were thrown into a fire. These feelings cannot be concealed, and all those present recognize the dangerous condition of such a person, although they cannot see what is happening within the person. The soul, however, is aware that friends are near, but they, and all earthly things seem but shadows. If you should ever be in this state, you should know it is possible for your weakness and human nature to be of help to you. At times, when a soul seems to be dying from a desire for death that oppresses the soul with such grief that it appears on the point of leaving the body, the mind—terrified at the thought—tries to still its pain to keep death at bay. Evidently this fear arises from human infirmity, for the soul's longings for death do not abate, nor can its sorrows be stilled or calmed until God brings it comfort. This He usually does by a deep trance, or by some vision. The true Comforter consoles and strengthens the heart, which then becomes resigned to live as long as He wills.

Effects of the Dart of Love

This gift brings great suffering, but leaves most precious graces within the soul, which loses all fear of any further crosses, for in comparison with the acute anguish it has gone through, all else seems as nothing. Considering what has been gained, the soul would gladly often endure the same pains, but can do nothing to help itself in the matter. There are no means of reaching that state again until God chooses to decree it, and if He does, none can resist or escape. The mind feels far deeper contempt for the world than before, realizing that nothing earthly can ease it in its torture. It is also more detached from people, having learned that no one but its Creator can bring consolation and strength. The soul is more anxious and careful not to offend God, seeing He can torment as well as comfort.

Two Spiritual Dangers

Two things in this spiritual state seem to me to endanger life, one is that which I just described, for it is a real peril. The other is an excessive gladness and a delight so extreme that the soul appears to swoon away to the point of leaving the body, which would bring no small joy.

Courage Required and Given by God

Now you see why I told you that courage was needed for these gifts, and when anyone asks for them from our Lord, He may well reply as He did to the sons of Zebedee in Matthew 20:22, "But Jesus answered and said, Ye know not what ye ask. Are ye able to drink of the cup that I shall drink of, and to be baptized with the baptism that I am baptized with?" I believe we should all answer, "Yes," for we know the Lord gives strength when He sees it's needed. He ever defends such souls and answers for them when they are persecuted and slandered as He did in Matthew 26:10—if not in words, at least in deeds. At last, ah, at last! Before they die He repays them for all they have suffered, as you shall now learn. May He be forever blessed and may all creatures praise Him. Amen.

THE SEVENTH MANSION

CHAPTER 1

Teaches on the sublime favors God bestows on souls that have entered the seventh mansion. The author shows the difference she believes to exist between Soul and Spirit.

You may think that so much has been said of this spiritual journey that nothing remains to be added. That would be a great mistake. God's immensity has no limits, neither have His works; therefore, who can recount His mercies and His greatness? It is impossible, so do not be amazed at what I write about them, for that is just a tiny amount of what remains untold concerning God. He has shown great mercy in communicating these mysteries to one who could describe them to us, for as we learn more of His interaction with His creature, we should praise Him more fervently, and esteem more highly the soul in which He so delights.

Each of us possesses a soul but we do not realize its value, as being made in the image of God; therefore, we fail to understand the important secrets it contains. May our Lord guide my pen and teach me to say somewhat of the much there is to tell of His revelations to the souls He leads into this mansion. I have begged Him earnestly to help me, since He sees that my object is to reveal His mercies for the praise and glory of His name. I hope He will grant this favor, if not for my own sake, at least for yours, so that you may discover how vital it is for you to put no obstacle in the way of the Spiritual Marriage of the Bridegroom with your soul. For, as you will learn, this brings very notable blessings with it.

St. Teresa Abashed at
Discussing Such Subjects

O great God, surely such a miserable creature as myself should tremble at the thought of speaking on such a subject so far beyond anything I deserve to understand. Indeed I feel dismay and doubt whether it would not be better to finish writing about this mansion in as few words as possible, lest people think I may be describing my own personal experience. I am overwhelmed with shame, for knowing what I am, it is an awesome undertaking. On the other hand, this fear seems but a temptation and weakness—even if I should be misjudged.. As long as God is even a little better praised and known, let all the world revile me. Besides, I may be dead before this book is seen. May He who lives and shall live through all eternity be praised. Amen.

Our Lord Introduces His Bride
into His Presence Chamber

When our Lord is pleased to take pity on the past and present sufferings of a soul that He has spiritually taken for His Bride—endured by her longing for Him—He, before consummating the celestial marriage, brings her into His mansion or presence chamber. This is the Seventh Mansion for as He has a dwelling place in Heaven, He also dwells in the soul where none but He may abide, and this may be termed a second Heaven.

Darkness of a Soul in Sin

It is important that we do not imagine the soul to be in darkness. As we are accustomed to believe there is no light but that which is exterior, we imagine the soul is wrapped in obscurity. This is indeed the case with a soul out of a state of grace. However, not through any defer in the Sun of Judgment that remains within it and gives it light, for the soul itself is incapable of receiving light, as I mentioned in the First Mansion. A certain person was given to understand that such unfortunate souls are, as it were, imprisoned in a gloomy dungeon, chained hand and foot and unable to perform any meritorious acts; they are also blind and cannot speak. We should have pity on them when we remember we were once in the same state, and God may show mercy on them also.

Intercession for Sinners

Let us be most zealously interceding for them and never neglect it. To pray for a soul in mortal sin is a far more profitable form of almsgiving than it would be to help a Christian whose hands are bound behind his back, tied to a post, and dying of hunger—not for want of food, for plenty of the choicest delicacies lay near him—but because he is unable to put them in his mouth, and he is exhausted and at the point of dying. Would it not be extreme cruelty of us to stand looking at him and give him nothing to eat? What if by your prayers you could loose his bonds? Now you understand.

The Soul as an Interior World

For the love of God, I implore you to constantly remember souls like this in your prayers. We are not speaking now of them, but of others who by the mercy of God have done penance for their sins and are in a state of grace. You must not think of the soul as insignificant and petty, but as an interior world containing the number of beautiful mansions you have seen, for in the center of the soul there is a mansion reserved for God Himself.

The Spiritual Nuptials

When His Majesty God deigns to bestow on the soul the grace of these divine nuptials, He brings it into His presence chamber and does not treat it as before when He put it into a trance. I believe He then united it to Himself as He did also during the prayer of union, but then only the superior part was affected, and the soul did not feel called to enter its own center as it does in this mansion. Here it matters little whether it is one way or the other.

Former Favors Differ from
Spiritual Nuptials

In the former gifts our Lord unites the spirit to Himself and makes it both blind and unable to speak like the Apostle Paul after his conversion. This prevents the soul from knowing from where or how it enjoy this grace, for the supreme delight of the spirit is to realize its nearness to God. During the actual moment of divine union the soul feels nothing, all its powers being entirely lost. But now He acts differently. In pity God removes the scales from the eyes letting it see and understand some of the grace received in a strange and wonderful manner in this mansion by means of an intellectual vision.

The Blessed Trinity
Revealed to the Soul

By some mysterious manifestation of the truth, the three Persons of the most Blessed Trinity reveal themselves, preceded by an illumination that shines on the spirit like a dazzling cloud of light. A sublime knowledge is infused into the soul, imbuing it with a certainty of the truth that the Three Persons, though distinct from one another, are of one substance, one power, one knowledge, and are the Triune God. Therefore, that which we hold as a doctrine of faith, the soul now understands by sight—though it sees the Blessed Trinity neither with the physical eyes nor of the soul, for this is not an imaginary vision. All Three Persons of the Trinity communicate themselves to the soul by speaking to it and making it understand the words of our Lord in the Gospel of John, where Jesus says that He and the Father and the Holy Ghost will come and make their abode with the soul that loves Him and keeps His commandments (John 14:17-23).

Permanent Presence of the Trinity
in the Soul

O, my God, how different from merely hearing and believing these words it is to realize their truth in this way! Day by day a growing amazement takes possession of the soul, for the Three Persons of the Blessed Trinity never seem to depart, and the soul sees with a clear certainty in the way I have described, that the Three Persons dwell deeply within the very depths of the center of the soul. The soul is now very conscious of the indwelling divine Companions, yet it cannot describe how it knows this for lack of words.

The Effects

You may imagine that such a person is so caught up in this experience that her mind is too inebriated to care about anything else. On the contrary, she is far more active than before in everything that concerns God's service. Only during leisure time does she enjoy the blessed companionship. Unless she first deserts God, I believe He will never cease to make her clearly aware of His presence, and that He will never allow her to lose this favor after He has bestowed it. At the same time, the soul is increasingly more careful to avoid offending Him in any way.

This Presence Is Not Always Realized

This presence is not always realized and so distinctly manifest to the person when God renews the favor, as it was the first time; otherwise the person could not possibly attend to anything else or live in society. Although this gift may not always be seen by so clear a light, yet whenever she thinks about it, she feels the companionship of the Blessed Trinity. For example, if we were with other people in a very well-lit room with windows and shutters and someone closed the source of light, we would still feel certain that the other people were still there even though we are unable to see them.

Beyond the Soul's Control

You may ask, could she not bring back the light and see the Trinity again? No, this is not in her power, only when our Lord chooses, He will open the shutters of the understanding. The Lord shows her great mercy in never leaving her and making her realize it so clearly. His divine Majesty seems to be preparing His Bride for greater things by this divine companionship that clearly promotes perfection in every way. It also causes her not to fear as she did when other graces were granted her.

The Center of the Soul Remains Calm

In spite of her trials and labors, the soul who received this favor found she had improved in all virtues, because the center of her soul never moved from its place of rest. In a way her soul appeared divided, because a short time after God had done her this favor she was undergoing great sufferings and complained of her soul like Martha did of Mary. She criticized the soul for enjoying solitary peace while leaving her so full of troubles and responsibilities to attend to that she could not keep it company.

The Soul and the Spirit Are
Distinct Though United

This may seem exaggerated to you, even though the soul is known to be undivided. This is not a fancy of the imagination; it is a fact, and it often occurs. These interior effects show for certain that there is a positive difference between the soul and the spirit, though they are one with each other. The distinction between them is extremely subtle, so they appear at times to be in opposition to one another. The same opposition appears in the knowledge given to them by God.

The Soul and It's Faculties Are Not Identical

It also seems to me that the soul and its faculties are not identical. There are many supernatural mysteries within us, and it would be presumptuous of me to attempt to explain them. By God's mercy we shall understand these secrets when we enter Heaven.

CHAPTER 2

Describes the difference between Spiritual Union and Spiritual Marriage using some very delicately drawn comparisons.

The divine favor of spiritual nuptials cannot be received in all its perfection during our present life. The first time God bestows this grace He uses a vision of His most sacred Humanity, revealing himself to the soul so that it may understand and be aware of the sovereign gift it is receiving. He may manifest himself in different ways to others. The person I mentioned in the last chapter saw the Lord after receiving Holy Communion. He appeared to her in all His splendor, beauty, and majesty, as He was after His resurrection. He told her that from then on she was to attend to His affairs as if they were her own and He would care for hers. He spoke other things to her understanding but did not give her the words to describe them to others. This may not seem like anything new, for the Lord had revealed himself to her at other times, yet this was very different because it left her bewildered and amazed at the vividness of what she saw and the words she heard—also because it took place in the interior of the soul where no other vision had been seen, with the exception of the one last mentioned.

Spiritual Betrothal and Marriage Differ

You must understand there is a vast difference between the visions seen in former mansions and this one. There is the same distinction between spiritual espousals and spiritual marriage as there is between people who are engaged to be married and those already united in holy matrimony. I use this as a comparison because there is no other more suitable, yet this betrothal is no more related to our physical condition than if the soul was a disembodied spirit. This is even truer of the spiritual marriage, for this secret union takes place in the innermost center of the soul where God himself must dwell. I believe there is no door required to enter it—I use the words *no door required*—because everything I described before seems to enter through the senses and faculties, as must the representation of the Lord's humanity. But what passes in the union of the spiritual nuptials is very different. In the spiritual nuptials, God appears in the center of the soul, not by an imaginary vision but by an intellectual vision far more mystic than those seen before, just as He appeared to the Apostles without having entered through the door and said "Peace be unto you" (John 20:19).

Spiritual Marriage is Permanent

So mysterious is the secret and so sublime is the favor that God bestows instantaneously on the soul, that it feels supreme delight. This can only be described by saying that our Lord promises for the moment to reveal to the soul His own heavenly glory in a far more subtle way than by any vision or spiritual delight. As far as I can understand, the spirit of this soul is made one with God, who is a Spirit. He desires to show certain persons how far His love for us extends so we may praise His greatness. He then deigns to unite himself to His creature, binding himself as firmly as two human beings joined in wedlock and will never separate himself from her.

Spiritual Betrothal May Be Dissolved

Spiritual betrothal is different and like the grace of union is often dissolved, for though two things are made one by union, separation is still possible and each part is separate unto itself. This favor generally passes quickly and as far as it is aware, the soul remains without His company.

Soul Remains with God
in Spiritual Marriage

This is not so in spiritual marriage with our Lord, because the soul always remains in its center with God. For example, this union may be symbolized by two wax candles, the tips touch each other so closely that there is only one flame, the wick, wax, and the light became one, but the two candles can be separated from each other and remain distinct. But spiritual marriage is like rain falling from heaven into a river or stream, it becomes one and the same liquid, so the river and the rain water cannot be divided. It can also be likened to a small stream that flows into the ocean never to be disunited from it. This marriage may also be likened to a room into which a bright light enters through two windows, though divided when it enters the light becomes one and the same.

Apostle Paul and Spiritual Marriage

Perhaps when the Apostle Paul said, "But He that is joined unto the Lord is one spirit" (1Corinthians 6:17), he meant this sovereign marriage, which presupposes the Lord having been joined to the soul by union. The same Apostle said, "For me to live is Christ, and to die is gain" (Philippians 1:21). I think these words may be spoken by our soul now, because now the little butterfly dies with supreme joy, for Christ is her life.

The Soul's Joy in Union

The effects of this union become more manifest as time goes on, because the soul learns that it is God who gives it life. Her intuitive belief is so strong and keenly felt to be misunderstood, though impossible to describe. These effects cause such overwhelming emotions that the soul experiencing them cannot refrain from amorous exclamations, such as: "O, Life of my life and Power that upholds me!" and other exclamations of praise and adoration. Streams of milk then issue forth, bringing solace to the servants of this castle from the bosom of His Divinity, where God forever holds the soul in His firm clasp. I think He wishes them to share in some way the riches the soul is enjoying. Therefore, from the flowing river in which the little stream is swallowed up, some drops of water flow occasionally to sustain the bodily powers of the servants of the bride and Bridegroom.

The Soul's Assurance of
God's Indwelling

A person who is plunged unexpectedly into water is certainly aware of what has happened to him, and it is even more evident for the soul experiencing the indwelt God. A stream of water could not fall on us unless it came from some source, so the soul feels certain there is someone within that sends these piercing darts that stir its life, and that there is a Sun from where this brilliant light streams forth from the interior of the spirit to its faculties.

The Soul at Peace

The soul itself, as I said, never moves from this center nor loses the peace He can give. The same peace He spoke to the Apostles when they assembled together after His resurrection (John 20:19). I think this salutation of the Lord contains far deeper meaning than the words convey. He also spoke peace to Mary Magdalene outside His tomb (Luke 7:50). The words spoken by the Lord are alive and active within us, and in these cases they must have wrought their effect in the souls already desiring a cleansing from within of everything of the physical nature. They desire to retain only the spiritual so they can be joined in this celestial union with the Spirit of God. Without a doubt if we empty ourselves of all that belongs to the creature because of our love for God, He will fill us with himself.

Christ's Prayer for the Divine Union
of the Soul

Our Lord Jesus Christ prayed for His Apostles in John 17:21, "That they all may be one; as thou, Father, art in me, and I in thee, that they also may be one in us: that the world may believe that thou hast sent me." I do not know how love could be greater than this! Let not one of us draw back from entering here, because His Majesty Christ Jesus also said in John 17:20, "Neither pray I for these alone, but for them also which shall believe on me through their word;" and He declared in John 17:23, " I in them, and thou in me, that they may be made perfect in one; and that the world may know that thou hast sent me, and hast loved them, as thou hast loved me."

The Fulfillment

God help me! How true these words are, and they are clearly understood and fulfilled in the soul in this state of prayer. If these words are not being fulfilled in us; it is our own fault, because Jesus Christ, our King and our Lord, cannot fail. It is we who fail by not being obedient to His commands in John 14:23, "Jesus answered and said unto him, If a man love me, he will keep my words: and my Father will love him, and we will come unto him, and make our abode with him." [This is beautifully expressed in this poem written by St. Teresa]

Such is the power of love, O soul,
To paint thee in my heart
No craftsman with such art
Whate'er his skill might be,
 Could there thine image thus impart!
'Twas love that gave thee life—
Then, fair one, if thou be
Lost to thyself, thou'lt see
Thy portrait in my bosom stamped—
Soul, seek thyself in Me.

Soul Experiences Unalterable Peace
in Seventh Mansion

Returning to what I was saying, God places the soul in His own mansion in the very center of the soul. I have heard it said the sublime Heaven our Lord dwells in does not revolve, so the usual movements of the faculties and imagination do not appear to take place in any way that could injure the soul or disturb its peace.

The Soul is Safe Here Unless
It Offends God

I do not mean to imply that after God has brought the soul this far that it is certain to be saved and cannot fall into sin again. What I am saying is the soul seems safe and secure as long as the Lord holds it in His care and it does not offend Him. At any rate, she does not consider herself safe, even if she has been in this high state for several years. She will be increasingly careful to avoid committing the least offence against God. As I shall explain later on, she is most anxious to serve Him and feels a constant pain and confusion at seeing how little she can do to serve Him as she desires to. This is no light cross—it is a severe mortification—because the harder the penances she can perform, the better she is pleased. Her greatest penance is to be deprived by God of health and strength to perform any at all. I told you elsewhere what intense pain this causes her, and now it grieves her even more. This must be because she is like a tree grafted on a stock growing near a stream that makes it greener and more fruitful. Why should we marvel at the longings of this soul whose spirit has truly become one with the celestial water I described?

Struggles Outside the Seventh Mansion

Returning again to what I wrote about, it is not intended that the powers, senses, and passions should continually enjoy peace. The soul does so, indeed, but in the other mansions there are still times of struggle, suffering, and fatigue; however, as a general rule they do not lose their peace. This *center of the soul* or *spirit* is so hard to describe or even to believe in. I think my inability to explain my meaning saves you from being tempted to disbelieve me. It is difficult to understand how there can be crosses and sufferings to bear and yet peace in the soul.

Comparisons Explaining This

Let me give you one or two comparisons—God grant they may be useful to you. If not, just know what I say is true. A king resides in his palace; many wars and disasters take place in his kingdom but he remains on his throne. In the same way; though tumults and wild beasts rage with great uproar in the other mansions, none of it enters the seventh mansion or drives the soul out of it. The minds regrets the troubles, but they do not disturb or rob it of its peace. The passions are too subdued to dare enter here, because if they did they would suffer further defeat. Though the whole body is in pain the head does not suffer with it. I smile at these comparisons—they do not please me—but I can think of no others. Think what you will about it, I have told you the truth.

CHAPTER 3

Discussion of great fruits produced. The wonderful difference between these effects and those formerly described should be carefully studied and remembered.

The little butterfly has died with the greatest joy of having found rest at last, and Christ lives in her. Let us see the difference between her present and former life, because the effects will prove whether what I told you is true. One benefit is a self-forgetfulness so complete that she really appears not to exist, because there has been such a transformation in her that she no longer recognizes herself. She also does not remember that Heaven, life, or glory will be hers, but seems entirely occupied in seeking God's interests. Apparently the words spoken by the Lord have done their work: "that she was to care for His affairs, and He would care for hers."

The Soul Only Cares for God's Honor

She lives in such a strange oblivion and cares for nothing else, no matter what occurs or happens. She actually seems to no longer exist—in fact would willingly die. She does not want to be involved in anything else unless she sees it will advance the honor and glory of God.

The Soul Does Continue to Perform External Necessities

Please do not imagine I mean she neglects to eat and drink and perform her regular duties, but it does torment her. I am speaking of her inner life for the Lord when I say she cares for nothing else. Regarding her exterior actions there is little to say. Her chief suffering is that she has little strength to do anything, but there is nothing in the world she would willingly omit doing if it would honor the Lord.

Other Fruits of These Favors

The second fruit is a strong desire for suffering. It does not disturb her soul like it did before, because the fervent wish of such souls is for the fulfillment of God's will in their lives, so that makes them acquiesce in all He does. If He wants her to suffer, she is content; if He doesn't, that is all right with her also. She no longer torments herself to death about it as she once did. She feels a great interior joy when she is persecuted and is far more peaceful than in the former state under such circumstances. She bears no grudge against her enemies and does not wish them ill. Indeed she has a special love for them and is deeply grieved at seeing them in trouble. Therefore, she does all she can to help them by earnestly interceding with God on their behalf. She would be gladly forfeit the favors the Lord shows her if they might be given to her enemies to perhaps prevent their offending the Lord.

The Soul's Fervent Desire to Serve God

The most surprising thing to me is that the sorrow and distress these favored souls felt because they could not die and enjoy our Lord's presence, has now become a fervent desire to serve Him. To the utmost of their power they want to praise Him and teach others to praise Him also. Their love for others has increased as has their desire to help them. Not only do they no longer wish for death, but they desire a long life with most heavy crosses to bear, if this would bring any honor to the Lord. Even if they knew for certain that upon physical death they would leave their bodies and their souls would enjoy God, it makes no difference to them. The glory the saints are enjoying does not tempt them; there is no longing to join them. These souls feel that their glory consists in helping the crucified Lord Jesus Christ, especially when they see how little mankind cares for His honor and offends Him. It is true that souls in this state forget this at times and are seized with longings to enjoy God by leaving this earth. However, when they reflect on how they possess Him continually in their souls they return to their former state, realizing that the most costly oblation they can make is to live their lives in His service, and they willingly offer them to the Lord.

Christ Dwells Within This Soul

Death, like a wonderful trance, is no longer a fear in their lives. The fact is, that He who gave them these torturing desires of death has exchanged them for other desires. May He be ever blessed and praised! Amen. In fact, such persons no longer wish for consolations or delights because they have Christ living within them. It is evident that Jesus' life on earth was one of continual torment, and He may wish us to desire that for ourselves also. He leads us mercifully as our weakness requires, but when He sees we have a need, He imparts His strength to us.

Impetuous Desires Returned
Upon Negligence

The soul who is thoroughly detached from all worldly things wishes to be either always alone or occupied with things that benefit the souls of others. The soul feels no dryness or any inner troubles, just a constant recollection of our Lord whom she wishes to praise unceasingly. When she grows negligent, however, the Lord arouses her by bringing back the former impetuous desires. It is very evident these impulses come from the interior of the soul and not from the intellect or memory, as anyone who has been in this state will readily agree. No matter how large a fire may be, the flame never burns downward—always upward, it is the same with this movement that excites the soul; the power comes from the very center and moves upward. If nothing else was gained by this prayer except the knowledge of the special care God takes to communicate himself to us and how He pleads with us to abide with Him, I think for the sake of these sweet and penetrating touches of His love all our past pains are well spent.

God's Constant Care of Such Souls

You will learn this by experience, for when the Lord has brought us to the prayer of union, He watches over us in this way unless we neglect to keep His commandments. When these impulses are given to you, remember they come from Him in the innermost mansion where He dwells in our souls. Praise Him fervently, because it is He who sends you this message or love letter so tenderly written, and only you can understand what He asks. Never neglect to answer Him, even if you are occupied with someone in a conversation. Our Lord may often be pleased to show you this secret favor in public, and the reply from within you should be as Saint Paul's, "Lord, what wilt Thou have me to do?" (Acts 9:6).

207

Jesus will show you in many ways how to please Him. It is a propitious moment, because He seems to be listening to us, and the soul is nearly always willing by this delicate touch to respond with a great determination. The soul is always calm in this mansion, because the dryness and disturbance felt in the other mansions seldom enters here. The soul also does not fear that this sublime favor can be counterfeited by the devil. The soul perceives nothing by senses or faculties, because the Lord reveals himself to the spirit, which He has taken to be with him in a place where the devil cannot enter.

Graces Given in Peace and Silence

All of these graces are divinely bestowed on the soul for no reason if it's own, except the total abandonment of itself to God. These graces are given in peace and silence like the building of Solomon's Temple where no sound was heard. It is the same way with the temple of God—His mansion where He and the soul rejoice in each other alone and in profound silence. The mind is not active and does not search for anything, because the Lord who created it wishes it to be a rest and watch what passes within it. Sometimes for short intervals of time, the mind cannot see this happening. It is not because the powers are lost, but they are dazed and astonished and cease functioning temporarily.

Ecstasies [loss of self-control] Rarely Experienced in Seventh Mansion

I, too, am astonished at seeing that when the soul arrives at this state it does not lose self-control except on rare occasions. Even on that rare occasion they are not like the former trances and flight of the spirit, and unlike before, they do not occur in public. They are no longer produced by special calls to devotion, such as religious pictures, hearing a sermon, or by sacred music.

Probable Reasons for This
Peace and Rest

The soul is no longer anxious like the poor little butterfly taking flight at the slightest alarm. This may be because of the rest the spirit has found in its repose, or because it has seen and experienced such wonders in this mansion that nothing can frighten it. The most likely reason is because it is rejoicing in heavenly Company and no longer feels alone.

I honestly do not know the reason. However, I do know that as soon as God shows the soul what this mansion contains and brings it within its walls, the infirmity that was so troublesome and impossible to get over disappears at once. Perhaps this is because our Lord has strengthened, enlarged, and developed the soul. It could also be that He wishes to make public what He is doing in secret within these souls. What I know for certain is His judgments are beyond our comprehension in this life.

This Stage and Effects Are Alluded to
in Scripture

Along with all the other good fruits I have mentioned in the different degrees of prayer, these effects are given by God to the soul when it draws near Him to receive that "kiss of His mouth" the bride petitioned Him for. Here the overflowing waters are given to the wounded hart; here she delights in the tabernacles of God, and here the dove sent out by Noah has plucked the olive branch to show she has found firm land amongst the floods and tempests of this world. "O Jesus! Who knows how much in Holy Scripture refers to this peace of the soul? O My Lord, You do see how important this peace is to us. Please cause Christians to strive to gain it. In Your mercy never remove it from those You have bestowed it upon, because they will live in fear until You have given them true peace and brought them to the place where it never ends."

Watchfulness of These Souls

I do not mean that peace is not real on earth when I said "true peace," I was referring to those who lose their peace because they have forsaken God. What fear the souls in this mansion must feel knowing it is possible to lose so great a gift. The dread of this loss makes them more careful, and they gain strength from their weakness lest they miss an opportunity to please God. The greater the favors they have received from His Majesty, the more hesitant and mistrustful they are of themselves. The marvels they have witnessed have revealed very clearly to them their own miseries and the heinousness of their sins, so much so that they are like the publican in Luke 18:13, "And the publican, standing afar off, would not lift up so much as his eyes unto heaven, but smote upon his breast, saying, God be merciful to me a sinner."

Crosses Suffered in this State

Sometimes they long to die and be in safety, but then their love at once makes them wish to live in order to serve God. Therefore, they commit all that concerns them to His mercy. At times they are more crushed than ever by the thought of the many graces they have received, lest like an overloaded ship they might sink from the burden. I assure you, these souls have their cross to bear, but it does not trouble them or rob them of their peace, because it is gone swiftly like a wave or a storm that is followed by a calm. God's presence within them makes them soon forget everything else, may He forever be blessed and praised by all His creatures! Amen.

CHAPTER FOUR

This concluding chapter shows what appears to be the Lord's principal intention in conferring these sublime favors on souls. It also explains how necessary it is for Mary and Martha to work together.

The effects I have mentioned do not always exist to the same degree in these souls. Remember I told you that in most cases our Lord occasionally leaves such persons to the weakness of their nature. The venomous creatures from the moat around the castle and the other mansions unite to revenge themselves for the time they were deprived of their power.

Humility

True, this condition lasts for a short time—perhaps a day or so—but during this disturbance usually caused by some passing event, these persons learn the benefits they derive from the holy Company they are in. The Lord gives them such fortitude that they never leave His service or give up the good resolutions they have made. In fact, they seem to gain strength by trial, and their hearts remain steadfast, unmoved by any movement of the will. The Lord wants the soul to remember its natural condition so it may remain humble, praise Him, and better understand and appreciate His great grace and all He has done for it.

Souls Now Free from and Sins

Do not imagine that in spite of the strong desire and determination of these souls that they do not commit imperfections and even fall into many sins: not willfully, because they are given special grace from God on this point:

211

I'm speaking of unknown sins. As far as they know they are free from mortal sins, but they are not certain if they are guilty of sins of ignorance.

Fate of Solomon

This brings much grief to their hearts, especially as they witness souls perishing around them. They have strong hopes of not being among the lost, but they remember what they learned in the Scriptures about what happened to King Solomon, who had so much favor with God, and they cannot help fearing for themselves.

Holy Fear

Let any among you who feels confidence on this point fear the most. King David said, "Blessed is the man who feareth the Lord." May the Lord ever protect us. Let us beg Him to never allow us to offend Him, for that is our greatest safety. May He be forever praised! Amen.

These Favors Strengthen
Souls to Suffer

It would be good for me to tell you the reason why God bestows such favors on souls in this world. Although upon considering the effects, you may have already learned this. I will return to the matter so that none of you will think it is only for the sake of pleasure that someone feels this. If that is what you think, it is a great mistake, because the Lord can bestow no greater favor on us than to give us a life such as was led by His beloved Son. I have often said I feel certain these graces are sent to strengthen our weakness so we may share in His suffering.

Crosses Borne by the Saints

It is true that we always find those nearest to Christ our Lord bear the heaviest cross, think of what His Apostles and His mother Mary bore. Do you not think St. Paul went through such trials? We learn from his conduct, the fruits of genuine visions and contemplations that come from our Lord, not our imagination, or the devil's fraud. Do you suppose that St. Paul hid himself to enjoy these spiritual consolations at leisure and did nothing else? You know that he never took a day's rest as far as we know, and he could not have slept much because he worked all night long to earn his living (1 Thessalonians 2:9).

St. Peter Told by Christ
How He Would Die

Experience of St. Peter, when Christ Jesus told him how he would die. "'Verily, verily, I say unto thee, When thou wast young, thou girdest thyself, and walkedst whither thou wouldest: but when thou shalt be old, thou shalt stretch forth thy hands, and another shall gird thee, and carry thee whither thou wouldest not.' This spake he, signifying by what death he should glorify God. And when he had spoken this, he saith unto him, 'Follow me'" (John 21:18-19).

Fruits of These Favors

Oh, how forgetful of our ease, unmindful of honors, and far from seeking men's esteem should we be, whose soul God has chosen for His special dwelling place. If our mind is fixed on Him, as it should be, we must forget ourselves. All our thoughts should be of how to please Him, and show Him how much we love Him.

Why the Spiritual Marriage Takes Place

This is the end and the focal point of my prayer—this is the reason for the spiritual marriage whose children are always good works. Works are the unmistakable sign that shows these favors from God. It will do me little good to be deeply meditating when alone; performing actions of virtue, or planning and promising to do wonders in God's service, if afterwards when the occasions present themselves, I do just the opposite. I was wrong in saying, "It will do me little good," because all the time we spend with God does us great good. If afterwards we weaken and fail to perform our good intentions, God will find a way for us to practice them at a time He selects and perhaps to our regret. When He sees a very cowardly soul, He often sends it some great affliction, much against it's will. The benefit to the soul is that He will bring it through the trial with profit for itself. The soul that has learned this is less timid in offering itself to Him.

Love for Christ Proved by Our Deeds

In the prior statement I should have said, "will do us little good" in comparison with the far greater good we can gain when our works fulfill our aspirations and promises. Those who cannot do all this at once should do it little by little, because in this way we gradually dominate our will and gain fruit from our prayers. If we fix our eyes on the Crucified One, all will seem easier. The Lord proved His love for us by suffering stupendous labors and sufferings; therefore, how can we seek to please Him by words alone?

True Spirituality

Do you know what it means to be truly spiritual? It is for men to make themselves love slaves of God—branded with His mark, which is His cross. Since we lay no more claim to ourselves, He can, in a manner of speaking, sell us to the world to continue His work—what greater privilege could we have? You will not experience much progress until you make up your mind to do this, because as I said, humility is the foundation of the whole building. Unless you are truly humble, the Lord, for your own sake, will never permit you to build your building very high—in case it falls to the ground.

214

Humility and Virtues Combined
with Prayer

Therefore, take care to lay a firm foundation by seeking to be the least of all and the slave of others by watching how you can help and please them. It will benefit you, more than them. A building built on such strong rock will never go to ruin. I remind you again, your foundation must not consist of prayer and contemplation alone; you must receive the Christian virtues and praise Him for them. You will never grow in your spiritual life if you do not, and pray to God that nothing worse than lack of progress happens as a result. You know that to stop is to go backward—if you love, you will never be content to come to a standstill.

Zeal of Advanced Souls

Perhaps you think I am speaking of beginners in their Christian walk and if you are not a beginner you can rest. But, as I told you, the rest such souls feel is within them, they are not looking for outward rest. Why do you think the soul sends these inspiring messages from its center to the dwellers in the confines of the castle and the surrounding mansions? To send them to rest and sleep? No. no, no! The soul wages a fiercer war now than it did when it was in those other areas of the castle and mansions—to keep the powers, senses and the whole body from being idle. Formerly it did not understand the immense benefit its afflictions brought and how God may have been using them to advance it to this state.

Strengthened by the Divine
Presence Within

The soul is now enjoying the presence of the Lord and gaining far greater strength than ever before. King David said, "With the Holy, thou shalt be holy." By becoming one with the Lord, this sovereign union of Spirit with spirit gives strength to the soul to suffer and die. No doubt, with the power and strength gained, the soul can help all within the castle and the very body itself that often seems to have no feeling left in it. The vigor the soul receives from "the wine" drunk in the cellar where the Bridegroom brought her, overflows into the feeble body just like food that nourishes both the head and the whole frame.

Examples of Saints Strengthened

Indeed the body suffers much while alive in whatever work it does; the soul has energy for much greater tasks and goads the body on to do more, because what the body does seems as nothing to the soul. This must be the reason for the severe penances performed by many of the saints. I believe this is what caused St. Francis of Assisi, St. Dominic and Fr. Elias to draw many souls to God. I assure you, without thought for themselves, they must have passed through many trials.

This is why I urge us to strive to offer petitions and prayers not for our own pleasure, but to gain strength to serve God. Do not seek a new way, because we should be strangers to pathways of ease. It would be strange thing to imagine we could gain these graces by any other road than by the one that Jesus and all His saints have trod before. We should not even imagine such a thing. All of us have our labor times and times of prayer and learning.

Woman and the Alabaster Box
of Ointment

The woman that came to the home of Simon the Pharisee to anoint Jesus' feet never worried about going through the streets alone, because of her zeal. She entered the house of a stranger and bore the remarks of the Pharisees. What did Jesus do? "And he turned to the woman, and said unto Simon, Seest thou this woman? I entered into thine house, thou gavest me no water for my feet: but she hath washed my feet with tears, and wiped them with the hairs of her head. Thou gavest me no kiss: but this woman since the time I came in hath not ceased to kiss my feet. My head with oil thou didst not anoint: but this woman hath anointed my feet with ointment. Wherefore I say unto thee, Her sins, which are many, are forgiven; for she loved much: but to whom little is forgiven, the same loveth little. And he said unto her, Thy sins are forgiven" (Luke 7:44-48).

Christ's Food is to do the Will of God

Christ's food is that in every possible way we should draw souls to Him to be saved and praise Him forever. While here on earth Jesus said to His disciples, "Jesus saith unto them, 'My meat is to do the will of him that sent me, and to finish his work'" (John 4:34).

Suffering and Grief of Mary

I assure you, Mary won the better part after many crosses and mortifications. The mere sight of how men hated Christ must have been intolerable for her. Think of the terrible pain she endured at the Crucifixion and His absence from her.

Can We Lead Souls to God?

You may say that you have neither the power nor the means to lead souls to God. You are willing to, but you do not know how—because you cannot teach or preach as the Apostles did. I have often written an answer to this objection, though I cannot remember if I did so in this book. However, the difficulty probably often crosses your minds because of the desires the Lord gives you to do so. I will tell you again. I told you how the devil frequently fills our thoughts with great schemes, and instead of putting our hands to the work we can do to serve the Lord, we may feel satisfied with wishing to perform impossibilities.

Leading Souls to Christ
Who Values Our Prayers

Much will be accomplished by your prayers. Do not try to pray for the whole world. Pray for your companions and loved ones because no one can do that better than you can; you have a deep longing for their salvation. It is no trifling matter to humble yourself and pray, because your love for them and your love of God will be a fire that kindles your urgent prayers for their salvation. This is a great work and one most pleasing to the Lord. By doing all in your power to pray for them, you show the Lord your willingness to pray for even more souls, and He will reward you as you win Him many souls. The praise they give to God will please Him, and they in turn will pray for their neighbors.

Conclusion

May it please God, my brothers and my sisters, that we may all meet together where we may praise Him forever. I pray He will give me the grace to practice what I have taught you by the merits of His Son who lives and reigns forever. Amen. I beg you, for the sake of the Lord, not to forget this poor sinner in your prayers.

EPILOGUE

Before writing this book you will remember I told you that I felt reluctant to even begin this work. Well, now that it is finished, I am very glad I wrote it. My time and trouble have been well spent. The statement I made in the beginning has proven to be true—"obedience has the benefit of producing power that makes impossible things easy"—and I must confess my obedience has not been costly to me.

My sisters, in considering your strict enclosures, little recreation, and the lack of conveniences in some of your convents, I think it may console you to enjoy yourselves in your own interior castle. You can enter and walk about at any hour you please without seeking permission from your superiors. No matter how wonderful all the mansions may look to you, it is true that you cannot enter all the mansions by your own power, you must wait until the Lord of the castle Himself admits you.

Therefore, I advise you to use no violence in forcing your entrance if you meet with an obstacle, for that would displease Him so much that He may never give you admittance to them. The Lord dearly loves humility. If you think yourself unworthy to enter the third mansion, He will grant you the favor of entering the fifth mansion instead. Then, if you serve Him well there, He will draw you into the mansion where He himself dwells, and where you never have to leave unless you are called away to perform your regular duties. If your duties keep you away from His presence chamber, He will await your return and hold the door open for you.

When you have learned how to enjoy this castle, you will always find rest. No matter how painful your trials may be, you have the hope of returning to the presence of the Lord, and that, no one can prevent. Although I have only mentioned seven mansions, each of them has many rooms. All of the mansions have gardens, fountains, and maze-like passages to explore. There are so many delightful things that you will wish to spend all your time in praising God who has created your soul.

If you find anything in this book that helps you to know Him better, you can be certain that it was sent by the Lord to encourage you. If you find anything amiss within its pages, you will know it is from me. In return for my strong desire to aid you in serving Him—my God and my Lord—I implore you, praise His Majesty fervently in my name whenever you read this. Beg Him to prosper His Church and give light to those who are lost.

I finished writing this book in the convent of St. Joseph of Avila, in the year 1577, on the Vigil of St. Andrew, for the glory of God, who liveth and reigneth forever and ever! Amen.

The Way of Perfection

CHAPTER 4

Exhorts the nuns to keep their Rule and names three things which are important for the spiritual life. Describes the first of these three things, which is love of one's neighbor, and speaks of the harm which can be done by individual friendships.

Now, daughters, you have looked at the great enterprise that we are trying to carry out. What kind of persons shall we have to be if we are not to be considered over-bold in the eyes of God and of the world? It is clear that we need to labor hard, and it will be a great help to us if we have sublime thoughts so that we may strive to make our actions sublime also. If we endeavor to observe our Rule and Constitutions in the fullest sense, and with great care, I hope in the Lord that He will grant our requests. I am not asking anything new of you, my daughters—only that we should hold to our profession, which, as it is our vocation, we are bound to do, although there are many ways of holding to it.

Our Primitive Rules tell us to pray without ceasing. Provided we do this with all possible care (and it is the most important thing of all), we shall not fail to observe the fasts, disciplines, and periods of silence that the Order commands; for, as you know, if prayer is to be genuine it must be reinforced with these things—prayer cannot be accompanied by self-indulgence.

It is about prayer that you have asked me to say something to you. As an acknowledgment of what I shall say, I beg you to read frequently and with a good will what I have said about it thus far, and to put this into practice. Before speaking of the interior life—that is, of prayer—I shall speak of certain things that those who attempt to walk along the way of prayer must of necessity practice. So necessary are these that, even though not greatly given to contemplation, people who have them can advance a long way in the Lord's service. But unless they have them, they cannot possibly be great contemplatives, and, if they think they are, they are much mistaken. May the Lord help me in this task and teach me what I must say, so that it may be to His glory. Amen.

Do not suppose, my friends and sisters, that I am going to charge you to do a great many things; may it please the Lord that we do the things that our holy Fathers ordained and practiced, and by so doing they merited that name. It would be wrong of us to look for any other way or to learn from anyone else.

There are only three things that I will explain at some length and which are taken from our Constitution itself. It is essential that we should understand how very important they are to us in helping us to preserve that peace, both inward and outward, which the Lord so earnestly recommended to us. One of these is love for each other; the second, detachment from all created things; the third, true humility, which, although I put it last, is the most important of the three and embraces all the rest.

With regard to the first—namely, love for each other— this is of very great importance; for there is nothing, however annoying, that cannot easily be borne by those who love each other, and anything that causes annoyance must be quite exceptional. If this commandment were kept in the world, as it should be, I believe it would take us a long way toward the keeping of the rest. But, what with having too much love for each other or too little, we never manage to keep it perfectly. It may seem that for us to have too much love for each other cannot be wrong, but I do not think anyone who had not been an eye-witness of it would believe how much evil and how many imperfections can result from this.

The devil sets many snares here that the consciences of those who aim only in a rough-and-ready way at pleasing God seldom observe—indeed, they think they are acting virtuously—but those who are aiming at perfection understand what they are very well: little by little they deprive the will of the strength that it needs if it is to employ itself wholly in the love of God.

This is even more applicable to women than to men and the harm that it does to community life is very serious. One result of it is that all the nuns do not love each other equally: some injury done to a friend is resented; a nun desires to have something to give to her friend or tries to make time for talking to her, and often her object in doing this is to tell her how fond she is of her, and other irrelevant things, rather than how much she loves God. These intimate friendships are seldom calculated to make for the love of God. I am more inclined to believe that the devil initiates them so as to create factions within religious Orders. When a friendship has for its object the service of His Majesty, it at once becomes clear that the will is devoid of passion and indeed is helping to conquer other passions.

Where a convent is large I should like to see many friendships of that type; but in this house, where there are not—and can never be—more than thirteen nuns, all must be friends with each other, love each other, be fond of each other, and help each other. For the love of the Lord, refrain from making individual friendships, however holy, for even among brothers and sisters such things are apt to be poisonous and I can see no advantage in them. When they are between other relatives, they are much more dangerous and become a pest.

Believe me, sisters, though I may seem to you extreme in this, great perfection and great peace come of doing what I say, and many occasions of sin may be avoided by those who are not very strong. If our will becomes inclined more to one person than to another (this cannot be helped, because it is natural—it often leads us to love the person who has the most faults if she is the most richly endowed by nature), we must exercise a firm restraint on ourselves and not allow ourselves to be conquered by our affection. Let us love the virtues and inward goodness, and let us always apply ourselves and take care to avoid attaching importance to externals.

Let us not allow our will to be the slave of any, sisters, save of Him Who bought it with His blood. Otherwise, before we know where we are, we shall find ourselves trapped and unable to move. God help me! The puerilities [immature actions] that result from this are innumerable. Because they are so trivial, only those who see how bad they are will realize and believe it. There is no point in speaking of them here except to say that they are wrong in anyone, and, in a prioress, pestilential [pernicious, harmful].

In checking these preferences we must be strictly on the alert from the moment that such a friendship begins, and we must proceed diligently and lovingly rather than severely. One effective precaution against this is that the sisters should not be together except at the prescribed hours, and that they should follow our present custom in not talking with one another, or being alone together, as is laid down in the Rule: each one should be alone in her cell. There must be no workroom at Saint Joseph's; for, although it is a praiseworthy custom to have one, it is easier to keep silence if one is alone, and getting used to solitude is a great help to prayer. Since prayer must be the foundation on which this house is built, it is necessary for us to learn to like whatever gives us the greatest help in it.

Returning to the question of our love for one another. It seems quite unnecessary to commend this to you. For where are there people so brutish as not to love one another when they live together, are continually in one another's company, indulge in no conversation or association with any outside their house, and believe that God loves us and that they themselves love God, since they are leaving everything for His Majesty? More especially is this so since virtue always attracts love, and I hope in God that, with the help of His Majesty, there will always be love in the sisters of this house.

It seems to me, therefore, that there is no reason for me to commend this to you any further.

With regard to the nature of this mutual love and what is meant by the virtuous love that I wish you to have here, and how we shall know when we have this virtue—which is a very great one, since Our Lord has so strongly commended it to us and so straightly enjoined it upon His Apostles—about all this I should like to say a little now as well as my lack of skill will allow me. If you find this explained in great detail in other books, take no notice of what I am saying here, for it may be that I do not understand what I am talking about.

There are two kinds of love which I am describing. The one is purely spiritual and apparently has nothing to do with sensuality or the tenderness of our nature, either of which might stain its purity. The other is also spiritual, but mingled with it are our sensuality and weakness; yet it is a worthy love, which, as between relatives and friends, seems lawful. Of this I have already said enough.

It is of the first kind of spiritual love that I would now speak. It is untainted by any sort of passion, for such a thing would completely spoil its harmony. If it leads us to treat virtuous people, especially confessors, with moderation and discretion, it is profitable. But if the confessor is seen to be tending in any way towards vanity, he should be regarded with grave suspicion, and, in such a case, conversation with him, however edifying, should be avoided. The sister should make her confession briefly and say nothing more. It would be best for her, indeed, to tell the superior that she does not get on with him and go elsewhere. This is the safest way, providing it can be done without injuring his reputation.

In such cases, and in other difficulties with which the devil might ensnare us, so that we have no idea where to turn, the safest thing will be for the sister to try to speak with some learned person. If necessary, permission to do this can be given her, and she can make her confession to him and act in the matter as he directs her. For he cannot fail to give her some good advice about it, without which she might go very far astray.

How often people stray through not taking advice, especially when there is a risk of doing someone harm! The course that must on no account be followed is to do nothing at all. For when the devil begins to make trouble in this way, he will do a great deal of harm if he is not stopped quickly. The plan I have suggested, then, of trying to consult another confessor is the safest one if it is practicable, and I hope in the Lord that it will be so.

Reflect upon the great importance of this, for it is a dangerous matter, and can be a veritable hell, and a source of harm to everyone. I advise you not to wait until a great deal of harm has been done, but to take every possible step that you can think of and stop the trouble at the outset. This you may do with a good conscience. But I hope in the Lord that He will not allow persons who are to spend their lives in prayer to have any attachment except to one who is a great servant of God. And I am quite certain He will not unless they have a love for prayer and for striving after perfection in the way we try to do here. For unless they see that he understands their language and likes to speak to them of God, they cannot possibly love him, as he is not like them. If he is such a person, he will have very few opportunities of doing any harm, and, unless he is very simple, he will not seek to disturb his own peace of mind and that of the servants of God.

As I have begun to speak about this, I will repeat that the devil can do a great deal of harm here, which will long remain undiscovered, and thus the soul that is striving after perfection can be gradually ruined without knowing how. For if a confessor gives occasion for vanity through being vain himself, he will be very tolerant with it in others. May God, for His Majesty's own sake, deliver us from things of this kind. It would be enough to unsettle all the nuns if their consciences and their confessor should give them exactly opposite advice. And if it is insisted that they must have one confessor only, they will not know what to do, nor how to pacify their minds, since the very person who should be calming them and helping them is the source of the harm. In some places there must be a great deal of trouble of this kind. I always feel very sorry about it and so you must not be surprised if I attach great importance to your understanding this danger.

CHAPTER 6

Returns to the subject of perfect love, already begun.

I have digressed a great deal but no one will blame me who understands the importance of what has been said. Let us now return to the love that is lawful and good for us to feel. This I have described as purely spiritual. I am not sure if I know what I am talking about, but it seems to me that there is no need to speak much of it, since so few, I fear, possess it.

Let any one of you to whom the Lord has given it praise Him fervently, for she must be a person of the greatest perfection. It is about this that I now wish to write. Perhaps what I say may be of some profit, for if you look at a virtue, you desire it and try to gain it, and so become attached to it.

God grant that I may be able to understand this, and even more that I may be able to describe it, for I am not sure that I know when love is spiritual and when there is sensuality mingled with it, or how to begin speaking about it. I am like one who hears a person speaking in the distance and, though he can hear that he is speaking, cannot distinguish what he is saying. It is just like that with me. Sometimes I cannot understand what I am saying, yet the Lord is pleased to enable me to say it well. If at other times what I say is nonsensical, it is only natural for me to go completely astray.

Now it seems to me that when God has brought someone to a clear knowledge of the world, and of its nature, and of the fact that another world (or, let us say, another kingdom) exists, and that there is a great difference between the one and the other—the one being eternal and the other only a dream; and of what it is to love the Creator and what to love the creature (this must be discovered by experience, for it is a very different matter from merely thinking about it and believing it); when one understands by sight and experience what can be gained by the one practice and lost by the other; and what the Creator is and what the creature; and many other things that the Lord teaches to those who are willing to devote themselves to being taught by Him in prayer, or whom His Majesty wishes to teach—then one loves very differently from those of us who have not advanced thus far.

It may be, sisters, that you think it irrelevant for me to treat of this, and you may say that you already know everything that I have said. God grant that this may be so, and that you may indeed know it in the only way that has any meaning, and that it may be graven upon your innermost being, and that you may never for a moment depart from it. For if you know it, you will see that I am telling nothing but the truth when I say that he whom the Lord brings thus far possesses this love. Those whom God brings to this state are, I think, generous and royal souls; they are not content with loving anything so miserable as these bodies, however beautiful they be and however numerous the graces they possess. If the sight of the body gives them pleasure, they praise the Creator, but as for dwelling upon it for more than just a moment—no!

When I use that phrase "dwelling upon it," I refer to having love for such things. If they had such love, they would think they were loving something insubstantial and were conceiving fondness for a shadow, they would feel shame for themselves and would not have the effrontery to tell God that they love Him without feeling great confusion.

You will answer me that such persons cannot love or repay the affection shown to them by others. Certainly they care little about having this affection. They may from time to time experience a natural and momentary pleasure at being loved; yet as soon as they return to their normal condition, they realize that such pleasure is folly except when the persons concerned can benefit their souls, either by instruction or by prayer. Any other kind of affection wearies them, for they know it can bring them no profit and may well do them harm. Nevertheless, they are grateful for it and recompense it by commending those who love them to God. They take this affection as something for which those who love them lay the responsibility upon the Lord, from Whom, since they can see nothing lovable in themselves, they suppose the love comes, and think that others love them because God loves them. And so they leave His Majesty to recompense them for this and beg Him to do so, thus freeing themselves and feeling they have no more responsibility.

When I ponder it carefully, I sometimes think this desire for affection is sheer blindness, except when, as I say, it relates to persons who can lead us to do good so that we may gain blessings in perfection.

It should be noted here that when we desire anyone's affection, we always seek it because of some interest, profit, or pleasure of our own. Those who are perfect, however, have trodden all these things beneath their feet—and despise the blessings that may come to them in this world, and its pleasures and delights—in such a way that, even if they wanted to, so to say, they could not love anything outside God, or unless it had to do with God. What profit, then, can come to them from being loved themselves?

When this truth is put to them, they laugh at the distress that had been assailing them in the past as to whether their affection was being returned or not. Of course, however pure our affection may be, it is quite natural for us to wish it to be returned. But when we come to evaluate the return of affection, we realize that it is insubstantial, like a thing of straw, as light as air and easily carried away by the wind. For however dearly we have been loved, what is there that remains to us? Such persons, then, except for the advantage that the affection may bring to their souls (because they realize that our nature is such that we soon tire of life without love), care nothing whether they are loved or not.

Do you think that such persons will love none and delight in none save God? No! They will love others much more than they did, but with a more genuine love, with greater passion and with a love that brings more profit. That, in a word, is what love really is. And such souls are always much fonder of giving than of receiving, even in their relations with the Creator Himself. This, I say, merits the name of love, which name has been usurped from it by those other base affections.

Do you ask, again, by what they are attracted if they do not love things they see? They do love what they see and they are greatly attracted by what they hear, but the things that they see are everlasting. If they love anyone they immediately look right beyond the body (on which, as I say, they cannot dwell), fix their eyes on the soul and see what there is to be loved in that. If there is nothing, but still they see some suggestion or inclination that shows them that if they dig deep they will find gold within this mine, they think nothing of the labor of digging, since they have love.

There is nothing that suggests itself to them that they will not willingly do for the good of that soul since they desire their love for it to be lasting, and they know quite well that that is impossible unless the loved one has certain good qualities and a great love for God. I really mean that it is impossible, however great their obligations. And even if that soul were to die for love of them, and do them all the kind actions in its power; even had it all the natural graces joined in one, their wills would not have strength enough to love it nor would they remain fixed upon it. They know and have learned and experienced the worth of all this; no false dice can deceive them. They see that they are not in unison with that soul and that their love for it cannot possibly last. For unless that soul keeps the law of God, their love will end with life—they know that unless it loves Him they will go to different places.

Those into whose souls the Lord has already infused true wisdom do not esteem this love, which lasts only on earth, at more than its true worth—if, indeed, at so much. Those who like to take pleasure in worldly things, delights, honors and riches, will account it of some worth if their friend is rich and able to afford them pastime and pleasure and recreation. But those who already hate all this will care little or nothing for such things. So if they have any love for such a person, it will be a passion that he may love God so as to be loved by

231

Him. For, as I say, they know that no other kind of affection but this can last, and that this kind will cost them dear, for which reason they do all they possibly can for their friend's profit—they would lose a thousand lives to bring him a small blessing. Oh, precious love, forever imitating the Captain of Love, Jesus, our Good!

CHAPTER 7

Treats of the same subject of spiritual love and gives certain counsels for gaining it.

It is strange to see how impassioned this love is. How many tears, penances, and prayers it costs. How careful is the loving soul to commend the object of its affection to all who it thinks may prevail with God, and to ask them to intercede with Him for it. And how constant is its longing, so that it cannot be happy unless it sees that its loved one is making progress. If that soul seems to have advanced, and is then seen to fall some way back, her friend seems to have no more pleasure in life. She neither eats nor sleeps, is never free from this fear, and is always afraid that the soul whom she loves so much may be lost, and that the two may be parted for ever. She cares nothing for physical death, but she will not suffer herself to be attached to something that a puff of wind may carry away so that she is unable to retain her hold upon it. This, as I have said, is love without any degree whatsoever of self-interest. All that this soul wishes and desires is to see the soul it loves be enriched with blessings from Heaven. This is love, quite unlike our ill-starred earthly affections—to say nothing of illicit affections, from which may God keep us free.

These last affections are a very hell, and it is needless for us to weary ourselves by saying how evil they are, for the least of the evils that they bring are terrible beyond exaggeration. There is no need for us ever to take such things upon our lips, sisters, or even to think of them, or to remember that they exist anywhere in the world. You must never listen to anyone speaking of such affections, either in jest or in earnest, nor allow them to be mentioned or discussed in your presence. No good can come from our doing this, and it might do us harm even to hear them mentioned. But with regard to the lawful affections that, as I have said, we may have for each other, or for relatives and friends, it is different. Our whole desire is that they should not die. If their heads ache, our souls seem to ache, too. If we see them in distress, we are unable (as people say) to sit still under it, and so on. This is not so with spiritual affection.

Although the weakness of our nature may at first allow us to feel something of all this, our reason soon begins to reflect whether our friend's trials are not good for her, to wonder if they are making her richer in virtue, and how she is bearing them—then we shall ask God to give her patience so that they may win her merit. If we see that she is being patient, we feel no distress—indeed, we are gladdened and consoled. If all the merit and gain that suffering is capable of producing could be attributed to her, we should still prefer suffering her trial ourselves to seeing her suffer it, but we are not worried or disquieted.

I repeat once more that this love is a similitude and copy of that which was borne for us by the good Lover, Jesus. It is for that reason that it brings us such immense benefits, for it makes us embrace every kind of suffering, so that others, without having to endure the suffering, may gain its advantages. The recipients of this friendship, then, profit greatly, but their friends should realize that either this fellowship—I mean, this exclusive friendship—must come to an end or that they must prevail upon Our Lord that their friend may walk in the same way as themselves, as Saint Monica prevailed with Him for Saint Augustine.

Their heart does not allow them to practice duplicity: if they see their friend straying from the road, or committing any faults, they will speak to her about it—they cannot allow themselves to do anything else. And if after this the loved one does not amend, they will not flatter her or hide anything from her. Either she will amend or their friendship will cease; for otherwise they would be unable to endure it, nor is it in fact endurable. It would mean continual war for both parties. A person may be indifferent to all other people in the world and not worry whether they are serving God or not, since the person she has to worry about is herself. But she cannot take this attitude with her friends, for nothing they do can be hidden from her—she sees the smallest mote in them. This, I repeat, is a very heavy cross for her to bear.

Happy the souls that are loved by such as these! Happy the day on which they came to know them! O my Lord, wilt Thou not grant me the favor of giving me many who have such love for me? Truly, Lord, I would rather have this than be loved by all the kings and lords of the world.

And rightly so, for such friends use every means in their power to make us lords of the whole world and to have all that is in it subject to us. When you make the acquaintance of any such persons, sisters, the Mother Prioress should employ every possible effort to keep you in touch with them. Love such persons as much as you like. There can be very few of them, but none the less it is the Lord's will that their goodness should be known. When one of you is striving after perfection, she will at once be told that she has no need to know such people—that it is enough for her to have God. But to get to know God's friends is a very good way of "having" Him—as I have discovered by experience, it is most helpful. For, under the Lord, I owe it to such persons that I am not in hell. I was always very fond of asking them to commend me to God, and so I prevailed upon them to do so.

Let us now return to what we were saying. It is this kind of love that I should like us to have. At first it may not be perfect, but the Lord will make it increasingly so. Let us begin with the methods of obtaining it. In the beginning it may be mingled with emotion, but this, as a rule, will do no harm. It is sometimes good and necessary for us to show emotion in our love, and also to feel it, and to be distressed by some of our sisters, [and by] trials and weaknesses, however trivial they may be. For on one occasion as much distress may be caused by quite a small matter as would be caused on another by some great trial, and there are people whose nature it is to be very much cast down by small things.

If you are not like this, do not neglect to have compassion on others. It may be that Our Lord wishes to spare us these sufferings, and will give us sufferings of another kind that will seem heavy to us, though to the person already mentioned they may seem light. In these matters, then, we must not judge others by ourselves, nor think of ourselves as we have been at some time when, perhaps without any effort on our part, the Lord has made us stronger than they. Let us think of what we were like at the times when we have been weakest.

Note the importance of this advice for those of us who would learn to sympathize with our neighbors' trials, however trivial these may be. It is especially important for such souls as have been described, for, desiring trials as they do, they make light of them all.

They must, therefore, try hard to recall what they were like when they were weak, and reflect that if they are no longer so, it is not due to themselves. For otherwise, little by little, the devil could easily cool our charity toward our neighbors, and make us think that what is really a failing on our part is perfection. In every respect we must be careful and alert, for the devil never slumbers. And the nearer we are to perfection, the more careful we must be, since his temptations are then much more cunning because there are no others that he dare send us. And if, as I say, we are not cautious, the harm is done before we realize it. In short, we must always watch and pray, for there is no better way than prayer of revealing these hidden wiles of the devil and making him declare his presence.

Contrive always, even if you do not care for it, to take part in your sisters' necessary recreation and to do so for the whole of the allotted time, for all considerate treatment of them is a part of perfect love. It is a very good thing for us to take compassion on each others' needs. See that you show no lack of discretion about things that are contrary to obedience. Though privately you may think the prioress' orders harsh ones, do not allow this to be noticed or tell anyone about it (except that you may speak of it, with all humility, to the prioress herself), for if you did so you would be doing a great deal of harm. Get to know what are the things in your sisters that you should be sorry to see, and those about which you should sympathize with them. Always show your grief at any notorious fault that you may see in one of them.

It is a good proof and test of our love if we can bear with such faults and not be shocked by them. Others, in their turn, will bear with your faults, which, if you include those of which you are not aware, must be much more numerous. Often commend to God any sister who is at fault and strive for your own part to practice the virtue that is the opposite of her fault with great perfection. Make determined efforts to do this so that you may teach your sister by your deeds what perhaps she could never learn by words nor gain by punishment.

The habit of performing some conspicuously virtuous action through seeing it performed by another is one that very easily takes root. This is good advice—do not forget it. Oh, how true and genuine will be the love of a sister who can bring profit to everyone by sacrificing her own profit to that of the rest! She will make a great advance in each of the virtues and keep her Rule with great perfection. This will be a much truer kind of friendship than one that uses every possible loving expression (such as are not used, and must not be used, in this house): "My life!" "My love!" "My darling!" and suchlike things, one or another of which people are always saying.

Let such endearing words be kept for your Spouse, for you will be so often and so much alone with Him that you will want to make use of them all, and this His Majesty permits you. If you use them among yourselves they will not move the Lord so much; and, quite apart from that, there is no reason why you should do so. They are very effeminate, and I should not like you to be that, or even to appear to be that, in any way, my daughters. I want you to be strong men. If you do all that is in you, the Lord will make you so manly that men themselves will be amazed at you. And how easy is this for His Majesty, Who made us out of nothing at all!

It is also a very clear sign of love to try to spare others household work by taking it upon oneself, and also to rejoice and give great praise to the Lord if you see any increase in their virtues. All such things, quite apart from the intrinsic good they bring, add greatly to the peace and concord that we have among ourselves, as through the goodness of God, we can now see by experience. May His Majesty be pleased ever to increase it, for it would be terrible if it did not exist, and very awkward if, when there are so few of us, we got on badly together. May God forbid that.

If one of you should be cross with another because of some hasty word, the matter must at once be put right, and you must betake yourselves to earnest prayer. The same applies to the harboring of any grudge, or to party strife, or to the desire to be greatest, or to any nice point concerning your honor. (My blood seems to run cold, as I write this, at the very idea that this can ever happen, but I know it is the chief trouble in convents.) If it should happen to you, consider yourselves lost. Just reflect and realize that you have driven your Spouse from His home. He will have to go and seek another abode, since you are driving Him from His own house. Cry aloud to His Majesty and try to put things right. And if frequent confessions and communions do not mend them, you may well fear that there is some Judas among you.

For the love of God, let the prioress be most careful not to allow this to occur. She must put a stop to it from the very outset, and, if love will not suffice, she must use heavy punishments, for here we have the whole of the mischief and the remedy. If you gather that any of the nuns is making trouble, see that she is sent to some other convent and God will provide them with a dowry for her. Drive away this plague; cut off the branches as well as you can; and, if that is not sufficient, pull up the roots. If you cannot do this, shut up anyone who is guilty of such things and forbid her to leave her cell; far better this than that all the nuns should catch so incurable a plague.

Oh, what a great evil is this! God deliver us from a convent into which it enters. I would rather our convent caught fire and we were all burned alive. As this is so important I think I shall say a little more about it elsewhere, so I will not write at greater length here, except to say that, provided they treat each other equally, I would rather that the nuns showed a tender and affectionate love and regard for each other—even though there is less perfection in this than in the love I have described—than that there were a single note of discord to be heard among them. May the Lord forbid this, for His own sake. Amen.

CHAPTER 8

Treats of the great benefit of self-detachment, both interior and exterior, from all things created.

Let us now come to the detachment that we must practice, for if this is carried out perfectly it includes everything else. I say "it includes everything else" because, if we care nothing for any created things, but embrace the Creator alone, His Majesty will infuse the virtues into us in such a way that, provided we labor to the best of our abilities day by day, we shall not have to wage war much longer, for the Lord will take our defense in hand against the devils and against the whole world.

Do you suppose, daughters, that it is a small benefit to obtain for ourselves this blessing of giving ourselves wholly to Him, and keeping nothing for ourselves? Since, as I say, all blessings are in Him, let us give Him hearty praise, sisters, for having brought us together here, where we are occupied in this alone. I do not know why I am saying this, when all of you here are capable of teaching me, for I confess that, in this important respect, I am not as perfect as I should like to be and as I know I ought to be. And I must say the same about all the virtues and about all that I am dealing with here, for it is easier to write of such things than to practice them. I may not even be able to write of them effectively, for sometimes ability to do this comes only from experience—so if I have any success, it must be because I explain the nature of these virtues by describing the contraries of the qualities I myself possess.

As far as exterior matters are concerned, you know how completely cut off we are from everything. Oh, my Creator and Lord! When have I merited so great an honor? Thou seemest to have searched everywhere for means of drawing nearer to us. May it please Thy goodness that we lose not this through our own fault. Oh, sisters, for the love of God, try to realize what a great favor the Lord has bestowed on those of us whom He has brought here. Let each of you apply this to herself, since there are only twelve of us and His Majesty has been pleased for you to be one. How many people—what a multitude of people!—do I know who are better than myself and would gladly take this place of mine, yet the Lord has granted it to me who so ill deserves it!

Blessed be Thou, my God, and let the angels and all created things praise Thee, for I can no more repay this favor than all the others Thou hast shown me. It was a wonderful thing to give me the vocation to be a nun; but I have been so wicked, Lord, that Thou couldst not trust me. In a place where there were many good women living together, my wickedness would not perhaps have been noticed right down to the end of my life—I should have concealed it, as I did for so many years. So Thou didst bring me here, where, as there are so few of us that it would seem impossible for it to remain unnoticed, Thou dost remove occasions of sin from me so that I may walk the more carefully. There is no excuse for me, then, O Lord, I confess it, and so I have need of Thy mercy, that Thou mayest pardon me.

Remember, my sisters, that if we are not good we are much more to blame than others. What I earnestly beg of you is that anyone who knows she will be unable to follow our customs will say so. There are other convents in which the Lord is also well served, and she should not remain here and disturb these few of us whom His Majesty has brought together for His service. In other convents nuns are free to have the pleasure of seeing their relatives, whereas here, if relatives are ever admitted, it is only for their own pleasure. A nun who wishes to see her relatives in order to please herself, and does not get tired of them after the second visit, must, unless they are spiritual persons and do her soul some good, consider herself imperfect and realize that she is neither detached nor healthy, and will have no freedom of spirit or perfect peace. She needs a physician—and I consider that if this desire does not leave her, and she is not cured, she is not intended for this house.

The best remedy, I think, is that she should not see her relatives again until she feels free in spirit and has obtained this freedom from God by many prayers. When she looks upon such visits as crosses, let her receive them by all means, for then they will do the visitors good and herself no harm. But if she is fond of the visitors, if their troubles are a great distress to her and if she delights in listening to the stories that they tell her about the world, she may be sure that she will do herself harm and do them no good.

CHAPTER 10

Teaches that detachment from the things aforementioned is insufficient if we are not detached from our own selves and that this virtue and humility go together.

Once we have detached ourselves from the world, and from our kinsfolk, and are cloistered here in the conditions already described, it must look as if we have done everything and there is nothing left with which we have to contend. But, oh, my sisters, do not feel secure and fall asleep, or you will be like a man who goes to bed quite peacefully, after bolting all his doors for fear of thieves, when the thieves are already in the house. And you know there is no worse thief than one who lives in the house. We ourselves are the same. Unless we take great care and each of us looks well to it that she renounces her self-will, which is the most important business of all, there will be many things to deprive us of the holy freedom of spirit that our souls seek in order to soar to their Maker unburdened by the leaden weight of the earth.

It will be a great help towards this if we keep constantly in our thoughts the vanity of all things and the rapidity with which they pass away, so that we may withdraw our affections from things that are so trivial and fix them upon what will never come to an end. This may seem a poor kind of help, but it will have the effect of greatly fortifying the soul. With regard to small things, we must be very careful, as soon as we begin to grow fond of them, to withdraw our thoughts from them and turn them to God. His Majesty will help us to do this. He has granted us the great favor of providing that in this house most of it is done already. But it remains for us to become detached from our own selves, and it is a hard thing to withdraw from ourselves and oppose ourselves, because we are very close to ourselves and love ourselves very dearly.

It is here that true humility can enter, for this virtue and that of detachment from self, I think, always go together. They are two sisters who are inseparable. These are not the kinsfolk whom I counsel you to avoid. No, you must embrace them, and love them, and never be seen without them. Oh, how sovereign are these virtues, mistresses of all created things, empresses of the world, our deliverers from all the snares and entanglements laid by the devil—[these virtues are] so dearly loved by our Teacher, Christ, Who was never for a moment without them! He that possesses them can safely go out and fight all the united forces of Satan and the whole world and its temptations. Let him fear none, for his is the kingdom of the Heavens. There is none whom he need fear, for he cares nothing if he loses everything, nor does he count this as loss. His sole fear is that he may displease his God, and he begs Him to nourish these virtues within him lest he lose them through any fault of his own.

These virtues, it is true, have the property of hiding themselves from one who possesses them, in such a way that he never sees them nor can believe that he has any of them, even if he be told so. But he esteems them so much that he is forever trying to obtain them, and thus he perfects them in himself more and more. And those who possess them soon make the fact clear, even against their will, to any with whom they have fellowship. But how inappropriate it is for a person like myself to begin to praise humility and mortification, when these virtues are so highly praised by the King of Glory—a praise exemplified in all the trials He suffered. It is to possess these virtues, then, my daughters, that you must labor if you would leave the land of Egypt. For when you have obtained them, you will also obtain the manna. Then all things will taste well to you, and however much the world may dislike their savor, to you they will be sweet.

The first thing, then, that we have to do, and that at once, is to rid ourselves of love for this body of ours—and some of us pamper our natures so much that this will cause us no little labor, while others are so concerned about their health that the trouble these things give us (this is especially so of poor nuns, but it applies to others as well) is amazing. Some of us, however, seem to think that we embraced the religious life for no other reason than to keep ourselves alive, and each nun does all she can to that end. In this house, as a matter of fact, there is very little chance for us to act on such a principle, but I should be sorry if we even wanted to.

Resolve, sisters, that it is to die for Christ, and not to practice self-indulgence for Christ, that you have come here. The devil tells us that self-indulgence is necessary if we are to carry out and keep the Rule of our Order, and so many of us, indeed, try to keep our Rule by looking after our health. [We seem to worry that we will die if we haven't] kept it for as long as a month, perhaps even for a day. I really do not know what we are coming to.

No one need be afraid of our committing excesses here, by any chance—for as soon as we do any penances our confessors begin to fear that we shall kill ourselves with them. We are so horrified at our own possible excesses—if only we were as conscientious about everything else! Those who tend to the opposite extreme will I know, not mind my saying this, nor shall I mind if they say I am judging others by myself, for they will be quite right. I believe—indeed, I am sure—that more nuns are of my way of thinking than are offended by me because they do just the opposite. My own belief is that it is for this reason that the Lord is pleased to make us such weakly creatures—at least He has shown me great mercy in making me so. Since I was sure to be self-indulgent in any case, He was pleased to provide me with an excuse for this.

It is really amusing to see how some people torture themselves about it, when the real reason lies in themselves. Sometimes they get a desire to do penances, as one might say, without rhyme or reason. They go on doing them for a couple of days, and then the devil puts it into their heads that they have been doing themselves harm and so he makes them afraid of penances—after which they dare not do even those that the Order requires. [After all,] they have tried them once! They do not keep the smallest points in the Rule, such as silence, which is quite incapable of harming us. Hardly have we begun to imagine that our heads are aching than we stay away from choir, though that would not kill us either.

One day we are absent because we had a headache some time ago. Another day because our head has just been aching again. And on the next three days in case it should ache once more. Then we want to invent penances of our own, with the result that we do neither the one thing nor the other. Sometimes there is very little the matter with us, yet we think that it should dispense us from all our obligations and that if we ask to be excused from them we are doing all we need.

But why, you will say, does the Prioress excuse us? Perhaps she would not if she knew what was going on inside us. But she sees one of you wailing about a mere nothing as if your heart were breaking, and you come and ask her to excuse you from keeping the whole of your Rule, saying it is a matter of great necessity. And when there is any substance in what you say, there is always a physician at hand to confirm it or some friend or relative weeping at your side. Sometimes the poor Prioress sees that your request is excessive, but what can she do? She feels a scruple if she thinks she has been lacking in charity and she would rather the fault were yours than hers. She thinks, too, that it would be unjust of her to judge you harshly.

Oh, God help me! That there should be complaining like this among nuns! May He forgive me for saying so, but I am afraid it has become quite a habit. I happened to observe this incident once myself. A nun began complaining about her headaches and she went on complaining to me for a long time. In the end I made enquiries and found she had no headache whatever, but was suffering from some pain or other elsewhere.

These are things that may sometimes happen, and I put them down here so that you may guard against them, for if once the devil begins to frighten us about losing our health, we shall never get anywhere. The Lord give us light so that we may act rightly in everything! Amen.

CHAPTER 12

Teaches that the true lover of God must care little for life and honor.

We now come to some other little things that are also of very great importance, though they will appear trifling. All this seems a great task, and so it is, for it means warring against ourselves. But once we begin to work, God, too, works in our souls and bestows such favors on them that the most we can do in this life seems to us very little.

And we nuns are doing everything we can, by giving up our freedom for the love of God and entrusting it to another, and in putting up with so many trials—fasts, silence, enclosure, service in choir—that however much we may want to indulge ourselves we can do so only occasionally. Perhaps, in all the convents I have seen, I am the only nun guilty of self-indulgence. Why, then, do we shrink from interior mortification, since this is the means by which every other kind of mortification may become much more meritorious and perfect, so that it can then be practiced with greater tranquility and ease? This, as I have said, is acquired by gradual progress and by never indulging our own will and desire, even in small things, until we have succeeded in subduing the body to the spirit.

I repeat that this consists mainly or entirely in our ceasing to care about ourselves and our own pleasures, for the least that anyone who is beginning to serve the Lord truly can offer Him is his life. Once he has surrendered his will to Him, what has he to fear? It is evident that if he is a true religious and a real man of prayer and aspires to the enjoyment of Divine consolations, he must not turn back or shrink from desiring to die and suffer martyrdom for His sake. And do you not know, sisters, that the life of a good religious, who wishes to be among the closest friends of God, is one long martyrdom? I say "long" for, by comparison with decapitation, which is over very quickly, it may well be termed so, though life itself is short and some lives are short in the extreme. How do we know but that ours will be so short that it may end only one hour or one moment after the time of our resolving to render our entire service to God? This would be quite possible, and so we must not set store by anything that comes to an end, least of all by life, since not a day of it is secure. If a person thought that each hour might be his last, would he not spend it in labor?

Believe me, it is safest to think that this is so, for by so doing we shall learn to subdue our wills in everything. As I have said, if you are very careful about your prayer, you will soon find yourselves gradually reaching the summit of the mountain without knowing how. But how harsh it sounds to say that we must take pleasure in nothing, unless we also say what consolations and delights this renunciation brings in its train, and what a great gain it is, even in this life! What security it gives us! As you all practice this, you have done the principal part. So each of you must encourage and help the rest, and each of you must try to outstrip her sisters.

Be very careful about your interior thoughts, especially if they have to do with precedence. May Christ, by His Passion, keep us from expressing or dwelling upon such thoughts as these: "But I am her senior," "But I am older," "But I have worked harder," "But that other sister is being better treated than I am." If these thoughts come, you must quickly check them. If you allow yourselves to dwell on them, or introduce them into your conversation, they will spread like the plague—and in religious houses they may give rise to great abuses. Remember, I know a great deal about this.

If you have a prioress who allows such things, however trifling, you must believe that God has permitted her to be given to you because of your sins and that she will be the beginning of your ruin. Cry to Him, and let your whole prayer be that He may come to your aid by sending you either a religious or a person given to prayer. For if anyone prays with the resolve to enjoy the favors and consolations that God bestows in prayer, it is always well that he should have this detachment.

You may ask why I lay such stress on this and think that I am being too severe about it, and say that God grants consolations to persons less completely detached than that. I quite believe He does, for in His infinite wisdom He sees that this will enable Him to lead them to leave everything for His sake. I do not mean by "leaving" everything, "entering the religious life," for there may be obstacles to this, and the soul that is perfect can be detached and humble anywhere. It will find detachment harder in the world, however, for worldly trappings will be a great impediment to it. Still, believe me in this, questions of honor and desires for property can arise within convents as well as outside them, and the more temptations of this kind are removed from us, the more we are to blame if we yield to them. Though persons who do so may have spent years in prayer, or rather in meditation (for perfect prayer eventually destroys these attachments), they will never make great progress or come to enjoy the real fruit of prayer.

Ask yourselves, sisters, if these things that seem so insignificant mean anything to you, for the only reason you are here is that you may detach yourselves from them. Nobody honors you any the more for having them, and they lose you advantages that might have gained you more honor; the result is that you get both dishonor and loss at the same time. Let each of you ask herself how much humility she has and she will see what progress she has made. If she is really humble, I do not think the devil will dare to tempt her to take even the slightest interest in matters of precedence, for he is so shrewd that he is afraid of the blow she would strike him. If a humble soul is tempted in this way by the devil, that virtue cannot fail to bring her more fortitude and greater profit.

For clearly the temptation will cause her to look into her life, to compare the services she has rendered the Lord with what she owes Him and with the marvelous way in which He abased Himself to give us an example of humility, and to think over her sins and remember where she deserves to be on account of them. Exercises like this bring the soul such profit that on the following day Satan will not dare to come back again lest he should get his head broken.

Take this advice from me and do not forget it. You should see to it that your sisters profit by your temptations, not only interiorly (where it would be very wrong if they did not), but exteriorly as well. If you want to avenge yourself on the devil and free yourselves more quickly from temptation, ask the superior, as soon as a temptation comes to you, to give you some lowly office to do, or do some such thing, as best you can, on our own initiative, studying as you do it how to bend your will to perform tasks you dislike. The Lord will show you ways of doing so and this will soon rid you of the temptation.

God deliver us from people who wish to serve Him, yet who are mindful of their own honor. Reflect how little they gain from this. As I have said, the very act of desiring honor robs us of it, especially in matters of precedence—there is no poison in the world which is so fatal to perfection. You will say that these are little things that have to do with human nature and are not worth troubling about. But do not trifle with them, for in religious houses they spread like foam on water, and there is no small matter so extremely dangerous as are punctiliousness about honor and sensitiveness to insult.

Do you know one reason, apart from many others, why this is so? It may have its root, perhaps, in some trivial slight—hardly anything, in fact—and the devil will then induce someone else to consider it important, so that she will think it a real charity to tell you about it and to ask how you can allow yourself to be insulted so. She then will pray that God may give you patience and that you may offer it to Him, for even a saint could not bear more. The devil is simply putting his deceitfulness into this other person's mouth, and though you yourself are quite ready to bear the slight, you are tempted to vainglory because you have not resisted something else as perfectly as you should.

This human nature of ours is so wretchedly weak that even while we are telling ourselves that there is nothing for us to make a fuss about, we imagine we are doing something virtuous, and begin to feel sorry for ourselves, particularly when we see that other people are sorry for us too. In this way the soul begins to lose the occasions of merit that it had gained. It becomes weaker, and so opens a door to the devil by which he can enter on some other occasion with a temptation worse than the last. It may even happen that when you yourself are prepared to suffer an insult, your sisters come and ask you if you are a beast of burden, and say you ought to be more sensitive about things. Oh, my sisters, for the love of God, never let charity move you to show pity for another in anything to do with these fancied insults, for that is like the pity shown to holy Job by his wife and friends.

CHAPTER 17

How not all souls are fitted for contemplation and how some take long to attain it. True humility will walk happily along the road by which the Lord leads it.

I seem now to be beginning my treatment of prayer, but there still remains a little for me to say, which is of great importance because it has to do with humility, and in this house that is necessary. For humility is the principal virtue that must be practiced by those who pray, and, as I have said, it is very fitting that you should try to learn how to practice it often. That is one of the chief things to remember about it, and it is very necessary that it should be known by all who practice prayer. How can anyone who is truly humble think herself as good as those who become contemplatives? God, it is true, by His goodness and mercy, can make her so, but my advice is that she should always sit down in the lowest place, for that is what the Lord instructed us to do and taught us by His own example. Let such a one make herself ready for God to lead her by this road if He so wills. If He does not, the whole point of true humility is that she should consider herself happy in serving the servants of the Lord and in praising Him. For she deserves to be a slave of the devils in hell, yet His Majesty has brought her here to live among His servants.

I do not say this without good reason, for it is very important for us to realize that God does not lead us all by the same road, and perhaps she who believes herself to be going along the lowest of roads is the highest in the Lord's eyes. So it does not follow that because all of us in this house practice prayer, we are all destined to be contemplatives. That is impossible, and those of us who are not would be greatly discouraged if we did not grasp the truth that contemplation is something given by God. And since it is not necessary for salvation, and God does not ask it of us before He gives us our reward, we must not suppose that anyone else will require it of us. We shall not fail to attain perfection if we do what has been said here. We may, in fact, gain much more merit, because what we do will cost us more labor. The Lord will be treating us like those who are strong and will be laying up for us all that we cannot enjoy in this life. Let us not be discouraged, then, and give up prayer or cease doing what the rest do. For the Lord sometimes tarries long, and gives us as great rewards all at once as He has been giving to others over many years.

I myself spent over fourteen years without ever being able to meditate except while reading. There must be many people like this, and others who cannot meditate even after reading, but can only recite vocal prayers, in which they chiefly occupy themselves and take a certain pleasure. Some find their thoughts wandering so much that they cannot concentrate upon the same thing, but are always restless—to such an extent that if they try to fix their thoughts upon God, they are attacked by a thousand foolish ideas and scruples and doubts concerning the Faith. I know a very old woman, leading a most excellent life—I wish mine were like hers—a penitent and a great servant of God, who for many years has been spending hours and hours in vocal prayer. But she can get no help at all from mental prayer, the most she can do is to dwell upon each of her vocal prayers as she says them.

There are a great many other people just like this. If they are humble, they will not, I think, be any the worse off in the end, but very much in the same state as those who enjoy numerous consolations. In one way they may feel safer, for we cannot tell if consolations come from God or are sent by the devil. If they are not of God, they are the more dangerous, for the chief object of the devil's work on earth is to fill us with pride. If they are of God, there is no reason for fear, for they bring humility with them, as I explained in my other book at great length.

Others walk in humility, and always suspect that if they fail to receive consolations the fault is theirs, and are always most anxious to make progress. They never see a person shedding a tear without thinking themselves very backward in God's service unless they are doing the same, whereas they may perhaps be much more advanced.

For tears, though good, are not invariably signs of perfection; there is always greater safety in humility, mortification, detachment and other virtues. There is no reason for fear, and you must not be afraid that you will fail to attain the perfection of the greatest contemplatives.

Saint Martha was holy, but we are not told that she was a contemplative. What more do you want than to be able to grow to be like that blessed woman, who was worthy to receive Christ our Lord so often into her house, and to prepare meals for Him, and to serve Him and perhaps to eat at table with Him? If she had been absorbed in devotion [continually] as the Magdalen was, there would have been no one to prepare a meal for this Divine Guest. Now remember that this little community is Saint Martha's house, and that there must be people of all kinds here. Nuns who are called to the active life must not murmur at others who are very much absorbed in contemplation, for contemplatives know that, though they themselves may be silent, the Lord will speak for them, and this, as a rule, makes them forget themselves and everything else.

Remember that there must be someone to cook the meals and count yourselves happy in being able to serve like Martha. Reflect that true humility consists to a great extent in being ready for what the Lord desires to do with you and happy that He should do it, and in always considering yourselves unworthy to be called His servants. If contemplation, mental and vocal prayer, tending the sick, serving in the house, and working at even the lowliest tasks are of service to the Guest who comes to stay with us and to eat and take His recreation with us, what should it matter to us if we do one of these things rather than another?

I do not mean that it is for us to say what we shall do, but that we must do our best in everything, for the choice is not ours but the Lord's. If after many years He is pleased to give each of us her office, it will be a curious kind of humility for you to wish to choose. Let the Lord of the house do that, for He is wise and powerful and knows what is fitting for you and for Himself as well. Be sure that if you do what lies in your power and prepare yourself for high contemplation with the perfection aforementioned, then, if He does not grant it you (and I think He will not fail to do so if you have true detachment and humility), it will be because He has laid up this joy for you so as to give it to you in Heaven. And because, as I have said elsewhere, He is pleased to treat you like people who are strong and give you a cross to bear on earth like that which His Majesty Himself always bore.

What better sign of friendship is there than for Him to give you what He gave Himself? It might well be that you would not have had so great a reward from contemplation. His judgments are His own, and we must not meddle in them. It is indeed a good thing that the choice is not ours, for if it were we should think it the more restful life and all become great contemplatives. Oh, how much we gain if we have no desire to gain what seems to us best and so have no fear of losing, since God never permits a truly mortified person to lose anything except when such loss will bring him greater gain!

CHAPTER 19

Begins to treat of prayer. Addresses souls who cannot reason with the understanding.

It is a long time since I wrote the last chapter and I have had no chance of returning to my writing, so that, without reading through what I have written, I cannot remember what I said. However, I must not spend too much time at this, so it will be best if I go right on without troubling about the connection. For those with orderly minds, and for souls who practice prayer and can be a great deal in their own company, many books have been written, and these are so good and are the work of such competent people that you would be making a mistake if you paid heed to anything about prayer that you learned from me. There are books, as I say, in which the mysteries of the life of the Lord and of His sacred Passion are described in short passages, one for each day of the week. There are also meditations on the Judgment, on hell, on our own nothingness and on all that we owe to God, and these books are excellent both as to their teaching and as to the way in which they plan the beginning and the end of the time of prayer.

There is no need to tell anyone who is capable of practicing prayer in this way, and has already formed the habit of doing so, that by this good road the Lord will bring her to the harbor of light. If she begins so well, her end will be good also, and all who can walk along this road will walk restfully and securely, for one always walks restfully when the understanding is kept in restraint. It is something else that I wish to treat of and help you about if the Lord is pleased to enable me to do so. If not, you will at least realize that there are many souls who suffer this trial, and you will not be so much distressed at undergoing it yourselves at first, but will find some comfort in it.

There are some souls, and some minds, as unruly as horses not yet broken in. No one can stop them—now they go this way, now that way; they are never still. Although a skilled rider mounted on such a horse may not always be in danger, he will be so sometimes. And even if he is not concerned about his life, there will always be the risk of his stumbling, so that he has to ride with great care. Some people are either like this by nature or God permits them to become so. I am very sorry for them. They seem to me like people who are very thirsty and see water a long way off, yet when they try to go to it they find someone who all the time is barring their path—at the beginning of their journey, in the middle, and at the end. And when—after all their labor—and the labor is tremendous—they have conquered the first of their enemies, they allow themselves to be conquered by the second, and they prefer to die of thirst rather than drink water that is going to cost them so much trouble. Their strength has come to an end, their courage has failed them, and though some of them are strong enough to conquer their second enemies as well as their first, when they meet the third group their strength comes to an end, though perhaps they are only a couple of steps from the fountain of living water, of which the Lord said to the Samaritan woman that whosoever drinks of it shall not thirst again.

How right and how very true is that which comes from the lips of Truth Himself! In this life the soul will never thirst for anything more, although its thirst for things in the life to come will exceed any natural thirst that we can imagine here below. How the soul thirsts to experience this thirst! For it knows how very precious it is, and grievous though it be and exhausting, it creates the very satisfaction by which this thirst is allayed. It is, therefore, a thirst that quenches nothing but desire for earthly things and when God slakes it, satisfies in such a way that one of the greatest favors He can bestow on the soul is to leave it with this longing—so that it has an even greater desire to drink of this water again.

Water has three properties—three relevant properties that I can remember, that is to say, for it must have many more. One of them is that of cooling things. However hot we are, water tempers the heat, and it will even put out a large fire, except when there is tar in the fire, in which case, they say, it only burns the more. God help me! What a marvelous thing it is that when this fire is strong and fierce and subject to none of the elements, water should make it grow fiercer, and, though it's a contrary element, should not quench it but only cause it to burn the more! It would be very useful to be able to discuss this with someone who understands philosophy; if I knew the properties of things I could explain it myself; but though I love thinking about it, I cannot explain it—perhaps I do not even understand it.

You will be glad, sisters, if God grants you to drink of this water, as are those who drink of it now, and you will understand how a genuine love of God—if it is really strong, and completely free from earthly things, and able to rise above them—is master of all the elements and of the whole world. And as water proceeds from the earth, there is no fear of its quenching this fire, which is the love of God. Though the two elements are contraries, it has no power over it. The fire is absolute master, and subject to nothing.

You will not be surprised then, sisters, at the way I have insisted in this book that you should strive to obtain this freedom. Is it not a funny thing that a poor little nun of Saint Joseph's should attain mastery over the whole earth and all the elements? What wonder that the saints did as they pleased with them by the help of God? Fire and water obeyed Saint Martin; even birds and fishes were obedient to Saint Francis, and similarly with many other saints. Helped as they were by God, and themselves doing all that was in their power, they could almost have claimed this as a right. It was clear that they were masters over everything in the world, because they had striven so hard to despise it and subjected themselves to the Lord of the world with all their might. So, as I say, the water that springs from the earth has no power over this fire. Its flames rise high and its source is in nothing so base as the earth. There are other fires of love for God—small ones that may be quenched by the least little thing. But this fire will most certainly not be so quenched. Even should a whole sea of temptations assail it, they will not keep it from burning or prevent it from gaining the mastery over them.

Water that comes down as rain from Heaven will quench the flames even less, for in that case the fire and the water are not contraries, but have the same origin. Do not fear that the one element may harm the other, each helps the other and they produce the same effect. For the water of genuine tears—that is, tears which come from true prayer—is a good gift from the King of Heaven, for it fans the flames and keeps them alight, while the fire helps to cool the water. God bless me! What a beautiful and wonderful thing it is that fire should cool water! But it does, and it even freezes all worldly affections when it is combined with the living water that comes from Heaven, the source of the above-mentioned tears, which are given us and not acquired by our diligence. Certainly, then, nothing worldly has warmth enough left in it to induce us to cling to it unless it is something that increases this fire, the nature of which is not to be easily satisfied, but, if possible, to enkindle the entire world.

The second property of water is that it cleanses things that are not clean already. What would become of the world if there were no water for washing? Do you know what cleansing properties there are in this living water, this heavenly water, this clear water, when it is unclouded and free from mud and comes down from Heaven? Once the soul has drunk of it I am convinced that it makes it pure and clean of all its sins. For, as I have written, God does not allow us to drink of this water of perfect contemplation whenever we like. The choice is not ours. This Divine union is something quite supernatural, given that it may cleanse the soul and leave it pure and free from the mud and misery in which it has been plunged because of its sins. Other consolations, excellent as they may be, that come through the intermediacy of the understanding, are like water running all over the ground. This cannot be drunk directly from the source, and its course is never free from clogging impurities, so that it is neither so pure nor so clean as the other. I should not say that this prayer I have been describing, which comes from reasoning with the intellect, is living water—I mean so far as my understanding of it goes. For, despite our efforts, there is always something clinging to the soul, through the influence of the body and of the baseness of our nature, which we should prefer not to be there.

I will explain myself further. We are meditating on the nature of the world, and on the way in which everything will come to an end, so that we may learn to despise it, when almost without noticing it, we find ourselves ruminating on things in the world that we love. We try to banish these thoughts, but we cannot help being slightly distracted by thinking of things that have happened, or will happen, of things we have done and of things we are going to do. Then we begin to think of how we can get rid of these thoughts, and that sometimes plunges us once again into the same danger. It is not that we ought to omit such meditations, but we need to retain our misgivings about them and not to grow careless. In contemplation the Lord Himself relieves us of this care, for He will not trust us to look after ourselves. So dearly does He love our souls that He prevents them from rushing into things that may do them harm just at this time when He is anxious to help them. So He calls them to His side at once, and in a single moment reveals more truths to them and gives them a clearer insight into the nature of everything than they could otherwise gain in many years. For our sight is poor and the dust that we meet on the road blinds us, but in contemplation the Lord brings us to the end of the day's journey without our understanding how.

The third property of water is that it satisfies and quenches thirst. Thirst, I think, means the desire for something which is very necessary for us—so necessary that if we have none of it we shall die. It is a strange thing that if we have no water we die, and that we can also lose our lives through having too much of it, as happens to many people who get drowned. Oh, my Lord, if only one could be plunged so deeply into this living water that one's life would end! Can that be? Yes, this love and desire for God can increase so much that human nature is unable to bear it, and so there have been persons who have died of it. I knew one person who had this living water in such great abundance that she would almost have been drawn out of herself by raptures if God had not quickly succored her. She had such a thirst, and her desire grew so greatly, that she realized clearly that she might quite possibly die of thirst if something were not done for her. I say that she would almost have been drawn out of herself because in this state the soul is in repose. So intolerable does such a soul find the world that it seems to be overwhelmed, but it comes to life again in God. In this way His Majesty enables it to enjoy experiences that, if it had remained within itself, would perforce have cost it its life.

Let it be understood from this that as there can be nothing in our supreme Good which is not perfect, all that He gives is for our welfare, and however abundant this water that He gives may be, in nothing that He gives can there be superfluity [excessiveness]. For if His gift is abundant, He also bestows on the soul, as I have said, an abundant capacity for drinking, just as a glassmaker moulds his vessels to the size he thinks necessary, so that there is room for what he wishes to pour into them. As our desires for this water come from ourselves, they are never free from fault, and any good that there may be in them comes from the help of the Lord. But we are so indiscreet that as the pain is sweet and pleasant, we think we can never have too much of it. We have an immeasurable longing for it, and so far as is possible on earth, we stimulate this longing—sometimes this [nearly] goes so far as to cause death. How happy is such a death! And yet by living one might perhaps have helped others to die of the desire for it. I believe the devil has something to do with this. Knowing how much harm we can do him by living, he tempts us to be indiscreet in our penances and so to ruin our health, which is a matter of no small moment to him.

I advise anyone who attains to an experience of this fierce thirst to watch herself carefully, for I think she will have to contend with this temptation. She may not die of her thirst, but her health will be ruined, and she will involuntarily give her feelings outward expression, which ought at all costs to be avoided. Sometimes, however, all our diligence in this respect is unavailing and we are unable to hide our emotions as much as we should like. Whenever we are assailed by these strong impulses stimulating the increase of our desire, let us take great care not to add to them ourselves but to check them gently by thinking of something else. For our own nature may be playing as great a part in producing these feelings as our love. There are some people of this type who have keen desires for all kinds of things, even for bad things, but I do not think such people can have achieved great mortification, for mortification is always profitable. It seems foolish to check so good a thing as this desire, but it is not. I am not saying that the desire should be uprooted—only checked. One may be able to do this by stimulating some other desire that is equally praiseworthy.

In order to explain myself better I will give an illustration. A man has a great desire to be with God, as Saint Paul had, and to be loosed from this prison. This causes him pain, which yet is in itself a great joy, and no small degree of mortification will be needed if he is to check it—in fact, he will not always be able to do so. But when he finds it oppressing him so much, he may almost lose his reason. I saw this happen to someone not long ago. She was of an impetuous nature, but so accustomed to curbing her own will that, from what I had seen at other times, I thought her will was completely annihilated. Yet when I saw her for a moment, the great stress and strain caused by her efforts to hide her feelings had all but destroyed her reason. In such an extreme case, I think, even if the desire did come from the Spirit of God, it would be true humility to be afraid, for we must not imagine that we have sufficient charity to bring us to such a state of oppression.

I shall not think it at all wrong (if it be possible, I mean, for it may not always be so) for us to change our desire by reflecting that if we live we have more chance of serving God, and that we might do this by giving light to some soul that otherwise would be lost. As well as the fact that if we serve Him more, we shall deserve to enjoy Him more, and grieve that we have served Him so little. These are consolations appropriate to such great trials. They will allay our pain and we shall gain a great deal by them—if in order to serve the

Lord Himself, we are willing to spend a long time here below and to live with our grief. It is as if a person were suffering a great trial or a grievous affliction and we consoled him by telling him to have patience and leave himself in God's hands so that His will might be fulfilled in him. For it is always best to leave ourselves in God's hands.

And what if the devil had anything to do with these strong desires? This might be possible, as I think is suggested in Cassian's story of a hermit, leading the austerest of lives, who was persuaded by the devil to throw himself down a well so that he might see God the sooner. I do not think this hermit can have served God either humbly or efficiently, for the Lord is faithful and His Majesty would never allow a servant of His to be blinded in a matter in which the truth was so clear. But, of course, if the desire had come from God, it would have done the hermit no harm, for such desires bring with them illumination, moderation and discretion. This is fitting, but our enemy and adversary seeks to harm us wherever he can, and since he is not unwatchful, we must not be so either. This is an important matter in many respects. For example, we must shorten our time of prayer, however much joy it gives us, if we see our bodily strength waning or find that our head aches. Discretion is most necessary in everything.

Why do you suppose, daughters, that I have tried, as people say, to describe the end of the battle before it has begun and to point to its reward by telling you about the blessing that comes from drinking of the heavenly source of this living water? I have done this so that you may not be distressed at the trials and annoyances of the road and may tread it with courage and not grow weary. For, as I have said, it may be that when you have arrived and have only to stoop and drink of the spring, you may fail to do so and lose this blessing, thinking that you have not the strength to attain it and that it is not for you.

Remember, the Lord invites us all, and since He is Truth itself, we cannot doubt Him. If His invitation were not a general one, He would not have said: "I will give you to drink." He might have said: "Come, all of you, for after all you will lose nothing by coming; and I will give drink to those whom I think fit for it." But as He said we were all to come, without making this condition, I feel sure that none will fail to receive this living water unless they cannot keep to the path. May the Lord, Who promises it, give us grace, for His Majesty's own sake, to seek it as it must be sought.

CHAPTER 40

Describes how, by striving always to walk in the love and fear of God, we shall travel safely amid all these temptations.

Show us, then, O our good Master, some way in which we may live through this most dangerous warfare without frequent surprise.

The best way that we can do this, daughters, is to use the love and fear given us by His Majesty. For love will make us quicken our steps, while fear will make us look where we are setting our feet so that we shall not fall on a road where there are so many obstacles. Along that road all living creatures must pass, and if we have these two things we shall certainly not be deceived.

You will ask me how you can tell if you really have these two very, very, great virtues. You are right to ask, for we can never be quite definite and certain about it; if we were sure that we possessed love, we should be sure that we were in a state of grace.

But you know, sisters, there are some indications that are in no way secret but so evident that even a blind man, as people say, could see them. You may not wish to heed them, but they cry so loud for notice that they make quite an uproar, for there are not many who possess them to the point of perfection and thus they are the more readily noticed. Love and fear of God! These are two strong castles whence we can wage war on the world and on the devils.

Those who really love God love all good, seek all good, help forward all good, praise all good, and invariably join forces with good men and help and defend them. They love only truth and things worthy of love. Do you think it possible that anyone who really and truly loves God can love vanities, riches, worldly pleasures or honors? Can he engage in strife or feel envy? No, for his only desire is to please the Beloved. Such persons die with longing for Him to love them and so they will give their lives to learn how they may please Him better. Will they hide their love? No, if their love for God is genuine love they cannot. Why, think of Saint Paul or the Magdalen. One of these—Saint Paul—found in three days that he was sick with love. The Magdalen discovered this on the very first day. And how certain of it they were! For there are degrees of love for God, which shows itself in proportion to its strength. If there is little of it, it shows itself but little; if there is much, it shows itself a great deal. But it always shows itself, whether little or much, provided it is real love for God.

But to come to what we are chiefly treating now—the deceptions and illusions practiced against contemplatives by the devil—such souls have no little love, for had they not a great deal they would not be contemplatives, and so their love shows itself plainly and in many ways. Being a great fire, it cannot fail to give out a very bright light.

If they have not much love, they should proceed with many misgivings and realize that they have great cause for fear; and they should try to find out what is wrong with them, say their prayers, walk in humility and beseech the

Lord not to lead them into temptation—into which, I fear, they will certainly fall unless they bear this sign. But if they walk humbly and strive to discover the truth and do as their confessor bids them and tell him the plain truth, then the Lord is faithful, and as has been said, by using the very means with which he had thought to give them death, the devil will give them life, with however many fantasies and illusions he tries to deceive them. If they submit to the teaching of the Church, they need not fear; whatever fantasies and illusions the devil may invent, he will at once betray his presence.

But if you feel this love for God that I have spoken of, and the fear that I shall now describe, you may go on your way with happiness and tranquility. In order to disturb the soul and keep it from enjoying these great blessings, the devil will suggest to it a thousand false fears and will persuade other people to do the same. For if he cannot win souls he will at least try to make them lose something, and among the losers will be those who might have gained greatly had they believed that such great favors, bestowed upon so miserable a creature, come from God, and that it is possible for them to be thus bestowed, for sometimes we seem to forget His past mercies.

Do you suppose that it is of little use to the devil to suggest these fears? No, it is most useful to him, for there are two well-known ways in which he can make use of this means to harm us, to say nothing of others. First, he can make those who listen to him fearful of engaging in prayer, because they think that they will be deceived. Secondly, he can dissuade many from approaching God who, as I have said, see that He is so good that He will hold intimate converse with sinners. Many such souls think that He will treat them in the same way, and they are right: I myself know certain persons inspired in this way who began the habit of prayer and in a short time became truly devout and received great favors from the Lord.

Therefore, sisters, when you see someone to whom the Lord is granting these favors, praise Him fervently, yet do not imagine that she is safe, but aid her with more prayer, for no one can be safe in this life amid the engulfing dangers of this stormy sea. Wherever this love is, then, you will not fail to recognize it. Indeed, I do not know how it could be concealed. For they say that it is impossible for us to hide our love even for creatures, and that the more we try to conceal it, the more clearly is it revealed. And yet this is so worthless that it hardly deserves the name of love, for it is founded upon nothing at all—it is loathsome, indeed, to make this comparison. How then could a love like God's be concealed—so strong, so righteous, continually increasing, never seeing cause for ceasing to manifest itself, and resting upon the firm foundation of the love that is its [own] reward? As to the reality of this reward there can be no doubt, for it is manifest in Our Lord's great sorrows, His trials, the shedding of His blood and even the loss of His life.

Certainly then there is no doubt as to this love. It is indeed love and deserves that name of which worldly vanities have robbed it. God help me! How different must the one love be from the other to those who have experience of both!

May His Majesty be pleased to grant us to experience this before He takes us from this life, for it will be a great thing at the hour of death to realize that we shall be judged by One Whom we have loved above all things, and with a passion that makes us entirely forget ourselves. We shall not be going into a foreign land, but into our own country, for it belongs to Him Whom we have loved so truly and Who himself loves us. For this love of His, besides its other properties, is better than all earthly affection in that if we love Him we are quite sure that He loves us, too. Remember, my daughters, the greatness of the gain that comes from this love, and of our loss if we do not possess it, for in that case we shall be delivered into the hands of the tempter—hands so cruel and so hostile to all that is good, and so friendly to all that is evil.

What will become of the poor soul when it falls into these hands after emerging from all the pains and trials of death? How little rest it will have! How it will be torn as it goes down to hell! What swarms and varieties of serpents it will meet! How dreadful is that place! How miserable that lodging! Why a pampered person (and most of those who go to hell are that) can hardly bear to spend a single night in a bad inn. What, then, will be the feelings of that wretched soul when it is condemned to such an inn as this and has to spend eternity there? Let us not try to pamper ourselves, daughters. We are quite well off here—there is only a single night for us to spend in this bad inn. Let us praise God and strive to be holy in this life. It may be that we will begin to enjoy glory even in this world and will know no fear, but only peace.

Even if we do not attain to this, sisters, let us beseech God that if in due course we must suffer these pains [pains of this world], it may be with the hope of emerging from them. Then we shall suffer them willingly and lose neither the friendship nor the grace of God. May He grant us these in this life so that we may not unwittingly fall into temptation.

POETRY
BY SAINT TERESA OF AVILA

In the Hands of God

I am Yours and born of You,
What do You want of Me?

Majestic Sovereign,
Unending wisdom,
Kindness pleasing to my soul;
God sublime, one being good,
Behold this one so vile.
Singing of her love to You:
What do You want of me?

Yours, You made me,
Yours, You saved me,
Yours, You endured me,
Yours, You called me,
Yours, You awaited me,
Yours, I did not stray.
What do You want of Me?

Good Lord, what do You want of me,
What is this wretch to do?
What work is then,
This sinful slave, to do?
Look at me, Sweet Love,
Sweet Love, look at me,
What do You want of me?

In Your hand
I place my heart,
Body, life and soul,
Deep feelings and affections mine,
Spouse–Redeemer sweet,
Myself offered now to You,
What do You want of me?

Give me death, give me life,
Health or sickness,
Honor or shame,
War or swelling peace,
Weakness or full strength,
Yes, to these I say,
What do You want of me?

Give me wealth or want,
Delight or distress,
Happiness or gloominess,
Heaven or hell,
Sweet life, sun unveiled,
To You I give all,
What do You want of me?

Give me, if You will, prayer;
Or let me know dryness,
And abundance of devotion,
Or if not, then barrenness.
In You alone, Sovereign Majesty,
I find my peace,
What do You want of me?
Give me then wisdom.
Or for love, ignorance,
Years of abundance,
Or hunger and famine.

Darkness or sunlight,
Move me here to there:
What do You want of me?

If You want me to rest,
I desire it for love;
If to labor,
I will die working:
Sweet Love say
Where, how and when.
What do You want of me?

Calvary or Tabor give me,
Desert or fruitful land;
As Job in suffering
Or John at Your breast;
Barren or fruited vine,
Whatever be Your will:
What do You want of me?

Be it Joseph chained
Or as Egypt's governor,
David pained
Or exalted high,
Jonas drowned,
Or Jonas freed:
What do You want of me?

Silent or speaking,
Fruit-bearing or barren,
My wounds shown by the Law,
Rejoicing in the tender Gospel;
Sorrowing or exulting,
You alone live in me:
What do You want of me?

Yours I am, for You I was born:
What do You want of me?

You are Christ's Hands

Christ has no body now on earth by yours,
no hands but yours,
no feet but yours,
Yours are the eyes through which to look out
Christ's compassion to the world
Yours are the feet with which He is to go about
doing good;
Yours are the hands with which He is to
bless men now.

Oh, Exceeding Beauty

Oh, Beauty exceeding
All other beauties!
Paining, but You wound not
Free of pain You destroy
The love of creatures.

Oh, knot that binds
Two so different,
Why do You become unbound
For when held fast You strengthen
Making injuries seem good.
Bend the one without being
With being unending;
Finish, without finishing,
Love, without having to love,
Magnify our nothingness.

Let Nothing Disturb Thee

Let nothing disturb thee,
Nothing affright thee;
All thing are passing;
God never changeth;
Patient endurance
Attaineth to all things;
Who God possesseth
In nothing is wanting
Alone God sufficeth.

Let Mine Eyes See

Let mine eyes see Thee, sweet Jesus of Nazareth,
Let mine eyes see Thee, and then see death.
Let them see that can, Roses and Jasmine,
Seeing Thy face most fair, all blossom are therein.
Flower of seraphim, sweet Jesus of Nazareth.
Let mine eyes see Thee, and then see death.
Nothing I require, where my Jesus is;
Anguish all desire, saving only this;
All my help is His, He only succoureth.
Let mine eyes see Thee, and then see death.

If, Lord, Thy Love is Strong

If, Lord, thy love for me is strong
As this which binds me unto Thee,
What holds me from Thee, Lord, so long,
What holds Thee, Lord, so long from me?
O soul, what then desirest thou?
Lord, I would see Thee, who thus chose Thee.

What fears can yet assail thee now?
All that I fear is but to lose Thee.
Love's whole possession I entreat,
Lord make my soul Thine own abode,
And I will build a nest so sweet
It may not be too poor for God.

A soul in God hidden from sin,
What more desires for Thee remain,
Save but to love again,
And all on flame with love within,
Love on, and turn to love again.

God Alone is Enough

Let nothing upset you,
Let nothing startle you.

All things pass;
God does not change.

Patience wins
All it seeks.

Whoever has God
Lacks nothing:
God alone is enough.

STUDY GUIDE

Mansion One

1. What does St. Teresa mean when she exhorts the soul "to enter into yourself"?
2. Explain how the soul is compared to a tree.
3. How does self-knowledge bring humility to the soul?

Mansion 2

1. Why is perseverance essential?
2. How does reason convince the soul to continue its journey?
3. Explain the importance of choosing wise friends to accompany you on your journey.
4. How do we receive strength?
5. Explain the reason for vigilance on the pathway.
6. How do we conform to God's will?

Mansion Three

1. What is the primary reason for dryness in the prayer life?
2. What are some of the other reasons?
3. How do we give all to God?
4. Why does God test and try us?

5. Explain the importance of detachment when pursuing perfection.

6. What is the ointment for our wounds?

7. How does perfection grow?

Mansion Four

1. Why does Saint Teresa say the things in the Fourth Mansion are more difficult to explain?

2. Why are the poisonous reptiles useful in this mansion?

3. What is the difference between sweetness in prayer and spiritual comforts?

4. How are divine consolations shared by the soul and body?

Mansion Five

1. What is the soul's proof of union with God?

2. How is the silkworm used as a symbol of the soul?

3. What are the effects of divine union?

4. What is the basis for supernatural union with God?

5. What are the two things God commands us to do?

6. What is the sign that we are obeying His commands?

7. What is the benefit of fasting?

Mansion Six

1. Why does the soul who seeks perfection suffer resentment from others?

2. At what time is the fragrance of the Lord sensed?

3. When is the soul most aware of the Lord's presence?

4. Does the Lord bestow favors and graces only on the strong Christian?

5. What beneficial effects develop from these visions?

6. What benefit does Saint Teresa remind us of in 1 Corinthians 14:12?

7. Is there a time on this earth that the Christian will not have trials, temptations, and tests?

Mansion Seven

1. What is the difference between spiritual betrothal and marriage?

2. What are the benefits to the soul in the seventh mansion?

3. Why is the soul always calm in this mansion?

4. What is the foundation of our building?

5. What did the Lord tell the disciples his food was?

6. How can we help bring souls to Christ?

GLOSSARY

Abstraction – The act of removing.

Apostle Paul – A Christian missionary to the Gentiles; author of several Epistles in the New Testament; even though Paul was not present at the Last Supper he is considered an Apostle; Paul's name was Saul prior to his conversion to Christianity.

Archiepiscopal – Of or having to do with an archbishop or an archbishopric.

Areopagitical – Refers to Areopagus, which was the highest judicial and legislative council of ancient Athens.

Aridity – Used often in the writings of Saint Teresa of Avila and Saint John of the Cross; aridity has to do with spiritual dryness—a figurative desert experience when one does not feel close to God and does not appreciate spiritual things.

Asceticism – The practice of strict self-denial as a measure of spiritual discipline. An ascetic is one who chooses a path of simplicity, devotion, austerity, and poverty. Many ascetics are mystics as well.

Beatification – Roman Catholic Church to proclaim (a deceased person) to be one of the blessed and thus worthy of public religious veneration in a particular region or religious congregation.

Blessedness – Extreme happiness as a result of closeness to God. Blessedness brings the bliss of Heaven to the blessed on Earth.

Bollandists – The Jesuit editors of the "Acta Sanctorum," or "Lives of the Saints." Named from John Bolland, who began the work.

Calced – This is a division within the Carmelite Order of the Roman Catholic Church that has adapted the rules of the order to meet the needs of the times. Example: Such as the wearing of shoes, etc.

Carmelites – A mendicant order of the Roman Catholic Church that had its origins early in the Middle Ages on or near Mount Carmel in Palestine.

Christian – Professing belief in Jesus as Christ or following the religion based on the life and teachings of Jesus.

Cloisters – A place, especially a monastery or convent, devoted to religious seclusion.

Contemplation – Saint Teresa explains the difference between meditation and contemplation in her book *The Interior Castle*. Meditation relates to mental activity, and contemplation involves being totally focused on God and spiritual things that leads to a state of mystical awareness of God and His attributes. It requires detachment from the world and personal desires, purgation, and self-denial.

Contrition – Being contrite (sorry for one's sins and shortcomings) leads to contrition. It involves true grief over sin that leads to repentance.

Convent – A community, especially of nuns, bound by vows to a religious life under a superior.

Corporeal (Corporal) – Refers to the physical body and senses.

Detachment – Saint Teresa refers to *detachment* in her writings. It is a form of self-denial that makes one indifferent toward all worldly concerns, materialism, self-aggrandizement. It is a freeing of the soul to a higher state of spiritual happiness.

Devotions – Times of prayer and communion with God.

Discalced – This is a term given to the member of the Teresian Reform Movement within the Carmelite Order of the Roman Catholic Church. The term means *barefoot* or *shoeless*; it is a symbol of voluntary poverty, simplicity of lifestyle, devotion and detachment of discalced Carmelites who live simple and austere lives in their quest for total union with God.

Duchess of Alba – Member of the House of Alba, an aristocratic family of Alba de Tormes, Spain.

Foundress – A female founder; a woman who founds, establishes, or endows with a fund.

Fr. Ignatius Loyala – Founded the Company of Jesus.

Fr. Peter of Alcantara – Franciscan Monk who became Spiritual Director to St. Teresa of Avila in 1560.

God – Creator.

God's Elect – Chosen of God.

Good Works – Christian acts.

Grano salis – "With a grain of salt" is a literal translation of a Latin phrase, *cum grano salis*. A pinch of salt may also be used.

Habit – distinctive dress or costume, especially of a religious order.

Holy Spirit – The Spirit of God and Third Person of the Triune Godhead.

Illusive Vision – A product of the imagination.

281

Imaginary Vision – A vision in the mind.

Incarnation – This is a direct reference to Jesus Christ, who came to earth in the form of man. (See John 1:14.)

Intellectual Vision – This is a vision that makes the recipient aware of the closeness of the Lord, not by physical sight, but by a sensed Presence.

Intercession – Interceding in prayer for someone or something

Interior Life – The life of prayer.

Jesus Christ – Son of God.

Judas – An apostle of Jesus Christ, who betrayed Jesus for thirty pieces of silver.

Keep – The stronghold or innermost fortified part of the castle.

King David – King of Israel, wrote the Palms of David.

Locution(s) – A particular word, phrase, or expression, especially one that is used by a particular person or group.

Lot's Wife – (Old Testament) when God destroyed Sodom and Gomorrah, Lot and his family were told to flee without looking back; Lot's wife was disobedient and was immediately changed into a pillar of salt.

Lukewarmness – Lack of passion.

Manna – In the Bible, the food miraculously provided for the Israelites in the wilderness during their flight from Egypt.

Mary and Martha – Followers of Christ Jesus, and sisters of Lazarus, whom Jesus raised from the dead.

Mary Magdalene – Sinful woman Jesus healed of evil spirits; she became a follower of Jesus.

Meditation – Meditation involves mindfulness of the things of God, but it is mainly intellectual. It is thinking about or meditating on God or the things of God and will lead the believer to the next step, which is contemplation.

Mercy – God's unmerited favor.

Monastery – A community of persons, especially monks, bound by vows to a religious life and often living in partial or complete seclusion.

Mortification – This noun involves death; it is the putting to death of the flesh and all its appetites and desires. It is dying to self and living for God.

Moses – Old Testament Prophet who led the Israelites out of Egypt.

Mystic, Mystical, Mysticism – A mystic is a believer who wants to always be close to God, to hear His voice, and to have an intimate relationship with Him. To be mystical is to be intensely spiritual. Saint John of the Cross and Saint Teresa of Avila were devoted mystics, who experienced mystical union with God through direct knowledge of Him, supernatural visions, revelations, and holy communion.

Obloguy – Abusively detractive language or utterance; calumny.

Penance – An act of contrition, self-deprivation, abasement, mortification and self-denial related to one's devotion to God. It is also a sacramental rite that is practiced in the Roman Catholic Church.

Perfect – Matthew 5:48: *Be ye therefore perfect, even as your Father which is in Heaven is perfect.*

John 17:23: *I in them, and thou in me, that they may be made perfect in one; and that the world may know that thou hast sent me, and hast loved them, as thou hast loved me.*

Perfection – Is the final condition of the Church, without spot or wrinkle, when everything that is of God will be brought together in the Lord Jesus Christ, and presented to God the Father.

Pool of Bethesda – In John 5 in the Bible, Jesus healed a man at the Pool of Bethesda.

Prayer – Communing with God.

Prioress – The Superior of a group of nuns.

Raptures – The state of being transported by a lofty emotion; religious ecstasy.

Recondite – Not easily understood.

Revelation – Is an uncovering or disclosure via communication from the divine of something that has been partially or wholly hidden or unknown.

River of Life – And he shewed me a pure river of water of life, clear as crystal, proceeding out of the throne of God and of the Lamb (Revelation 22:1).

Saint Dominic – Founder of a religious order.

Saint Francis – Founder of a religious order.

Saint Ursula – Founder of a religious order.

Satan – The profoundly evil adversary of God and humanity, often identified with the leader of the fallen angels; the devil.

Saul – Old Testament King of Israel.

Self-Abandonment – Abandoning oneself and one's will to the will of God.

Sin – Disobedience to God.

Sodom – Old Testament) an ancient city near the Dead Sea that (along with Gomorrah) was destroyed by God for the wickedness of its inhabitants.

Solomon – King of Israel.

Spiritual Counselor – A mature Christian, knowledgeable in the Word of God, or a Minister, Priest, or Rabbi.

St. John of the Cross – Well known for his mystical writings and poetry. He was closely associated with Satin Teresa in her work of founding the reformed.

St. Peter – Disciple and Apostle of Jesus Christ.

Summa Theologica – The most famous theological work of Thomas Aquinas.

Temporal – Relating to, or limited by time: a temporal dimension; temporal and spatial boundaries.

Trances – Detachment from one's physical surroundings, as in religious contemplation.

Tree of Life – *And out of the ground made the LORD God to grow every tree that is pleasant to the sight, and good for food; the tree of life also in the midst of the garden, and the tree of knowledge of good and evil* (Genesis 2:9).

Trinity – The Triune Godhead; The Father, The Son, and The Holy Spirit.

Unitive – Serving to unite; tending to promote unity.

Virtue – Moral excellence and righteousness; goodness.

Worldliness – Of, relating to, or devoted to the temporal world.

INDEX

Pure Gold Classics

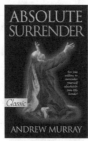
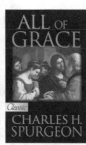

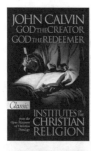
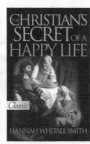
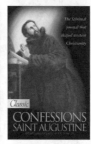

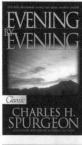

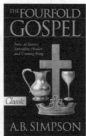

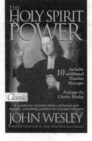

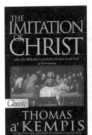

The Imitation of Christ — Thomas à'Kempis

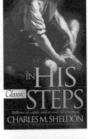

In His Steps — Charles M. Sheldon

Interior Castle — Teresa of Avila

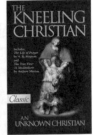

The Kneeling Christian — An Unknown Christian

Madame Jeanne Guyon

Morning by Morning — Charles H. Spurgeon

The Overcoming Life — D.L. Moody

The Pilgrim's Progress — John Bunyan

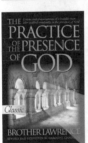

The Practice of the Presence of God — Brother Lawrence

Power, Passion & Prayer — Charles G. Finney

Secret Power — D.L. Moody

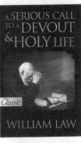

A Serious Call to a Devout & Holy Life — William Law

Sinners in the Hands of an Angry God — Jonathan Edwards

The Sovereignty of God — A.W. Pink

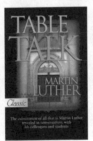

Table Talk — Martin Luther

Tozer — Fellowship of the Burning Heart

Tozer on the Holy Spirit — A.W. Tozer

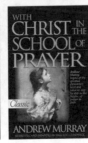

With Christ in the School of Prayer — Andrew Murray

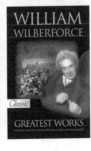

William Wilberforce — Greatest Works